POSTCARD HISTORY SERIES

South Dakota 1900–1930

IN VINTAGE POSTCARDS

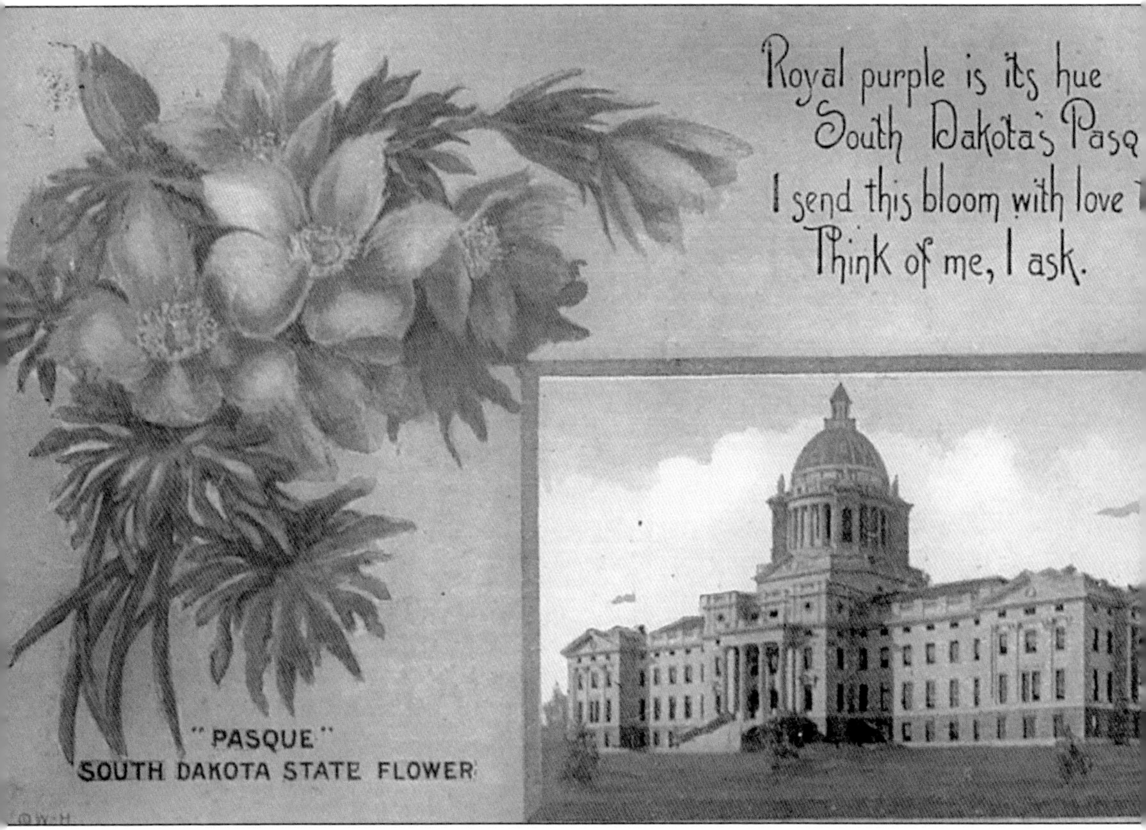

This full-color postcard was mailed shortly after the new capitol building was completed in 1910.

POSTCARD HISTORY SERIES

South Dakota 1900–1930

IN VINTAGE POSTCARDS

Richard L. Popp

ARCADIA PUBLISHING

ISBN 978-0-7385-1877-0

Published by Arcadia Publishing
Charleston, South Carolina

Printed in the United States of America

Library of Congress Catalog Card Number: 2001089686

For all general information contact Arcadia Publishing at:
Telephone 843-853-2070
Fax 843-853-0044
E-mail sales@arcadiapublishing.com
For customer service and orders:
Toll-Free 1-888-313-2665

Visit us on the Internet at www.arcadiapublishing.com

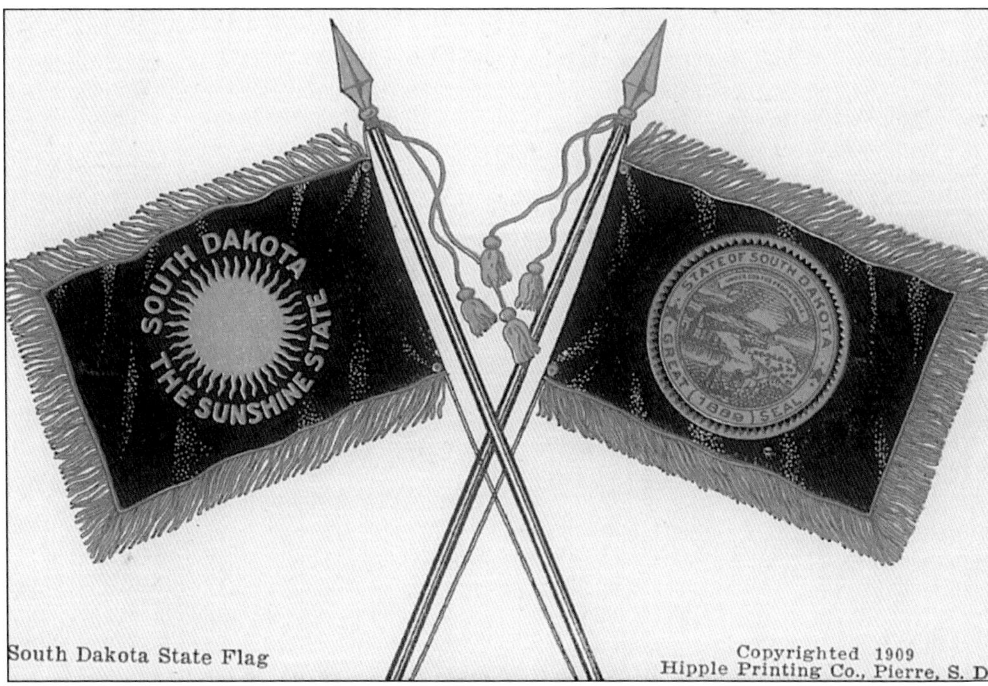

Ida M. Anding, who was then a stenographer in the State Department of History, designed South Dakota's flag in 1909. In 1963, to save production costs, the state seal was inserted into the center of the blazing sun so that the flag could be printed on one side only. The flag was changed again in 1992, when the state's motto became "The Mount Rushmore State."

Contents

ACKNOWLEDGMENTS

The postcards in this book came from many sources, often collected from the states to which they were sent. Thanks to Wendy for her patience while I sorted through box after box of cards at antique shops and postcard shows. Thanks also to Ken Stewart and Hazel Kalkbrenner for their encouragement, to Bob Kolbe for some of the better items, and to the staff and collections of the South Dakota State Historical Society for much of the background information. Although this book does not contain footnotes, it is completely dependent on the work of many South Dakota historians, and to them I express my deepest gratitude.

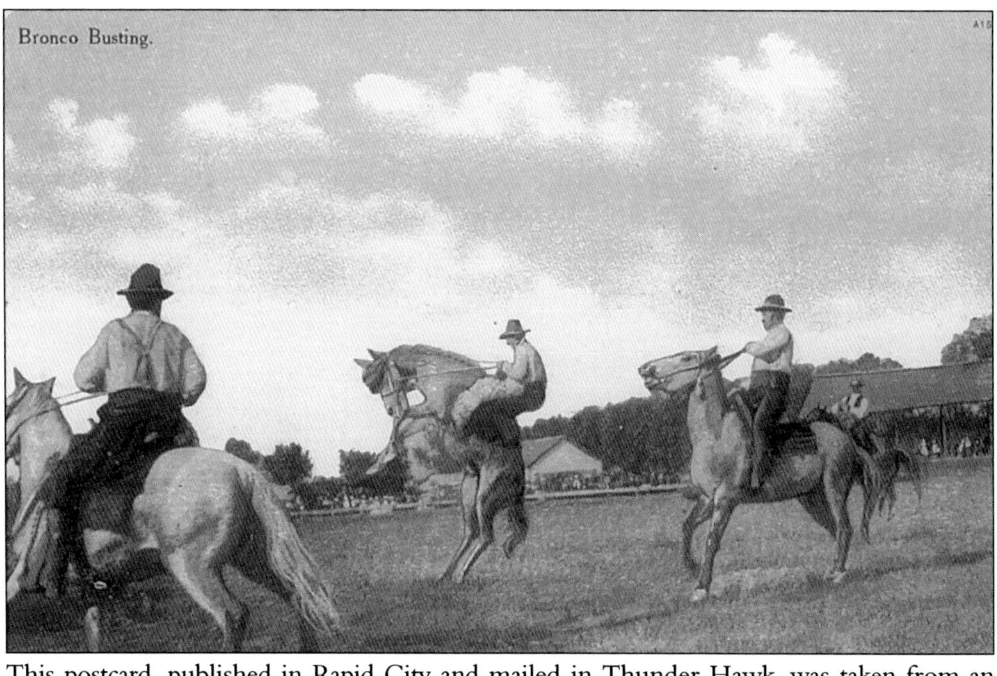

This postcard, published in Rapid City and mailed in Thunder Hawk, was taken from an original photograph by O.S. Leeland of Mitchell.

INTRODUCTION

Ever since their invention more than a century ago, picture postcards have been popular with travelers and tourists to let family and friends catch a glimpse of faraway places for themselves. Even after telephones became available, postcards performed an essential service—connecting people in isolated prairie towns. A penny postcard and a penny stamp were both cheaper than a letter, which cost 2¢ postage plus stationery. With a little knowledge of train schedules, South Dakota homesteaders could send postcards to friends 10 or 100 miles away and know exactly when their messages would arrive.

This book focuses on the "golden age" of postcards, which began in 1898 and continued through the 1920s. Some obvious postcard topics are missing, such as Wall Drug and the Crazy Horse Memorial. These attractions arrived later. By 1930, George Washington's head was just beginning to emerge from the rock on Mount Rushmore. Some tourists were already visiting the state at the turn of the century, and were already buying and mailing views of the Black Hills, the Badlands, and the Corn Palace. However, most of the cards in this volume were used by local people for personal communications between small towns, or with family members in distant places like Minnesota, Nebraska, and Iowa.

Many early photographers produced photos on paper with pre-printed postcard backs. These "real photo" postcards are often the best visual evidence we have of life in small towns—showing main streets, homesteads, parades, child and family portraits, fires, and train wrecks. Most small towns had a photo studio, and photographers produced postcard prints to sell locally, for tourists and visitors, and as advertising for local businesses. Even in a sparsely populated state such as South Dakota, the total number of postcards produced is not known, and probably never will be. The black-and-white photos from 100 years ago often remain sharp and clear, while our modern Polaroids fade to purple, and videotapes are destroyed by dirty tape heads.

Until recently, postcards have been overlooked as historical resources, in part because they were so ubiquitous. Many cards were produced cheaply and poorly in order to keep them inexpensive. The fad of postcard collecting, popular in the early 1900s, dwindled in the 1920s as it became old-fashioned and printing quality declined throughout the industry. Collectors valued postcards more for the stamps, or even the postmarks, than for the images or personal messages they contained.

Antique postcards gained attention as prices skyrocketed for other types of photographs and works of art. Millions of them survive in closets and attics, they are small and easy to store, and best of all they usually carry identifying captions right on them. Unlike other material artifacts such as furniture and glassware, postcards often include a message that links them to a specific person, place, and time, helping us connect with a little bit of history.

For a historian, postcards from a hundred years ago are still easily obtainable, accessible, and relatively sturdy, and they come with their own stories. Although I added information to put the images into context, the pictures and messages have their own stories to tell, and that is as it should be. I tried to select postcards that would represent the entire state of South Dakota, and I am sorry I could not include every community and every type of lifestyle. I believe this is the first book based exclusively on South Dakota postcards, and I hope it won't be the last.

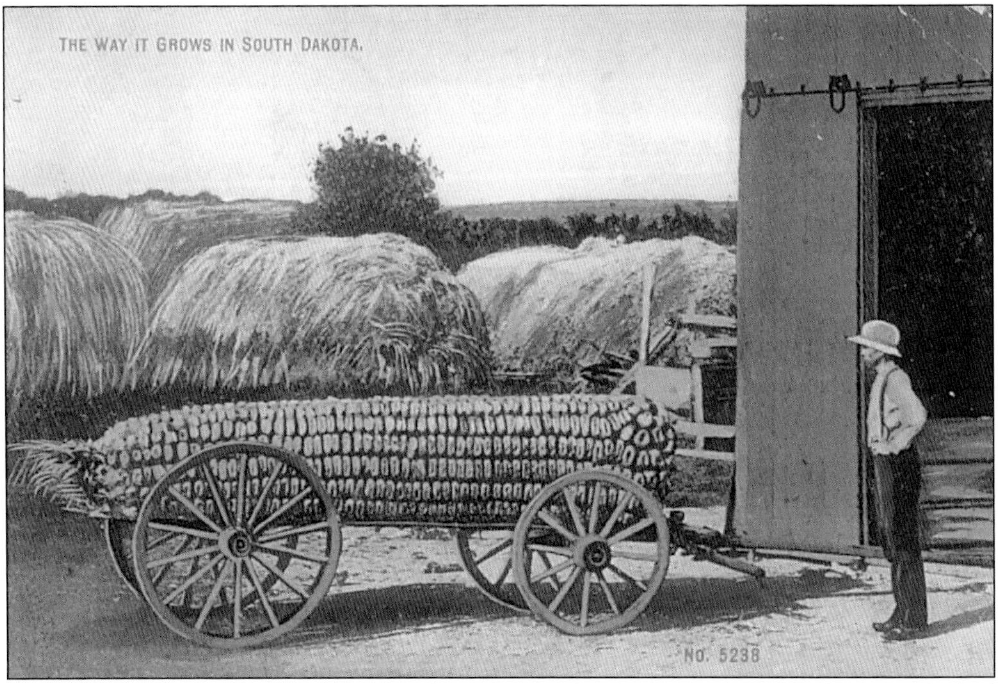

The sender of this postcard was hoping for a harvest like the picture. On April 7, 1910, he had finished sowing 70 acres of wheat, 27 acres of barley, and 40 acres of oats.

One

The Golden Age of Postcards

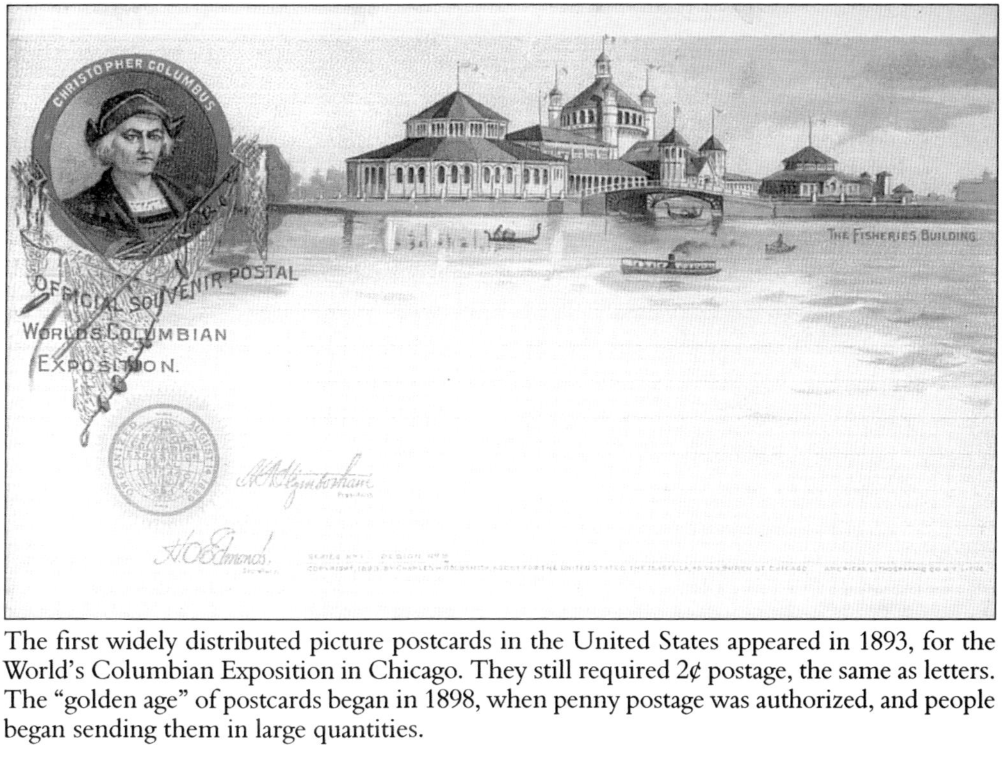

The first widely distributed picture postcards in the United States appeared in 1893, for the World's Columbian Exposition in Chicago. They still required 2¢ postage, the same as letters. The "golden age" of postcards began in 1898, when penny postage was authorized, and people began sending them in large quantities.

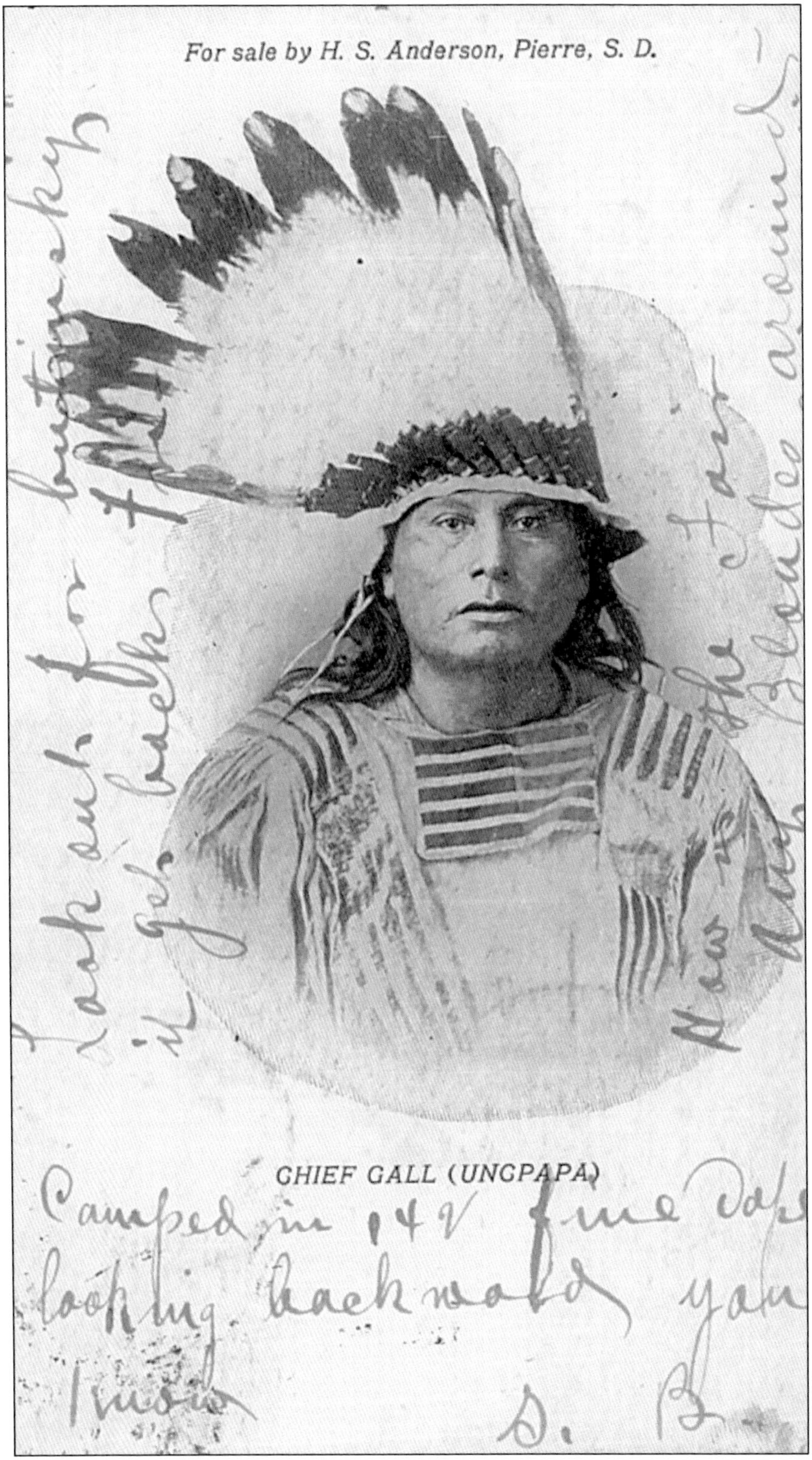

Until 1907, United States postal regulations reserved the back of postcards for the address only. Any personal messages had to be written around the picture on the front. This card was mailed from Pierre in 1906, with a cryptic message.

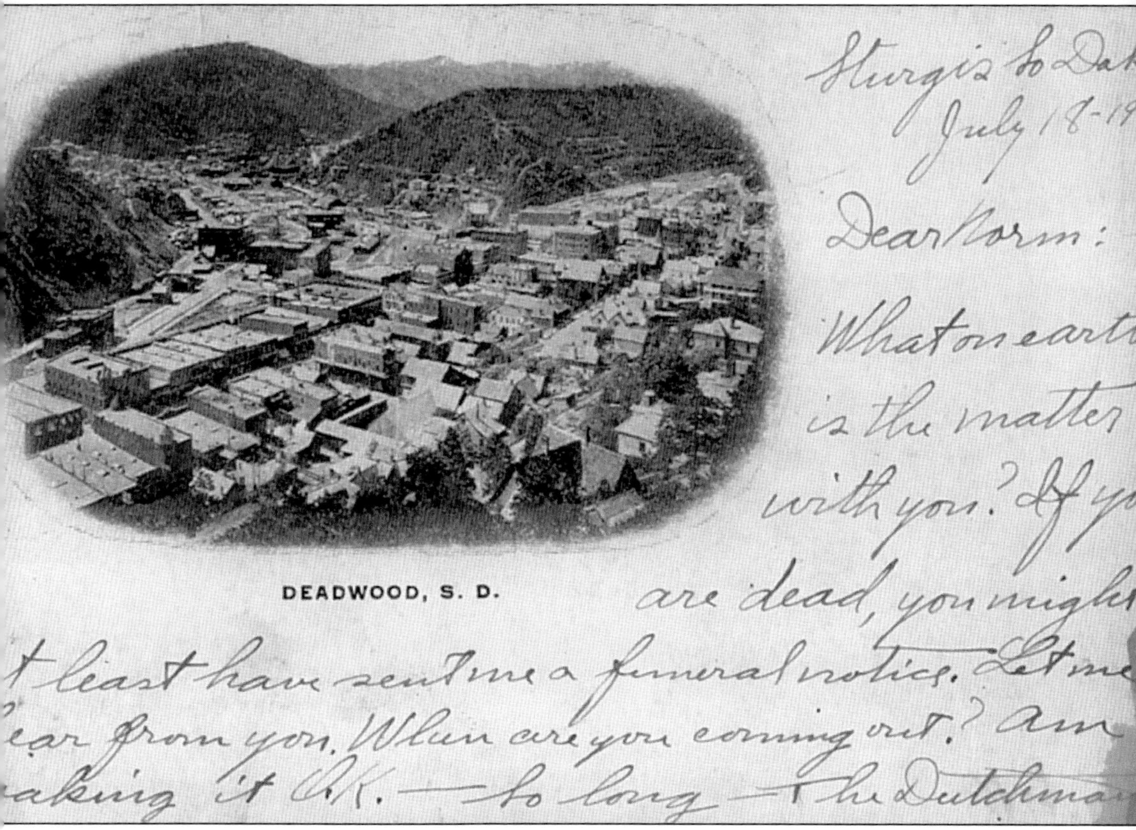

This view of Deadwood left enough room for an extended message, and the writer took advantage of the entire space.

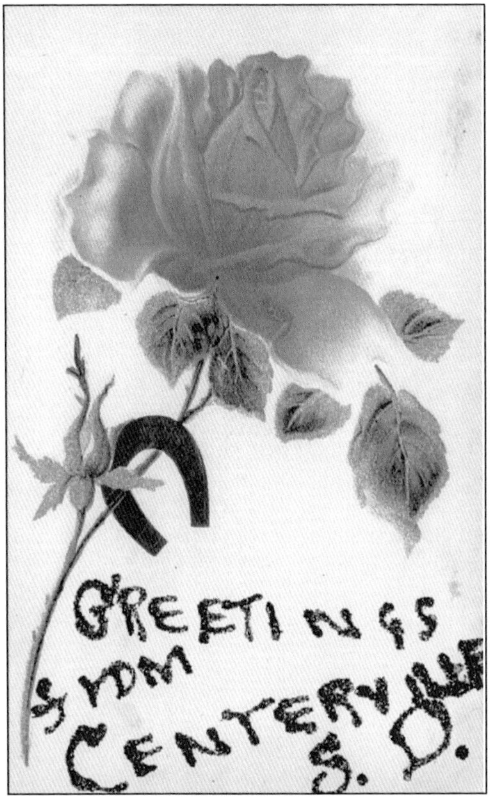

These cards with embossed flower designs have the words "Post Card" printed on the back in 14 different languages, so that they could be sold worldwide. Distributors provided glitter and glue for local stores to personalize the cards with greetings and their own town name.

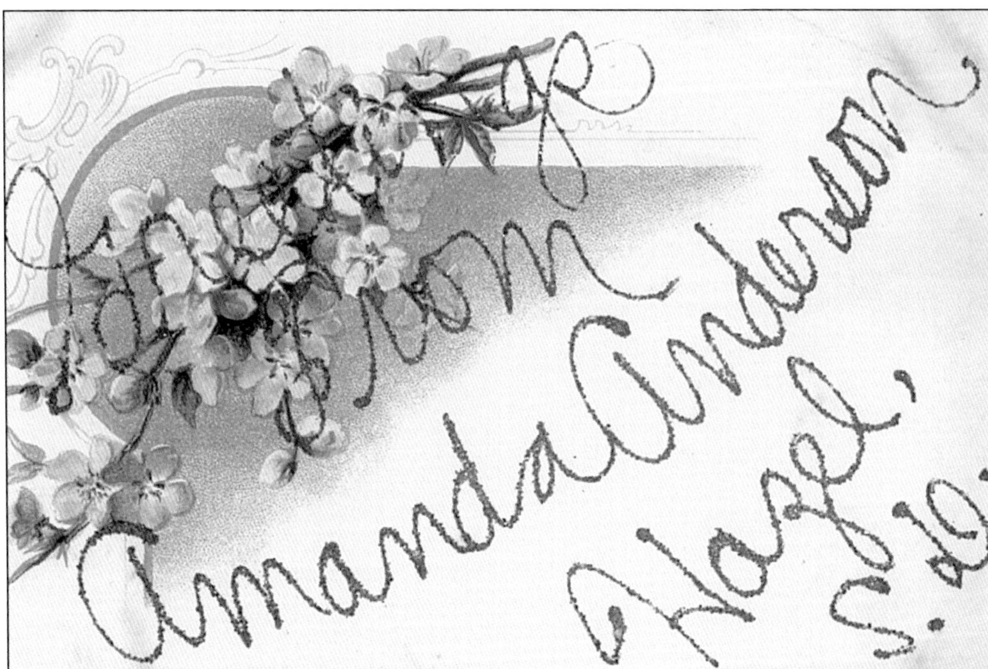

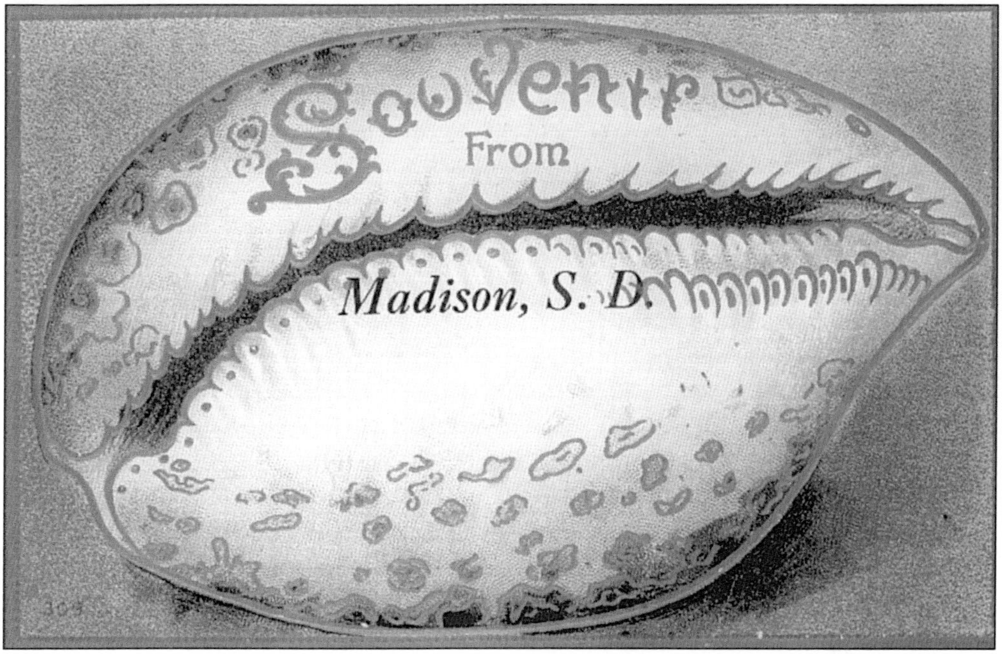

Seashells were popular postcard motifs nationwide, even in landlocked places like Madison and Seneca.

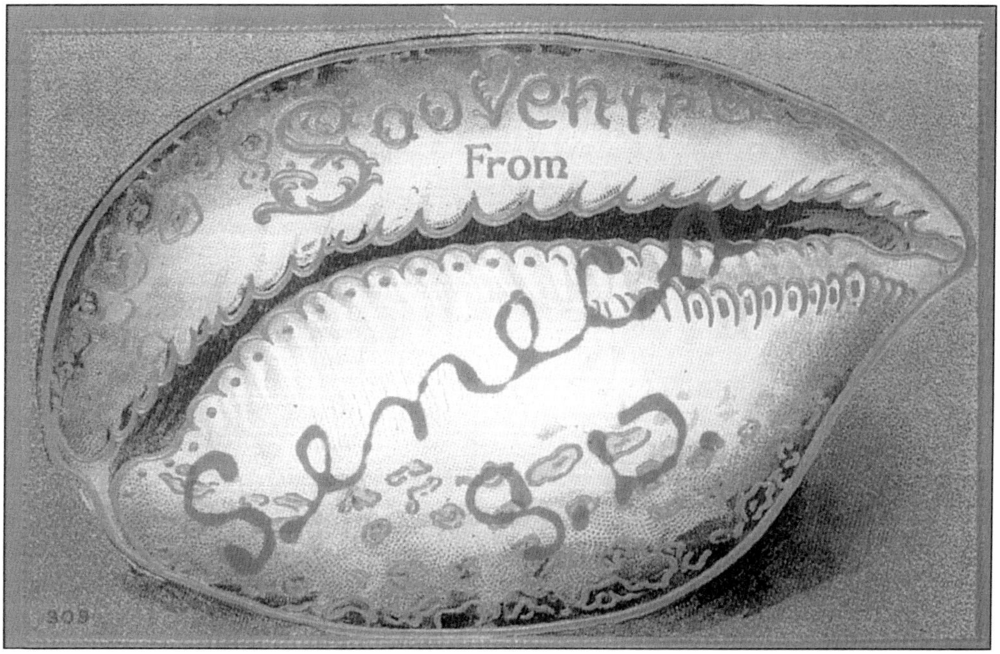

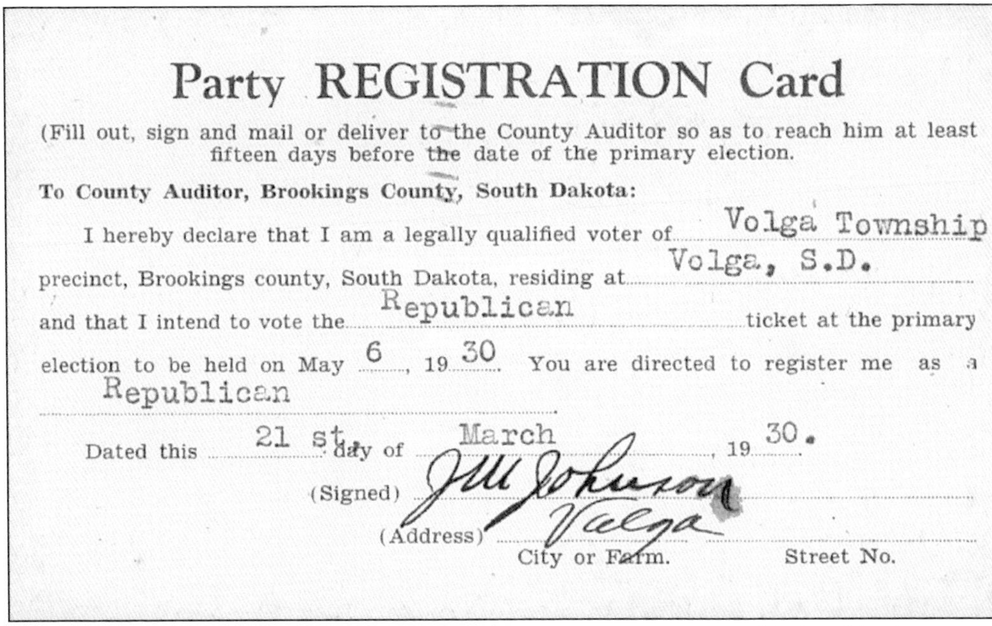

Party REGISTRATION Card

(Fill out, sign and mail or deliver to the County Auditor so as to reach him at least fifteen days before the date of the primary election.

To County Auditor, Brookings County, South Dakota:

I hereby declare that I am a legally qualified voter of Volga Township precinct, Brookings county, South Dakota, residing at Volga, S.D. and that I intend to vote the Republican ticket at the primary election to be held on May 6, 1930. You are directed to register me as a Republican

Dated this 21 st. day of March, 1930.

(Signed) J M Johnson

(Address) Volga

City or Farm. Street No.

Postcards provided an inexpensive and simple way to transact many kinds of business, and they didn't all have pretty pictures. Merchants, organizations, and government offices used preprinted postcards to send announcements, advertisements, and receipts.

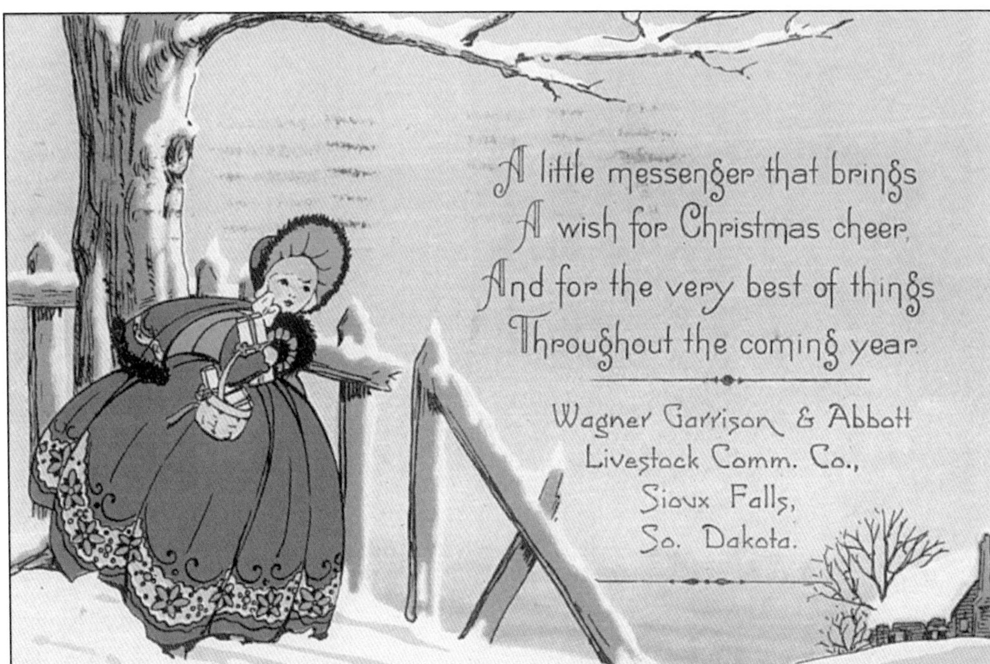

Businesses could have their names preprinted on a variety of holiday greetings or other stock images. This card was sent to a client in Worthing.

This comic postcard was designed with space to add the town name with a rubber stamp. It was sent to Roy Anderson in Grandfield with the message, "Roy is this the way you wash dishes for Mable?"

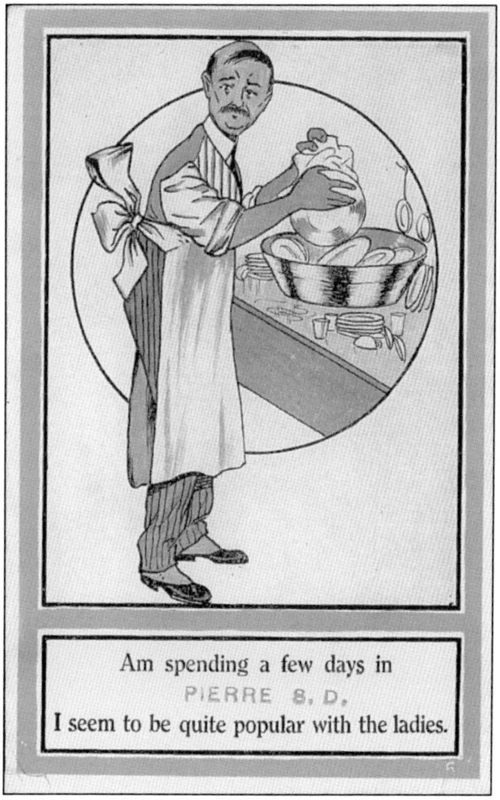

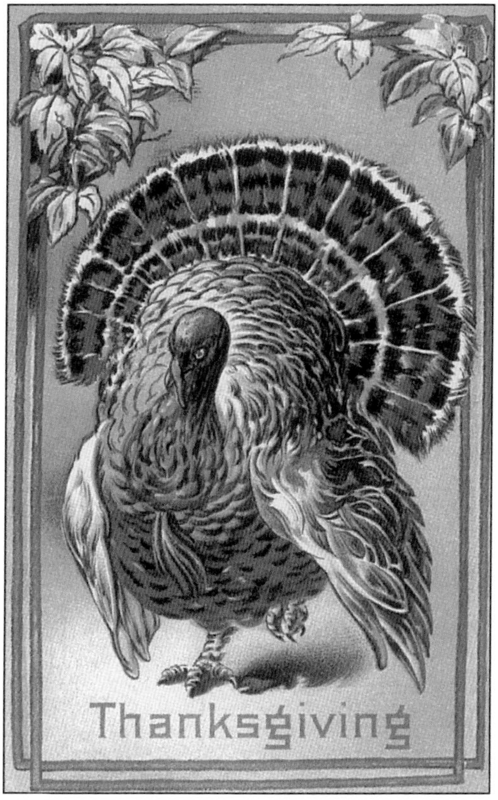

Holiday themes were popular for postcards. This card included a complete rundown of social events during Thanksgiving week in 1911, in the small community of LaDelle in Spink County: "Had a social at the town hall Friday evening. The people from Huron were up. Had a party for Jim M last Mon evening think we will have one for Helen Mc Friday night/from Cora & Ada."

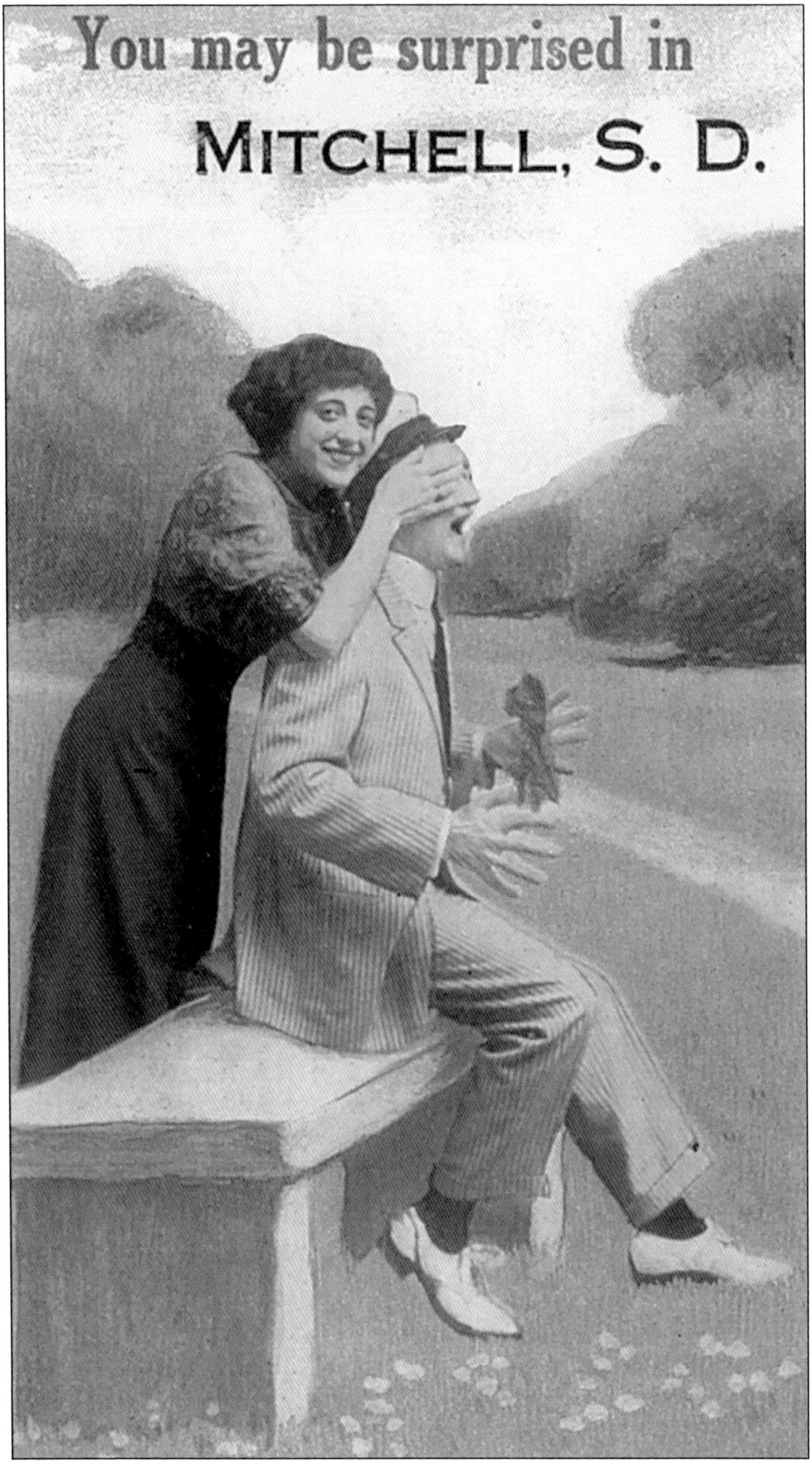

In 1907, the United States Post Office allowed the address side of postcards to be divided to provide additional space for messages. Publishers printed cards with all types of images to meet strong demand from consumers.

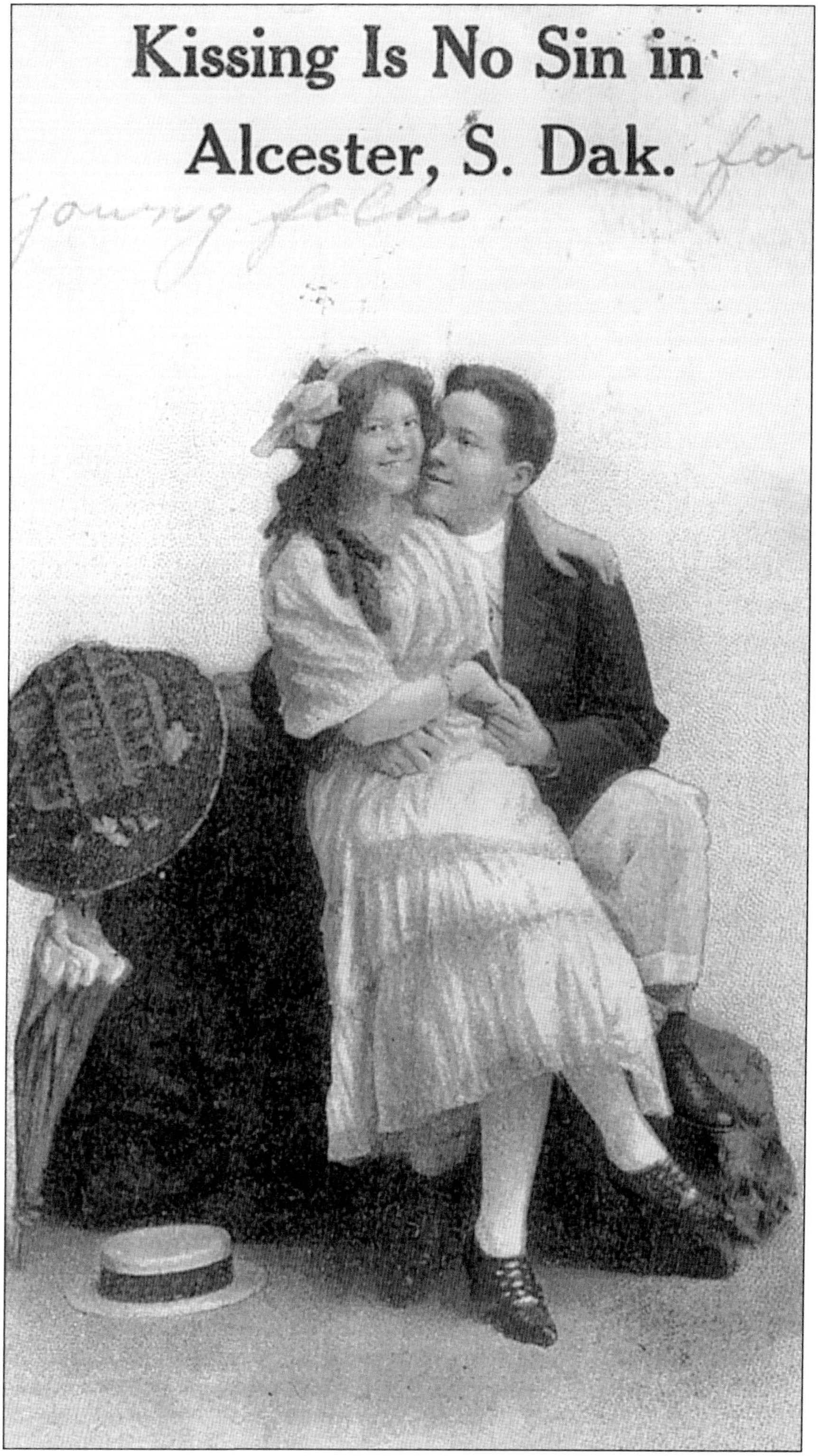

Romantic situations were popular postcard topics, and stock views could be ordered with any town name imprinted on them. The message on this card was revised by the sender, "for young folks."

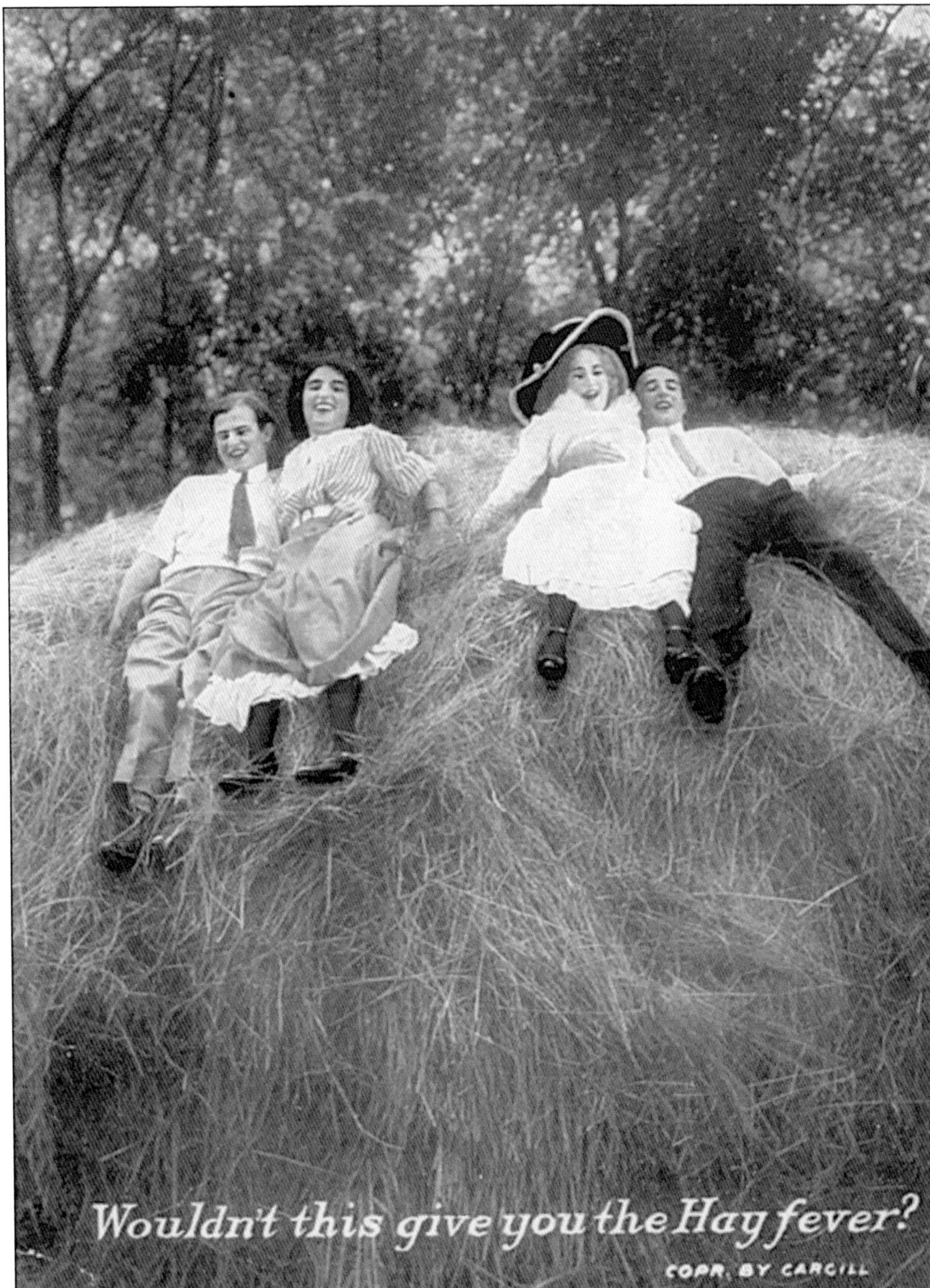

This fanciful view of harvest time was used by a writer in Ola to report the real business of farming to his cousin, Emil Anderson, in Mitchell in 1912: "Spose you ar Busy in the corn f[ields] every day. I finished Wensday am glad of It. Had Henry & Adolf C. To Help me. Corn south of hear is going from 35 to 50 bu. mine only went 25, but was glad to get that for such a dry summer as we had."

Two

Views of Nature

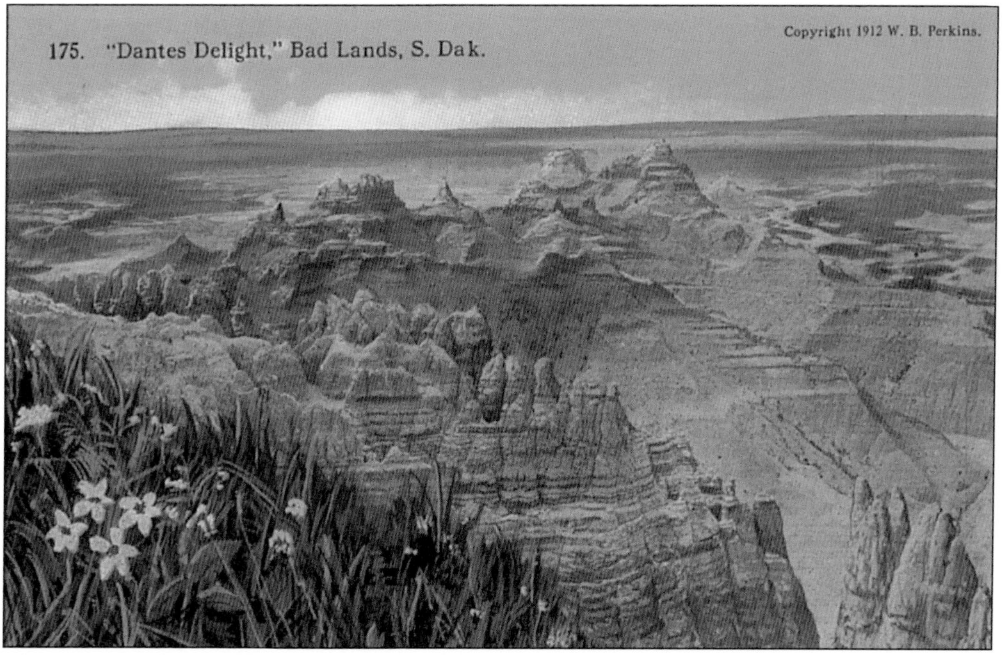

The strange otherworldly scenes in the Badlands were popular scenic spots long before they became a national monument in 1939. Both settlers and visitors admired the natural scenery of South Dakota, not only the Badlands and Black Hills, but also the rivers, lakes, bluffs, and wide open spaces throughout the state.

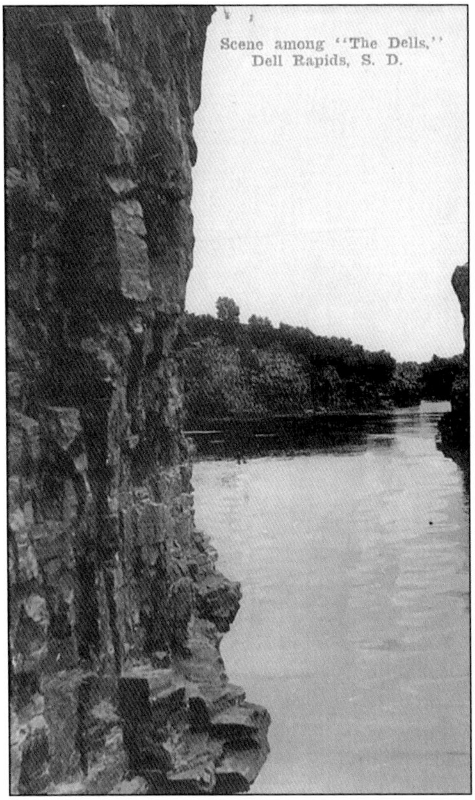

The Dells of the Big Sioux River drew settlers to the community of Dell Rapids and were often admired by photographers.

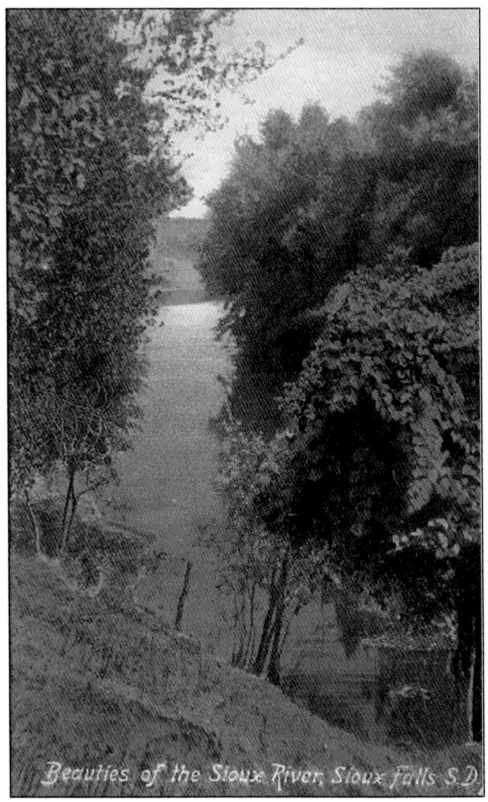

The sender used this card to thank a friend in Stillwater, Minnesota, for baby clothes, and she mentioned that her husband traveled to Mitchell to see presidential candidates William Jennings Bryan and William Howard Taft debate during the campaign of 1908.

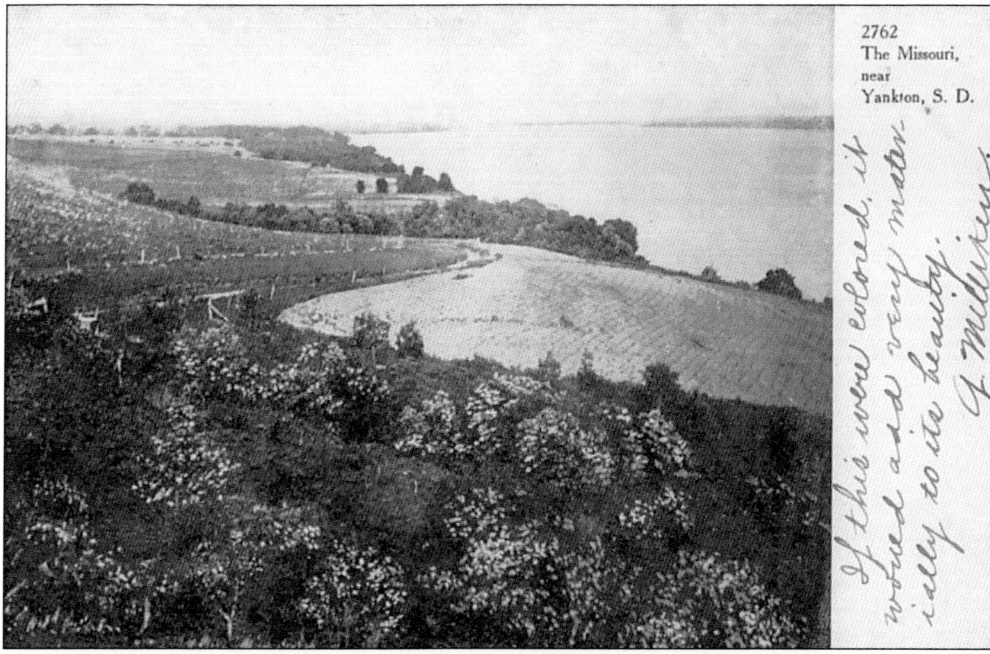

To many Americans at the turn of the 20th century, cultivated fields and orchards were more "beautiful" than the untamed wilderness. This view showed how the Missouri River near Yankton had been transformed into a beautiful place by the human touch.

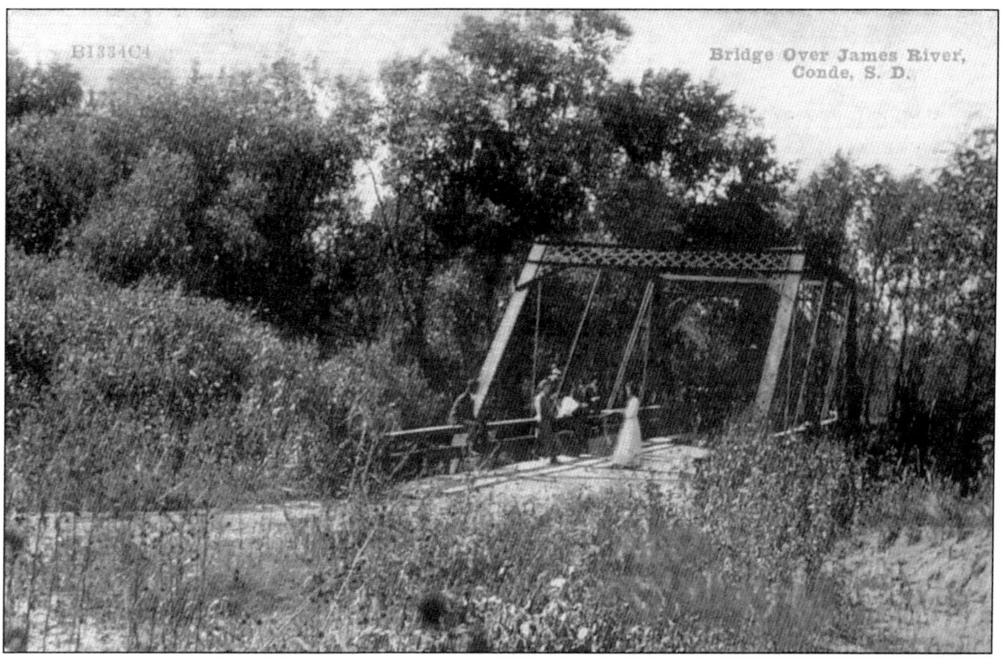

Wooded river bottoms, good roads, and sturdy bridges showed that South Dakota was a prosperous and comfortable place to live.

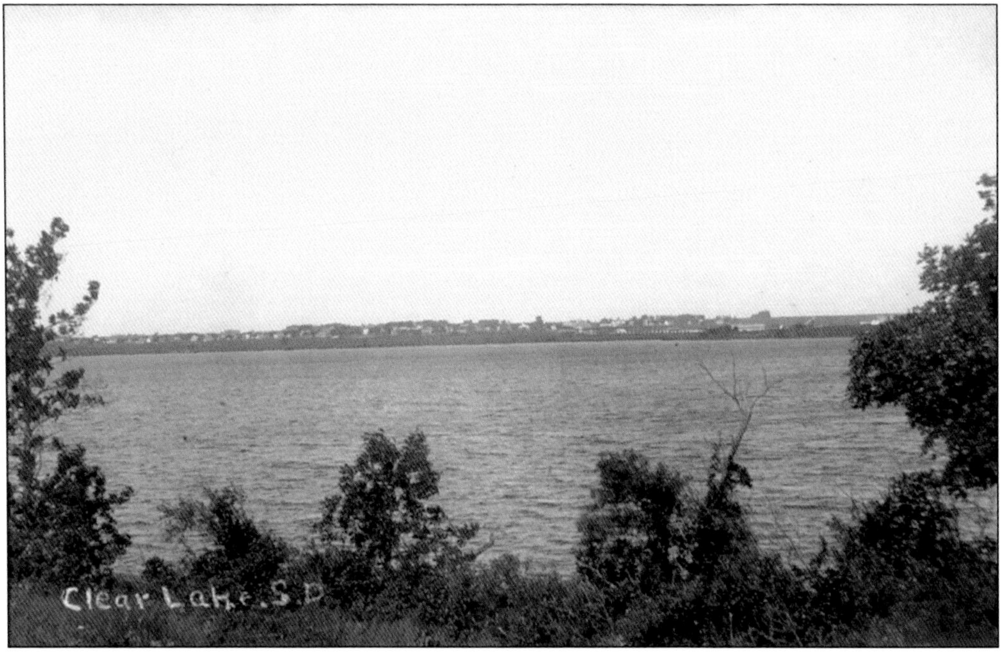

Postcards of lake and river scenes made South Dakota look fertile and well watered. The town of Clear Lake was photographed from across the water to make it look more inviting.

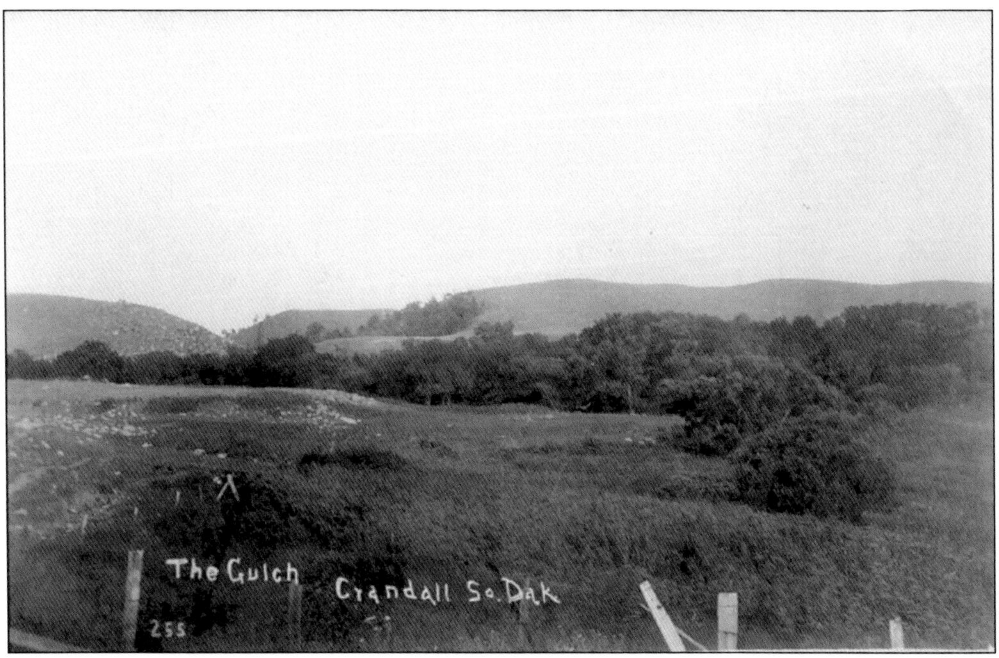

A somewhat more realistic view, this photograph still attempts to capture scenery and rolling hills to present the best possible image of the prairie in Day County.

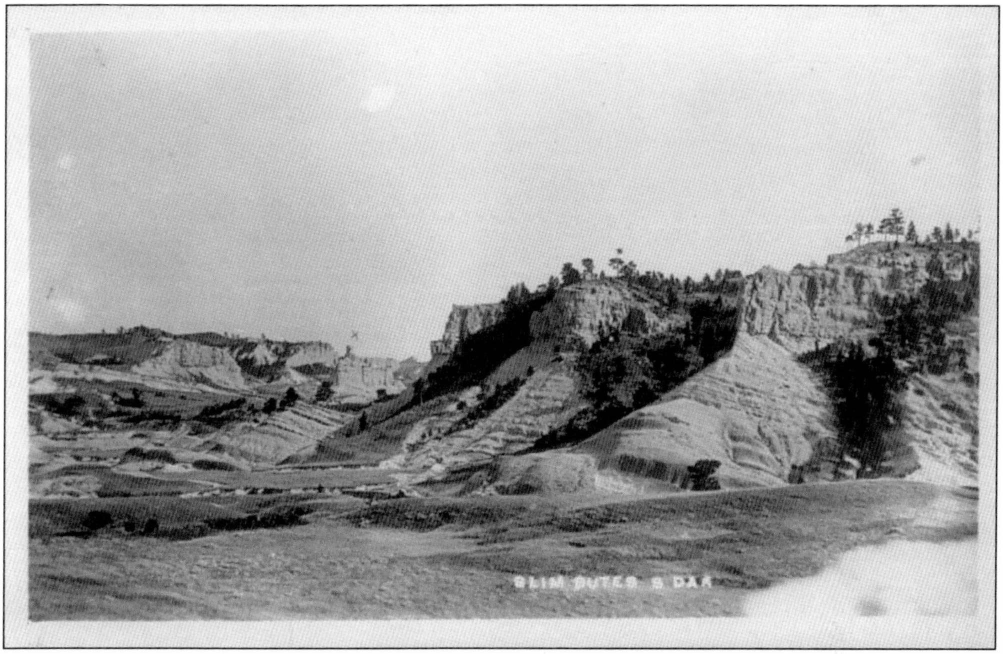

The sender of this card did not believe the photograph sufficiently captured the scene. "No picture can begin to show how beautiful a place it is, nor can any one describe it, for it is simply grand. Where I marked the small cross is one of the castles, formed from stone, most all the formations are white or real light sometimes cream or pink. Then to think of trees growing up on such places, one would wonder where they ever get moisture enough to live. We will have some pictures finished to send you, from those Esther took while out here."

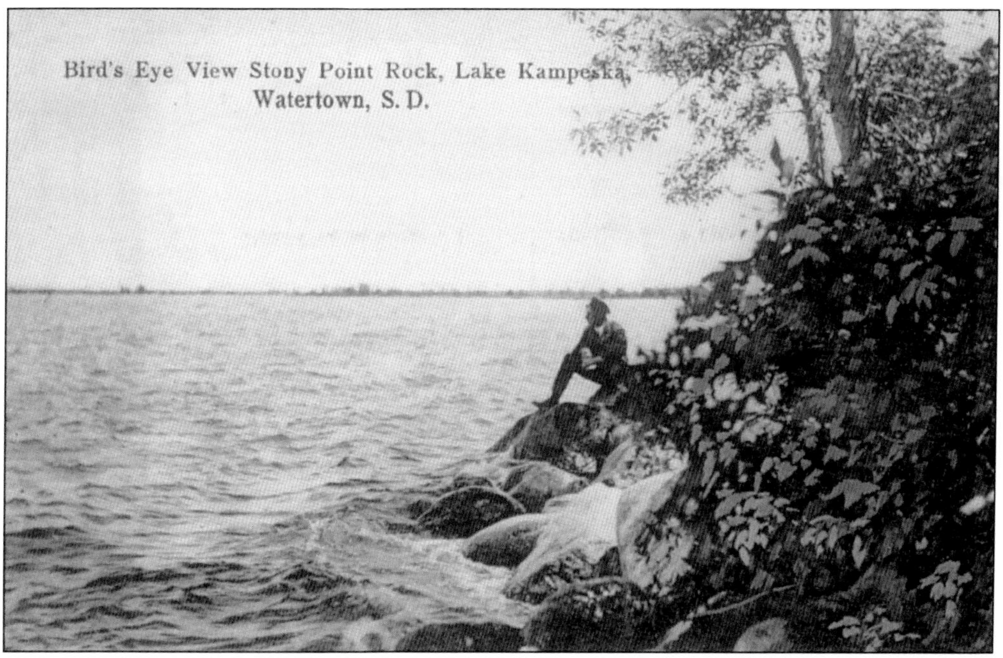

The rocky shoreline of Lake Kampeska near Watertown was a popular subject for early postcards.

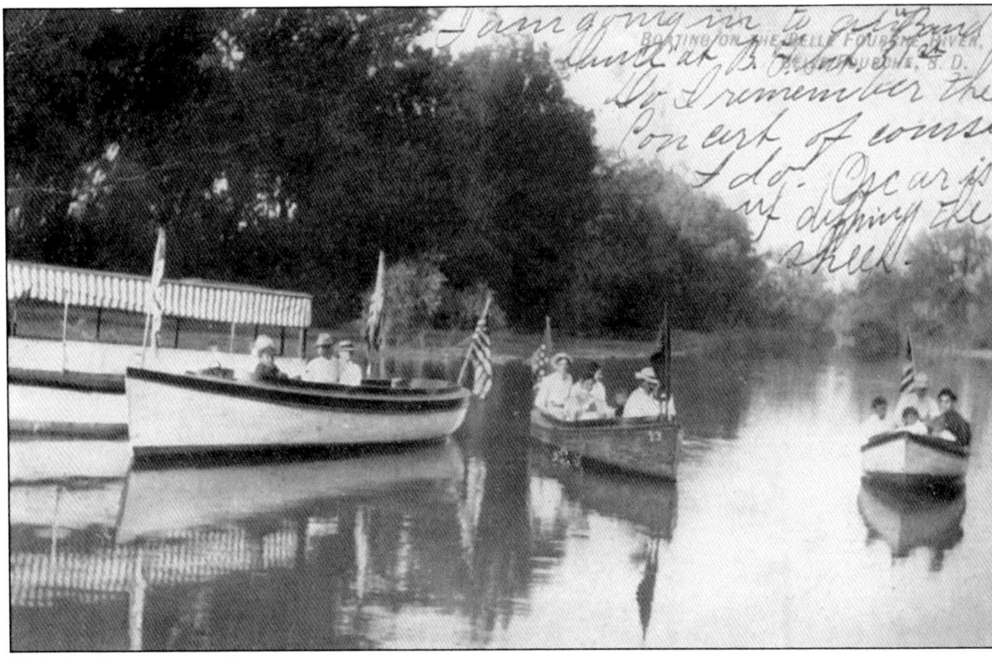

This idyllic scene on the Belle Fourche River includes the message, "I am going to our 'Band Dance' at B.F. [Belle Fourche] Sat. 31st Do I remember the Concert of course I do. Oscar is up dipping the sheep."

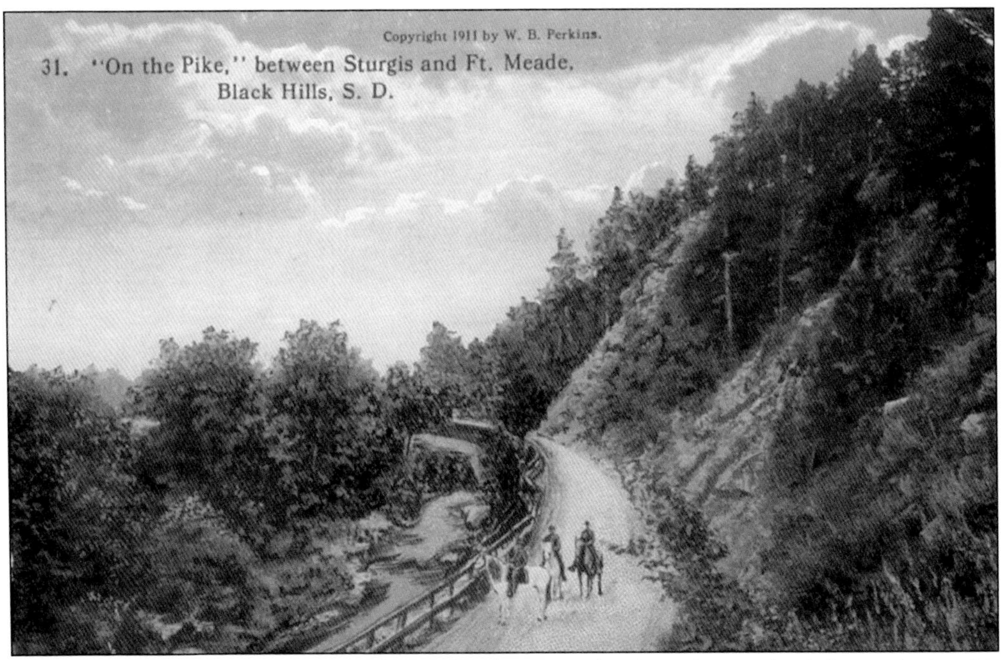

Although the photo was heavily redrawn for this reproduction, the sender, Myron, insisted it was a true representation of the place: "This is picture of the road we went over 1/2 hour ago," he wrote to his mother, Mary Godding, in Fountain, Colorado.

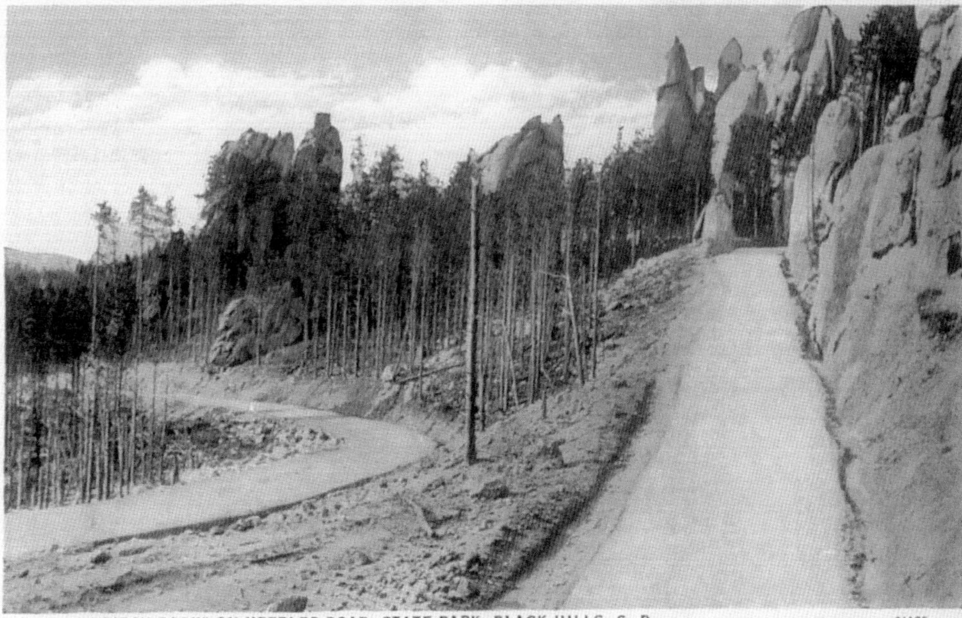

93. "SWITCH BACK" ON NEEDLES ROAD, STATE PARK, BLACK HILLS, S. D. 91195

Postcard publishers often added automobiles, people, and picturesque clouds to make their views more interesting and appealing, as two versions of this image show. Scenic photos from this period often included roads, train tracks, or bridges to show how nature had been improved.

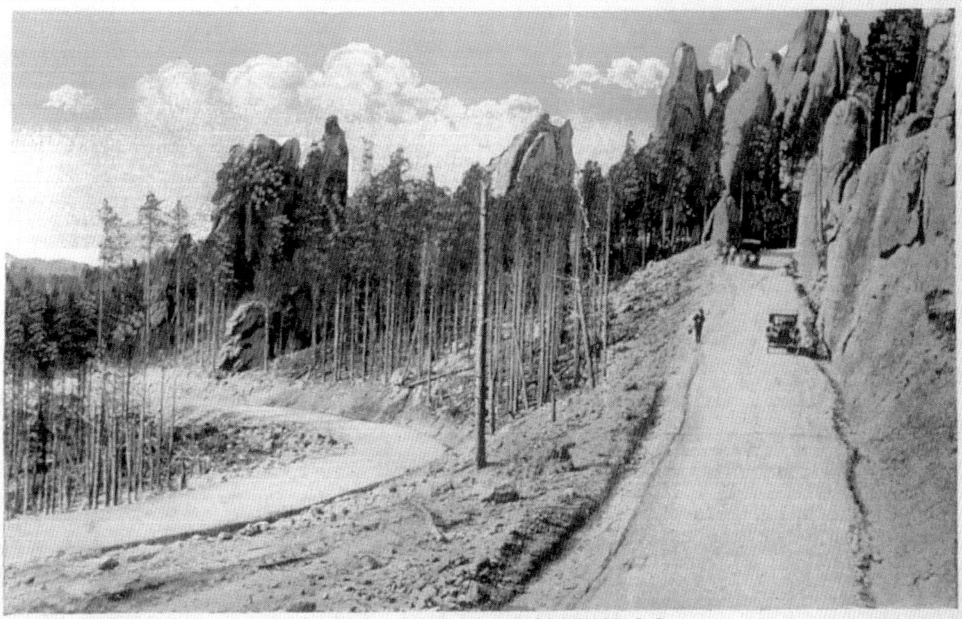

93. "SWITCH BACK" ON NEEDLES ROAD. STATE PARK, BLACK HILLS, S. D. 91195

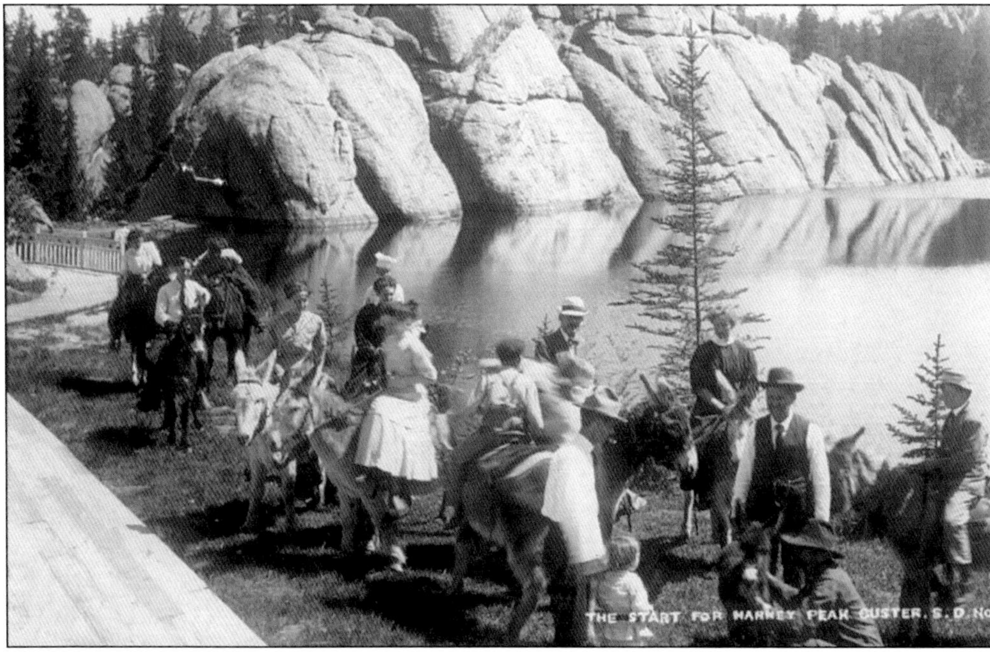

The Sylvan Lake resort was an early favorite for tourists. Mrs. Mary Griffith of Chokio, Minnesota, wrote to her daughter in 1911, "Here is the way we go to the top of Harney peak. Just imagine u hear the cowbells the little burros wear. We are having such a good time I wouldn't miss it for anything."

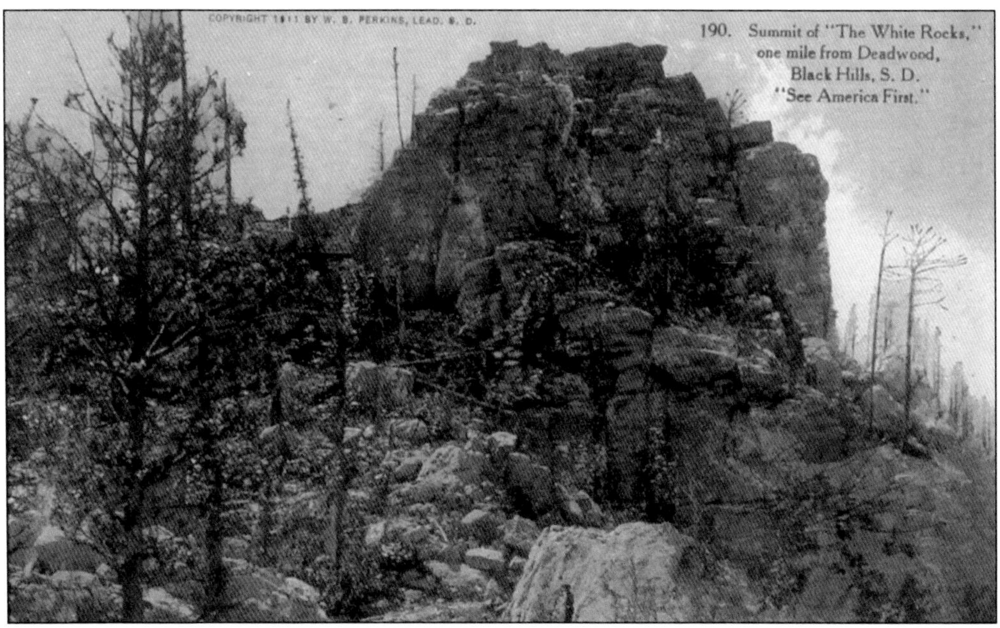

Hiking was a popular sport for some, but not for all, as evidenced in this note from Deadwood: "Walked 500 ft. to summit 11am 4-8-12. Above cemetery. E. not enthusiastic about mountain climbing, says too much like work."

Harney Peak, the highest point east of the Rocky Mountains, has long been a popular destination for hikers. This postcard was part of a series of scenic views sold by L.B. Hollister of Lead.

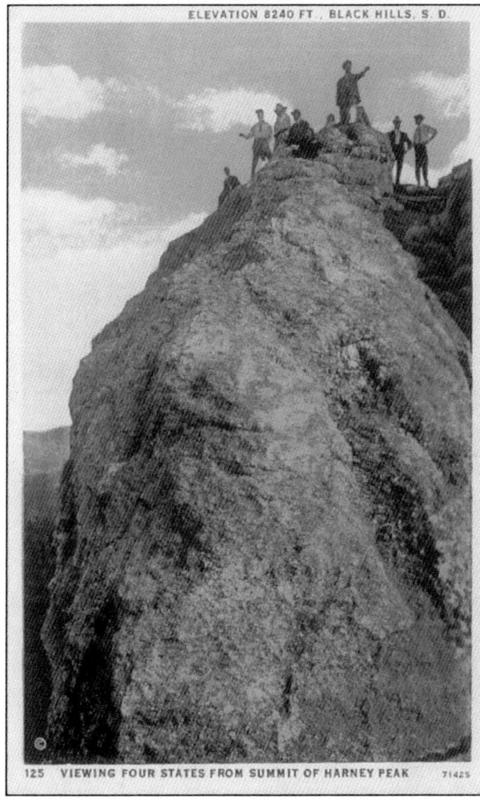

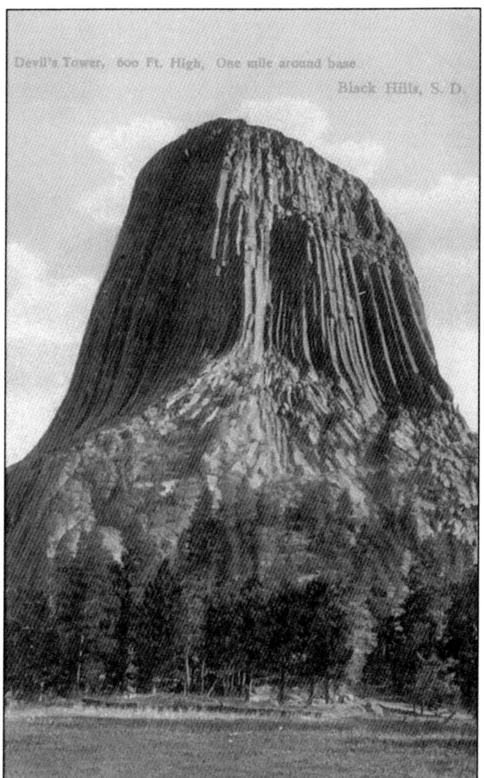

This well-known Wyoming landmark, on the western edge of the Black Hills, was frequently misplaced in South Dakota by foreign postcard publishers. This one was printed in Germany.

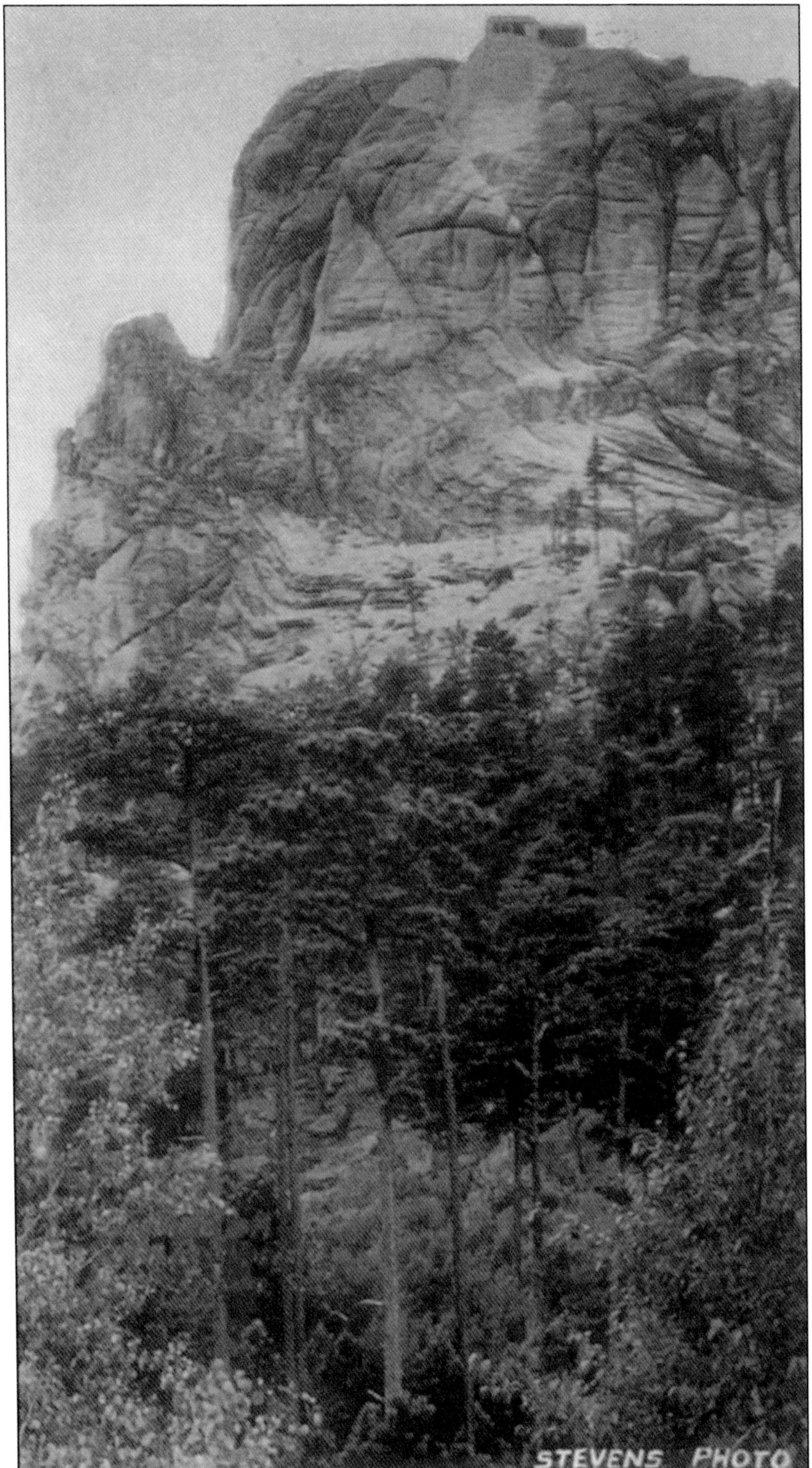

B121. Carving on Mt. Rushmore, Black Hills, S. D.

As early as 1924, state historian Doane Robinson suggested carving the rocks of the Needles into sculptures to improve the natural beauty of the Black Hills and to entice more tourists to visit the state. Sculptor Gutzon Borglum had been working in Georgia on the Stone Mountain memorial to Confederate generals, but when he visited Mount Rushmore, he immediately saw the potential for a project that would be truly national in scope. Blasting and carving Mount Rushmore into the figures of U.S. presidents began soon after President Calvin Coolidge dedicated the site in 1927.

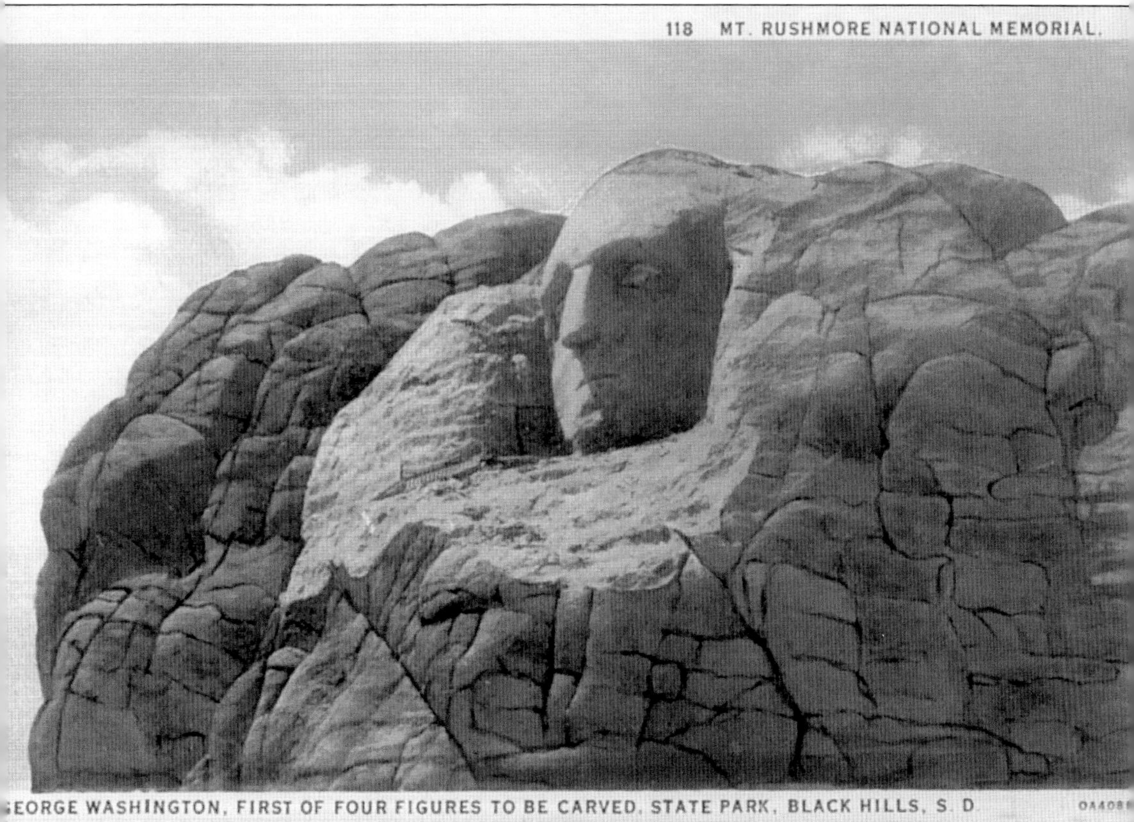

Washington's head was the first part of the Mount Rushmore Memorial to be completed, and it was unveiled on the Fourth of July in 1930. Work on Jefferson's head had started on Washington's right, but problems forced this part of the rock to be blasted away, and Jefferson was moved to the other side.

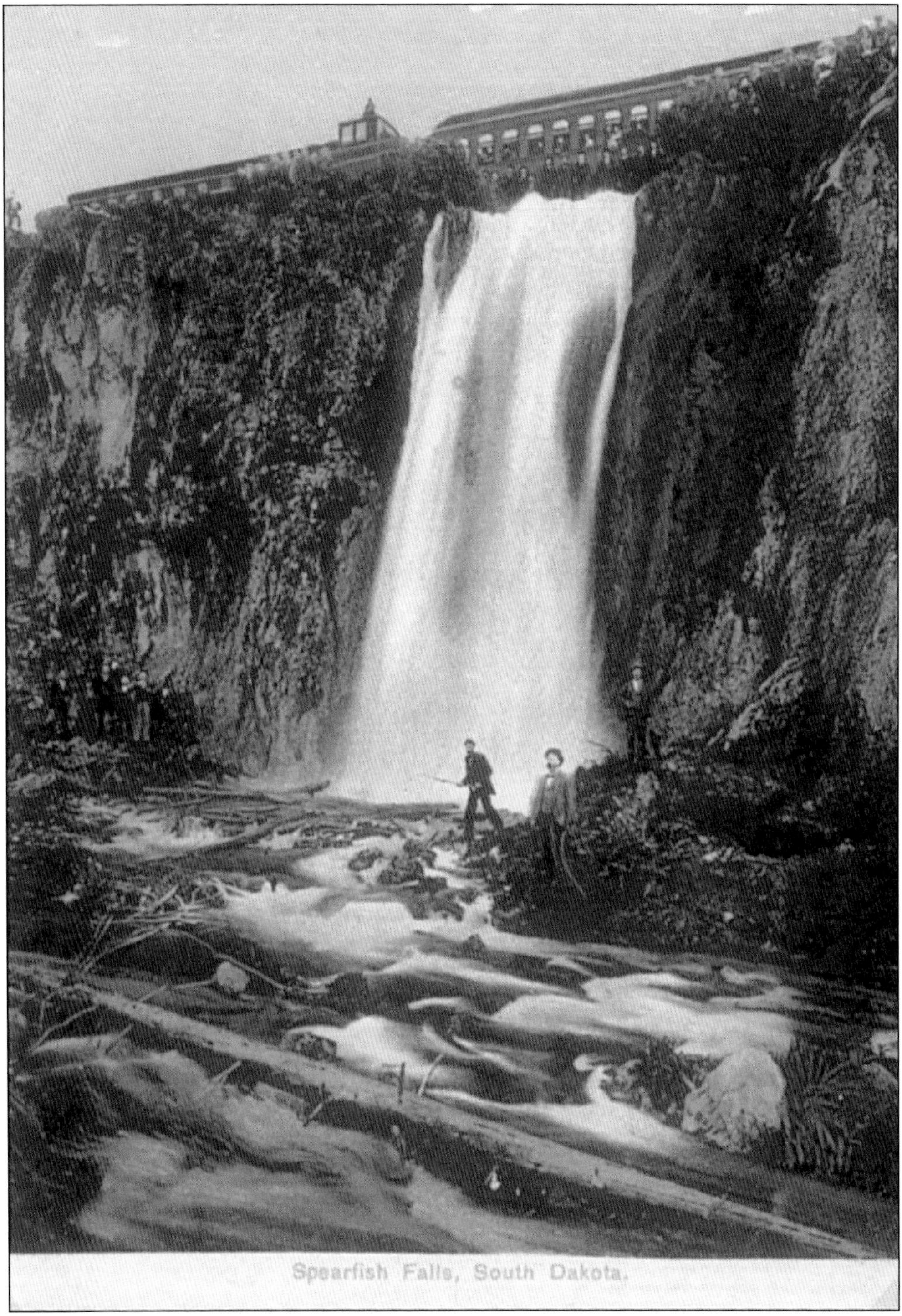

Excursion trains made travel possible for early tourists before roads and automobiles were widely available. Spearfish Falls was a popular spot until most of the water was diverted for use by the Homestake gold mills.

Three

SUBDUING THE LAND

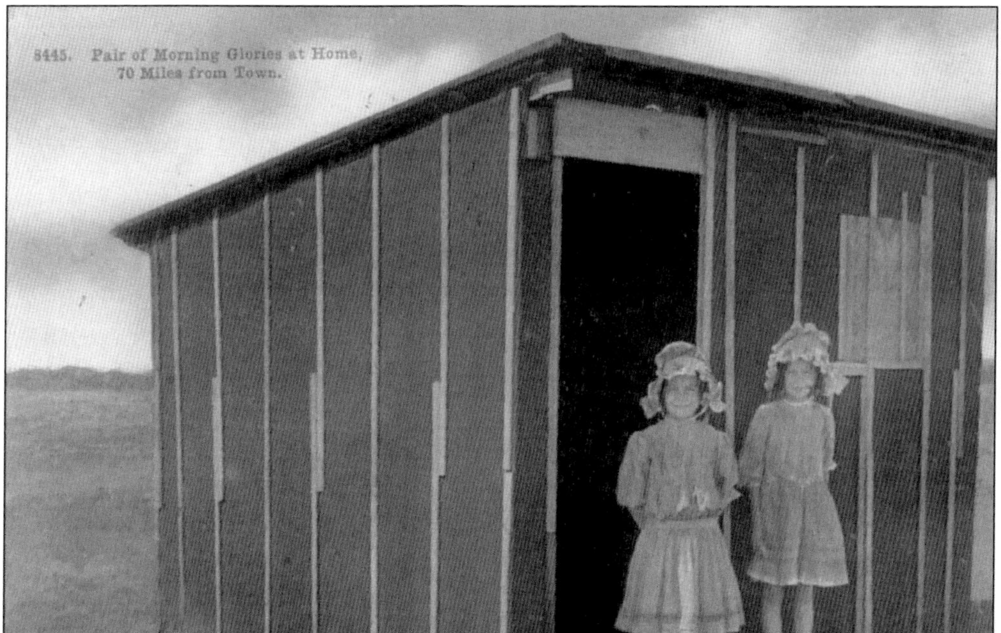

The homesteading frenzy brought many people to South Dakota who had no intentions of farming and no means to do so, but who only wanted to "prove up" and then resell the land. Many built claim shacks of tarpaper that met the barest minimum of the homesteading requirements, and then they only lived in them for the minimum number of days required.

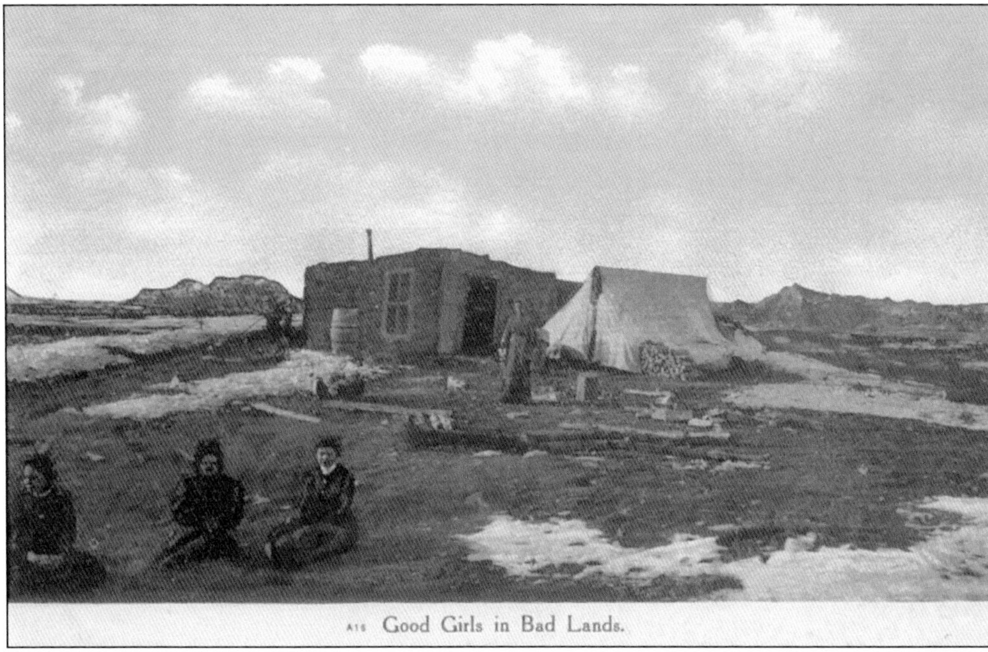

A substantial number of women claimed homesteads in South Dakota. Widows, divorcees, and single women saw opportunities in "free land," and some married women filed separate claims from their husbands, hoping to double their family lands.

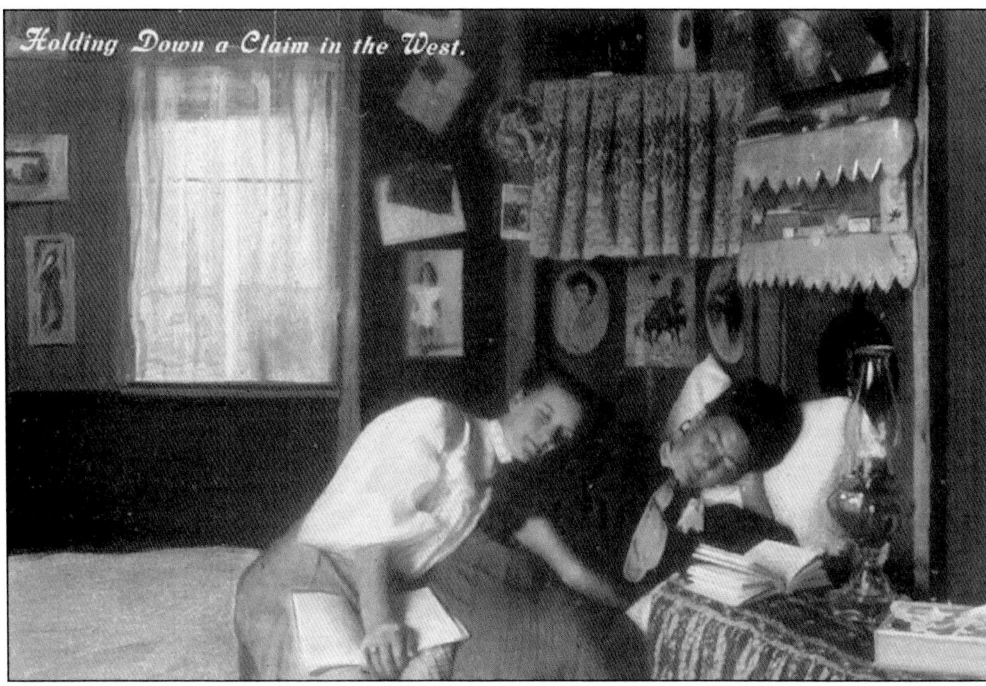

Claim shacks offered few amenities, but pictures cut from magazines, colored paper trimmed in scallops, and a few carefully chosen keepsakes helped make them livable.

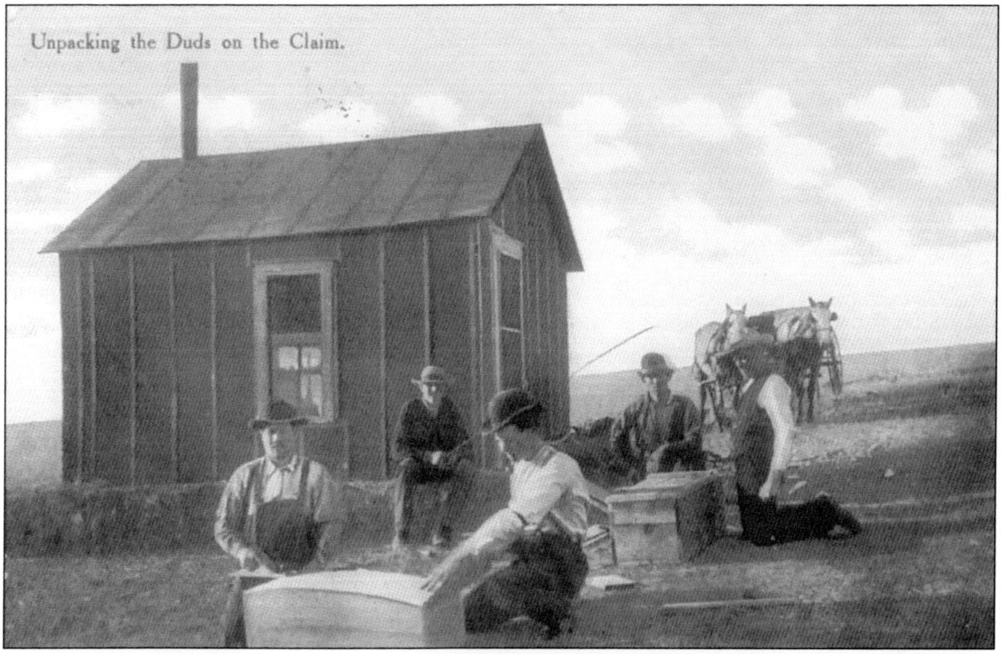

Even at the peak of the land boom with a family on each quarter section, many homesteaders had only a few neighbors within walking distance. Few came prepared for the loneliness and isolation of prairie life.

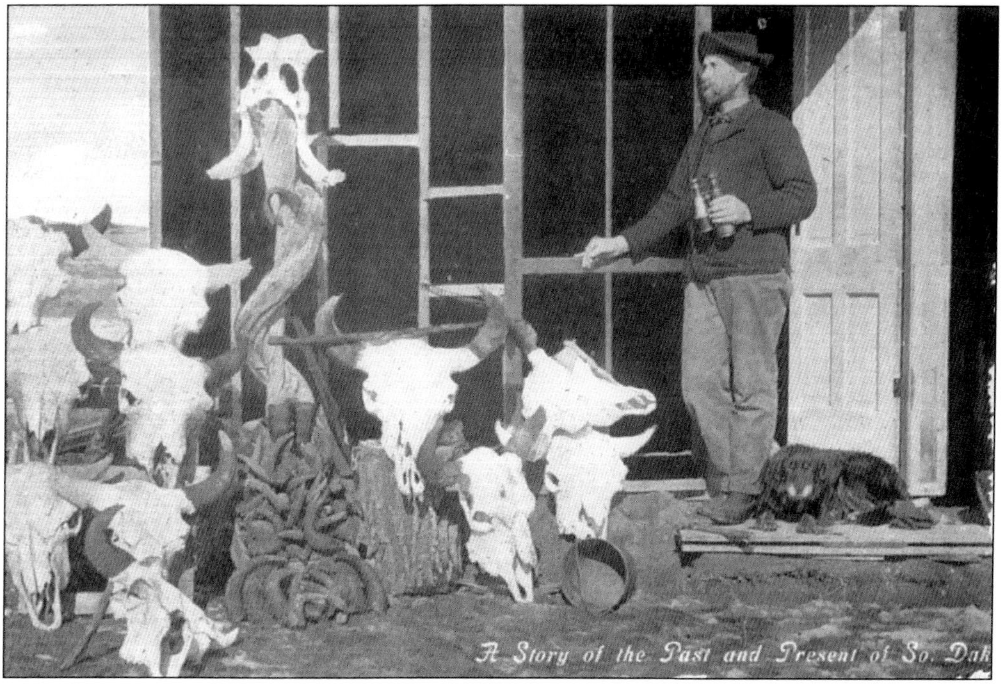

Some homesteaders survived their first few years on the plains by gathering buffalo bones and loading them onto train cars. The bones were shipped back east where they were ground into fertilizer.

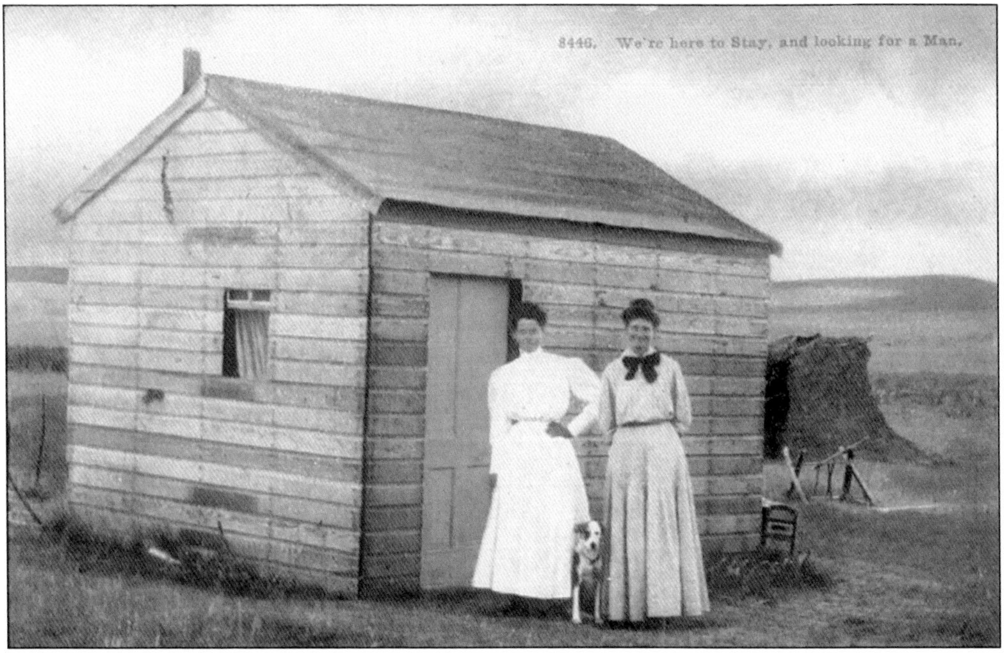

A woman writing from Dallas in 1911 expanded on the postcard caption to explain her situation: "I am not here to stay just yet but am hoping mighty hard that I shall have a chance to stay—like it fine."

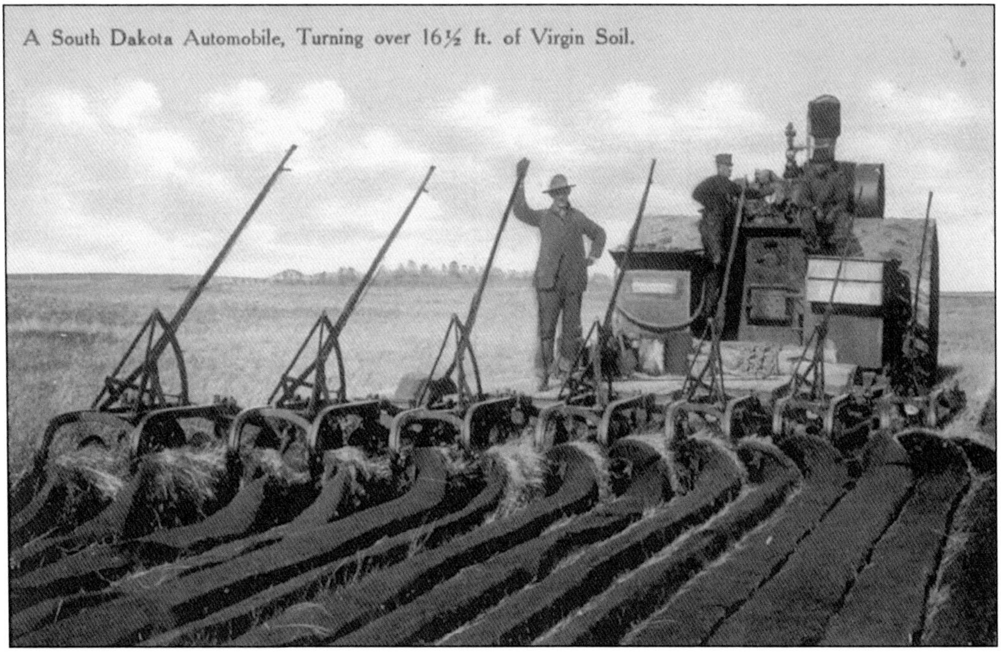

Immigrants marveled at the black fertile soil and flat fields that were easy to till, compared to the rocky, hilly farms back east. Most believed that "rain follows the plow," meaning that rainfall would literally increase as they turned the prairie into cultivated fields.

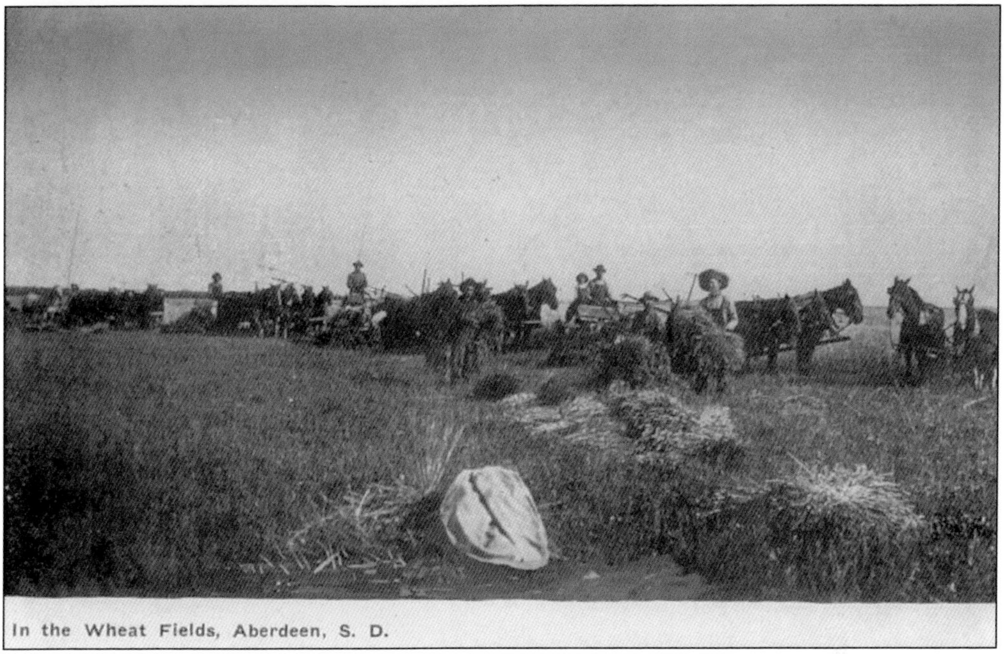

The wheat harvest needed many hands, and neighbors gathered along with itinerant workers to help bring in the crops.

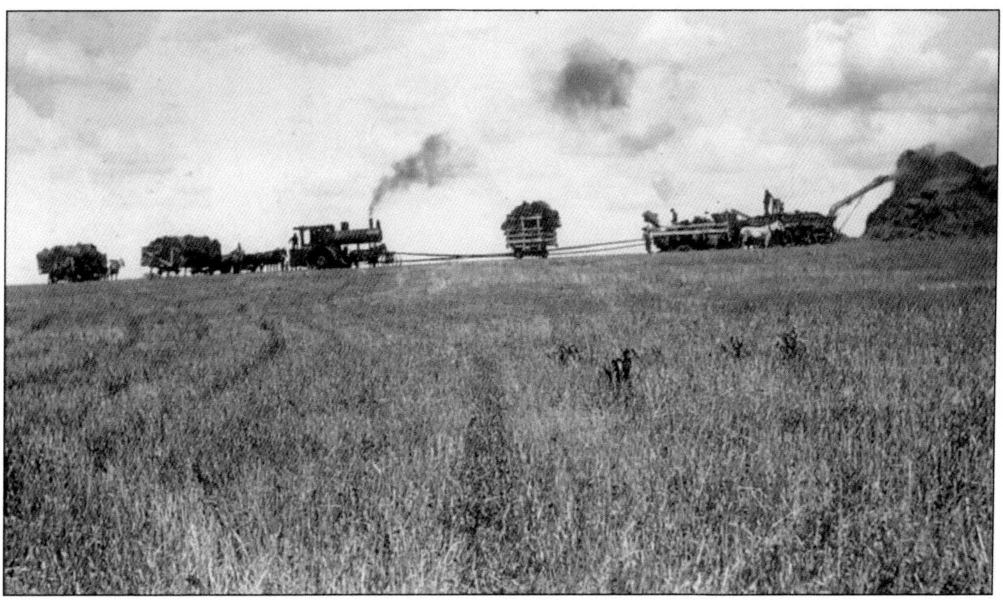

L.M. Whipple wrote from Armour to his wife in Minnesota in September 1909: "This is the rig I worked on for a few days, but you can't see me on the picture. You will hear from me at Rapid City."

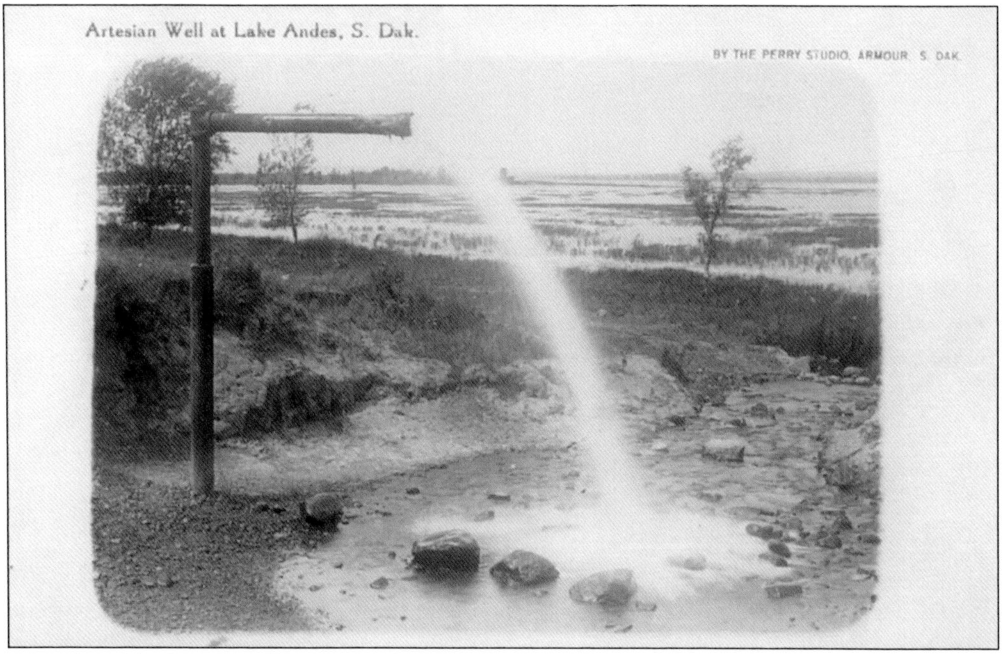

Water literally shot out of the ground when some of the first wells were dug in South Dakota. Promoters claimed that the water supply was endless and would turn the entire prairie green. As more wells were drilled, the water pressure decreased.

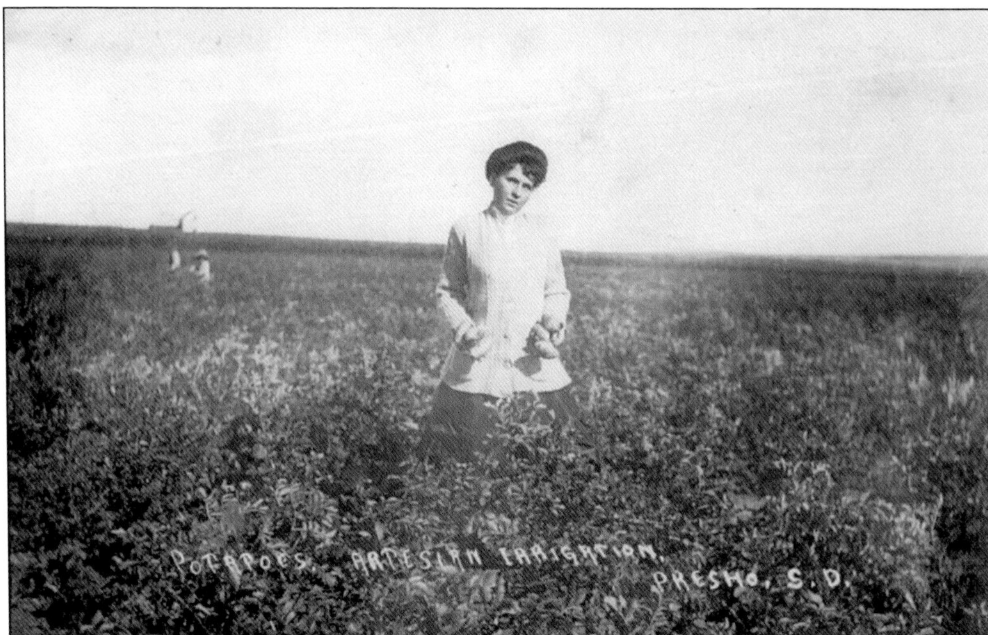

Prairie soil was fertile, when and if it was watered adequately. This potato field near Presho had an artesian well to keep it irrigated.

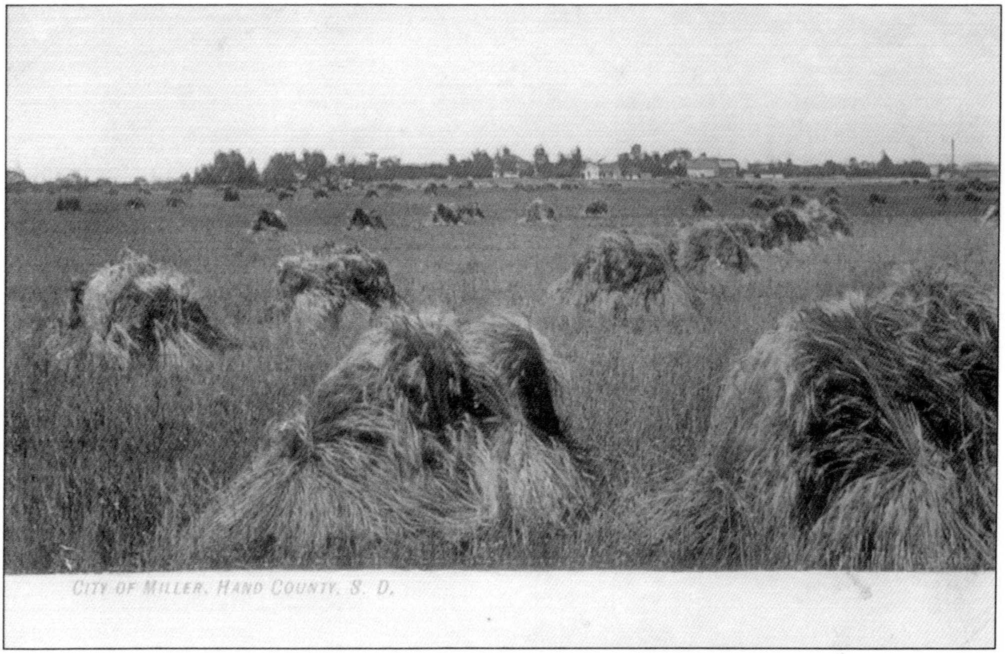

Gathered shocks of wheat with new homes and businesses of the town of Miller in the background provided visual evidence that the empty plains had been domesticated within only a few years.

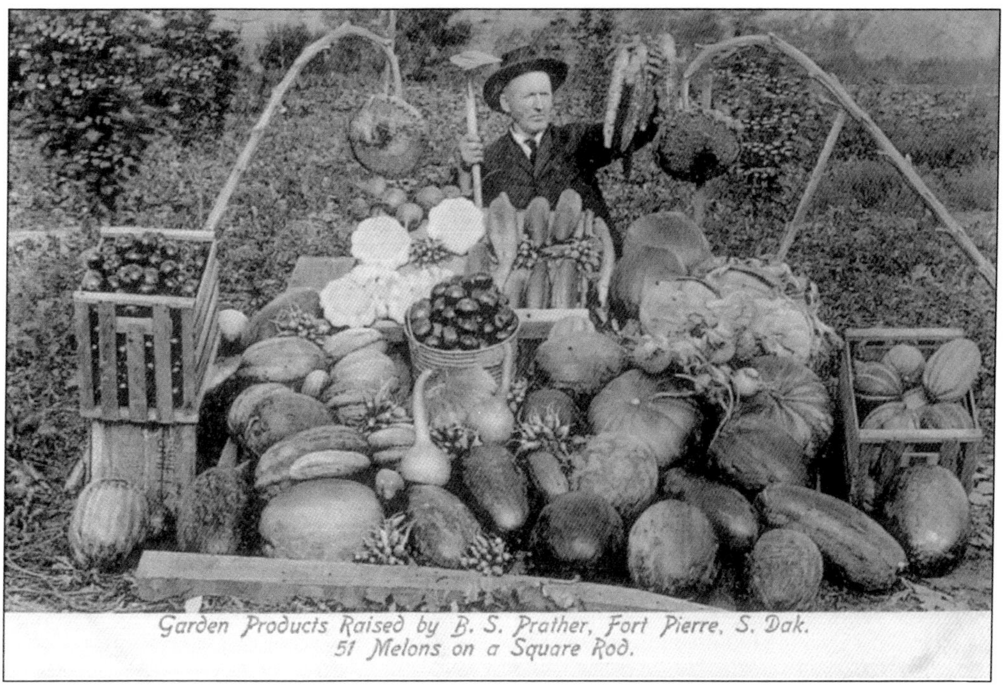

B.S. Prather of Fort Pierre was one of many South Dakotans who raised an incredible variety and quantity of vegetables and produce, and showed off how productive the land could be.

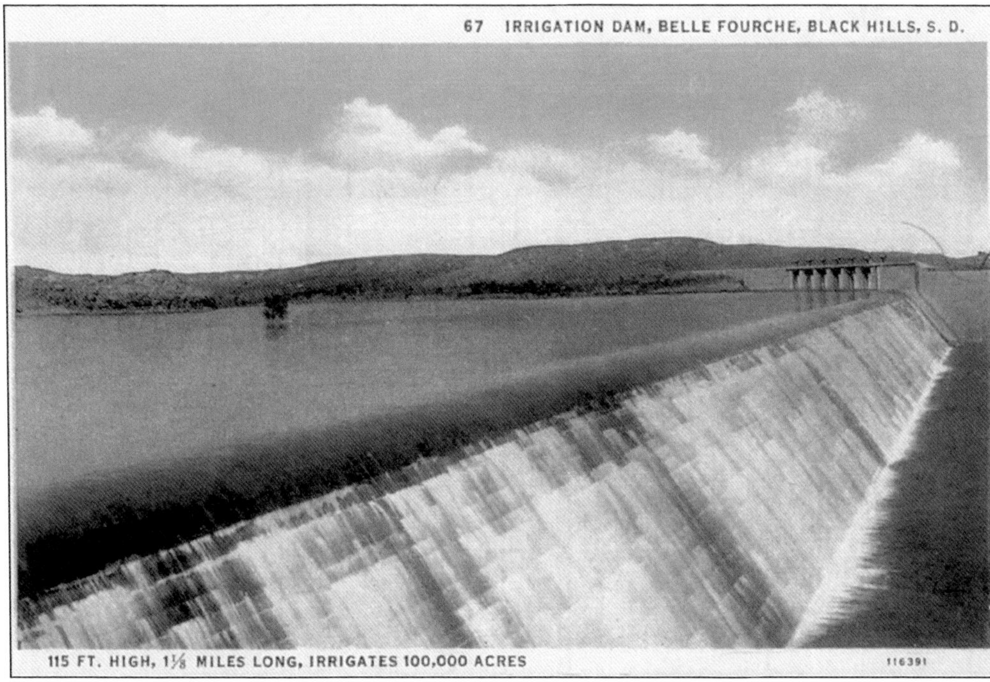

The Orman Dam, completed in 1910, brought water to a large section of western South Dakota. The sender explained the new sugar beet industry that sprang up in the area after the U & I Sugar Company processing plant arrived in Belle Fourche in 1927: "Sugar beet mill employs 300 night & day. Takes 12 to 18 hrs to turn a beet into sugar. Takes 1 lb of coal and 1/2 lb of limestone to refine 1 lb of sugar. 4500 sacks of sugar every 24 hrs."

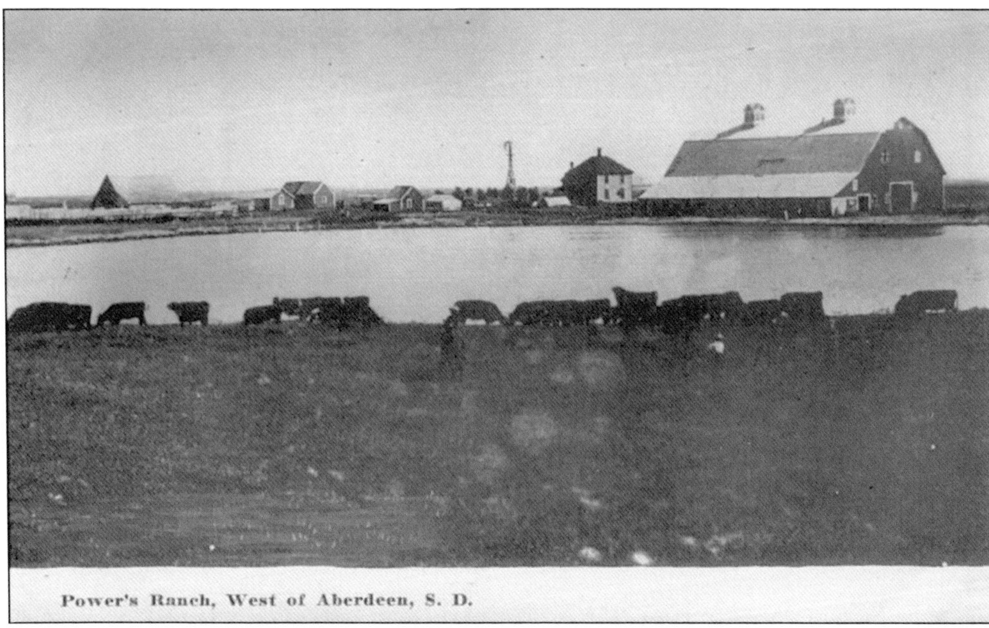

This prosperous Brown County ranch has water, cattle, numerous freshly painted buildings, and a windmill.

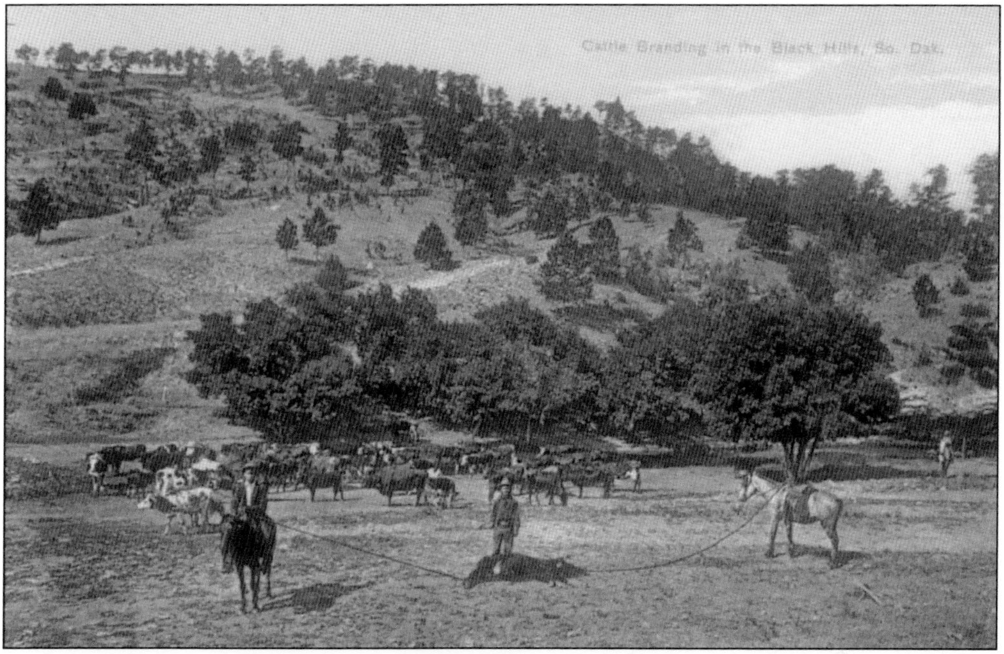

Texas cattle ranchers brought their herds north to the Dakotas and Montana searching for summer pasture. Although homesteaders eventually fenced off much of the open range, the western half of South Dakota was too dry for most crops, and cattle ranching remained a major industry.

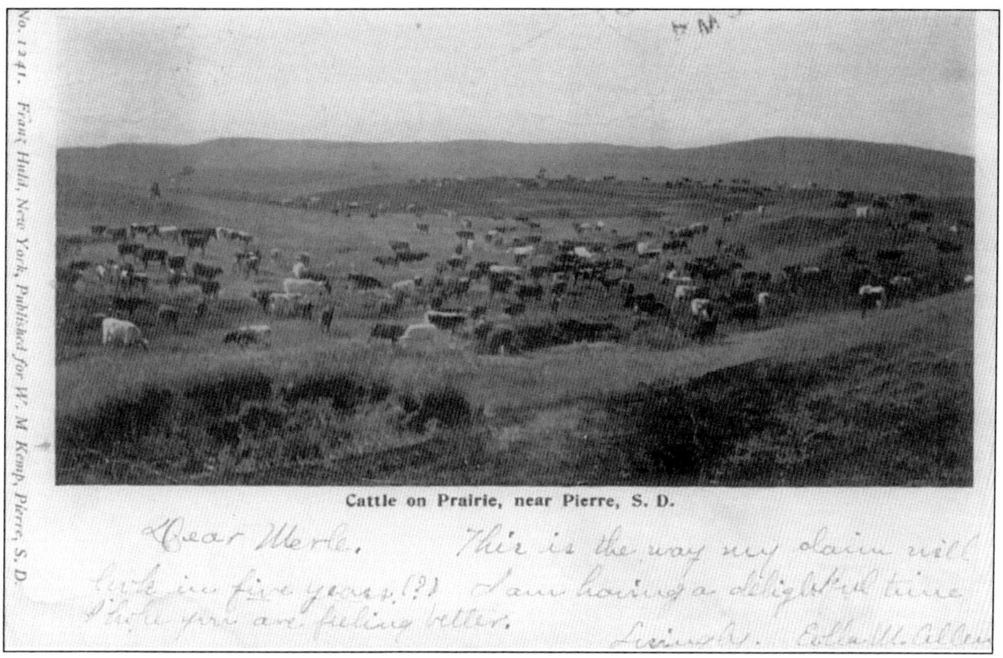

"This is the way my claim will look in five years (?)," wrote Ella M. Allen in 1905 to Merle Hubbard of Clear Lake, Iowa.

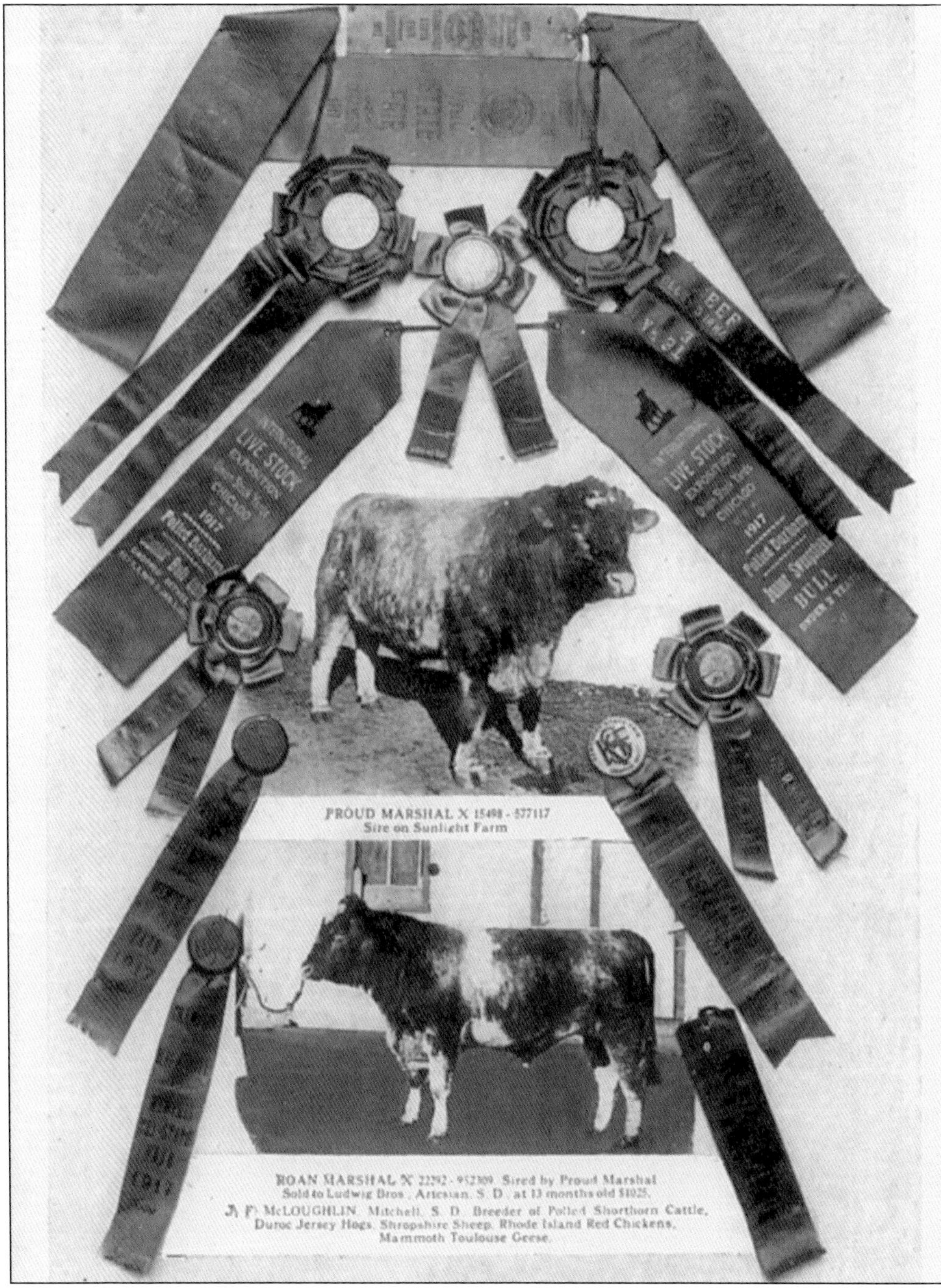

J.F. McLoughlin of Mitchell advertised himself as a "breeder of Polled Shorthorn Cattle, Duroc Jersey Hogs, Shropshire Sheep, Rhode Island Red Chickens, Mammoth Toulouse Geese." Ribbons came from state fairs in Kentucky, Ohio, and Tennessee, and from the Union Stock Yards in Chicago, all in 1917. Pictures show "Proud Marshal X 15498–577117, sire on Sunlight Farm," and "Roan Marshal X 22292–952309," sired by Proud Marshal and sold to Ludwig Brothers in Artesian at 13 months old for $1025.

Four

BUILDING TOWNS AND INSTITUTIONS

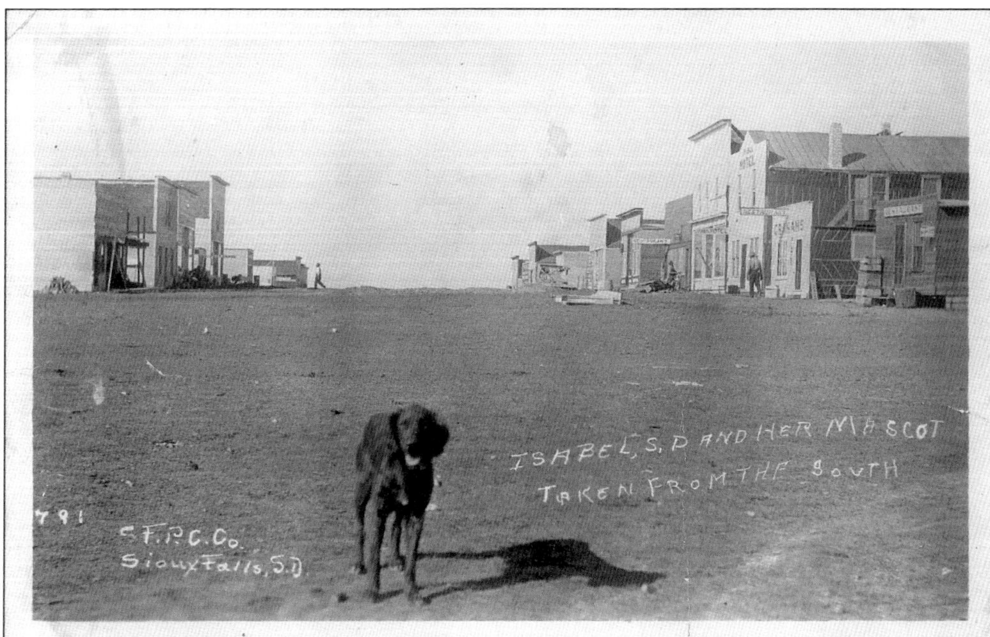

The town of Isabel was established in 1911, when the Milwaukee Road came through on its way west from the Missouri River. In addition to a good-looking mascot, this picture shows a new hotel and three restaurants.

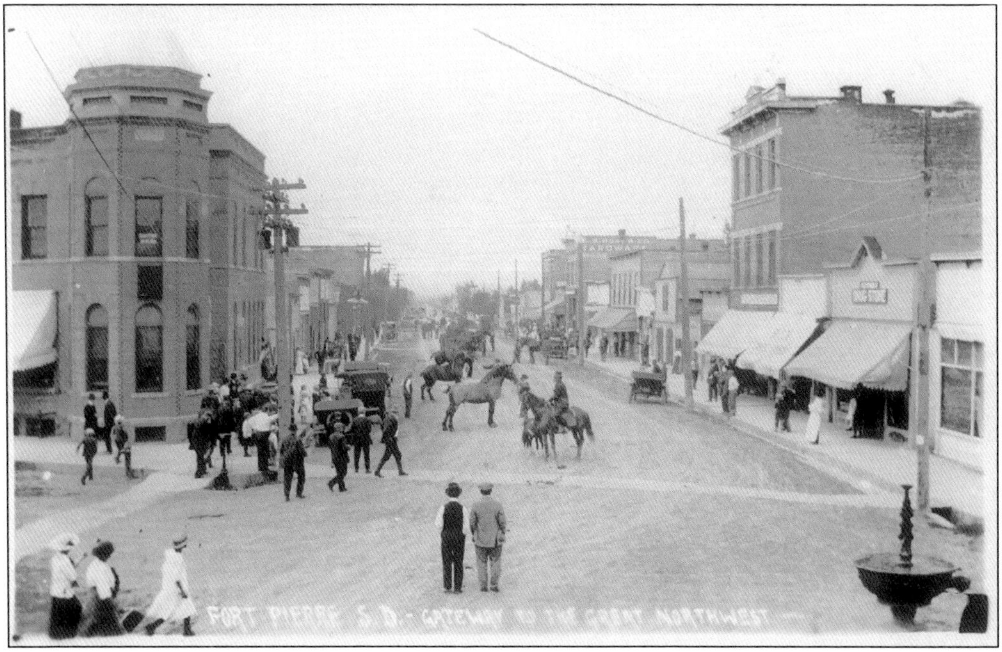

One of the oldest white settlements in South Dakota, Fort Pierre served as a trading post during the fur trading days, and after gold was discovered in the Black Hills, it connected goods arriving by steamboat and rail with the wagon trail to Deadwood. It was the largest city for hundreds of miles for many ranchers and homesteaders in western South Dakota.

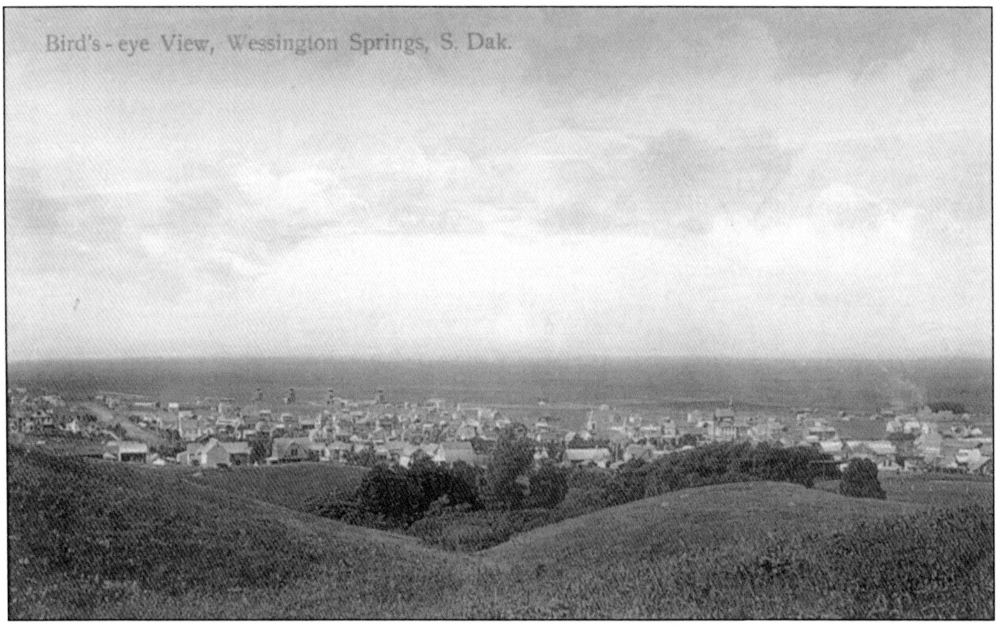

A series of natural springs along the Wessington Hills formed an early site for Indian camps, a rest stop for cattle herds moving through from Texas, and eventually a fully developed community. Unlike most towns in eastern South Dakota, Wessington Springs predated the coming of the railroad; the first white settlers arrived in the area in 1876.

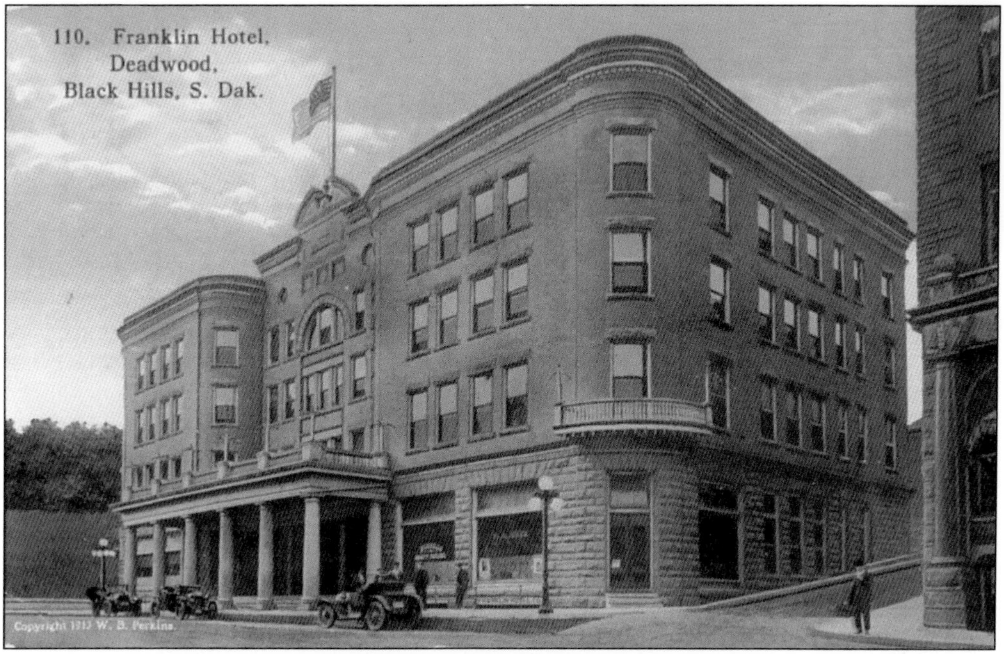

The Franklin Hotel, still a landmark in downtown Deadwood, was built in 1903 to show that Deadwood had matured and moved beyond its wild frontier days.

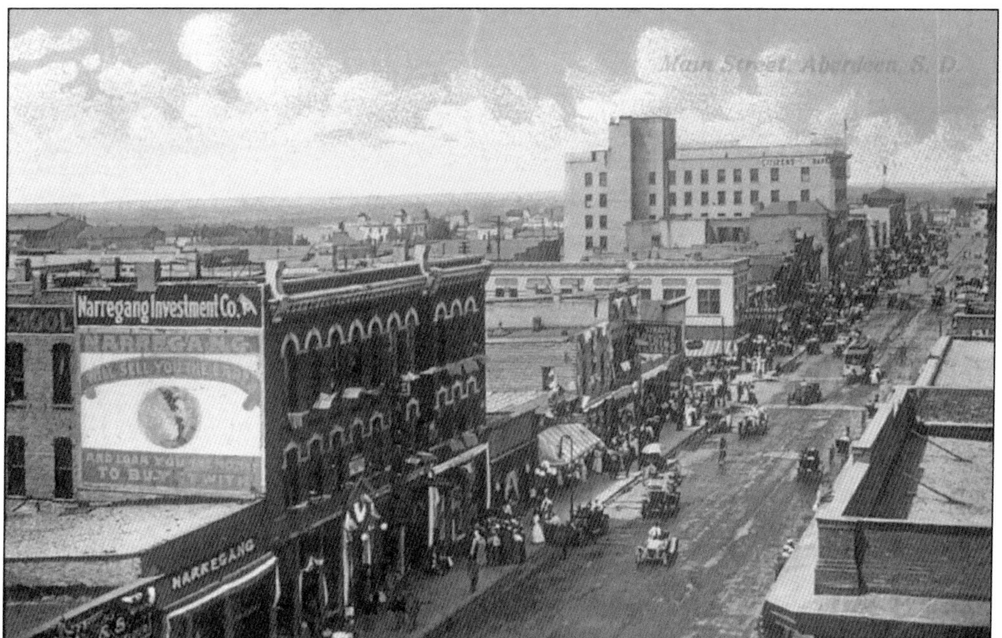

Horses and buggies share the road with automobiles and a streetcar on bustling Main Street in Aberdeen.

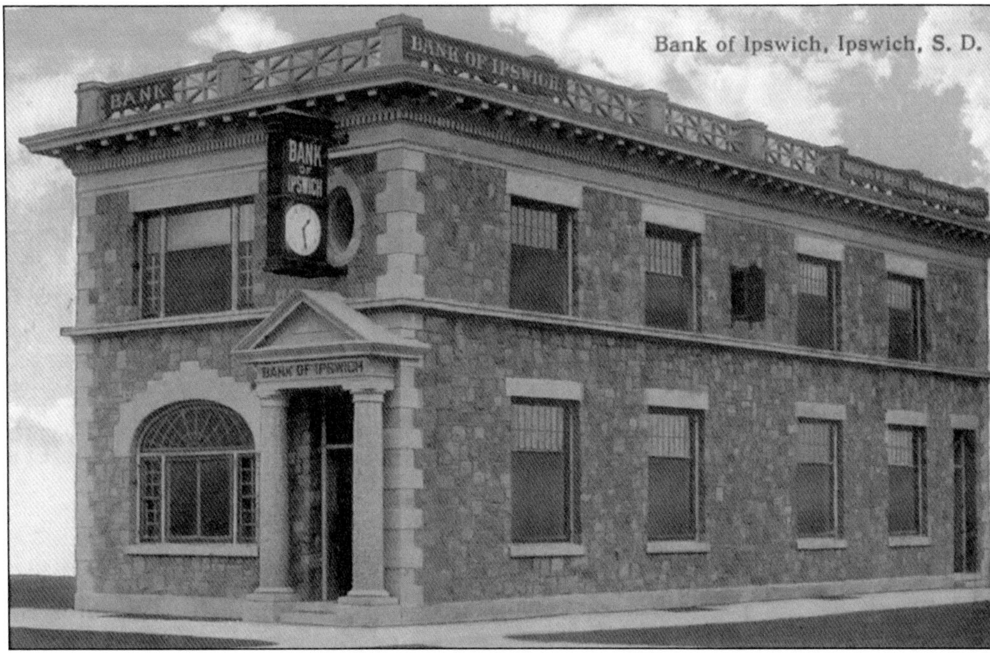

Banks needed to instill confidence in their depositors, and they often used solid traditional architecture to help make the point. The Bank of Ipswich featured Greek columns, elements from several other classical styles, and stone walls to show its stability to the community.

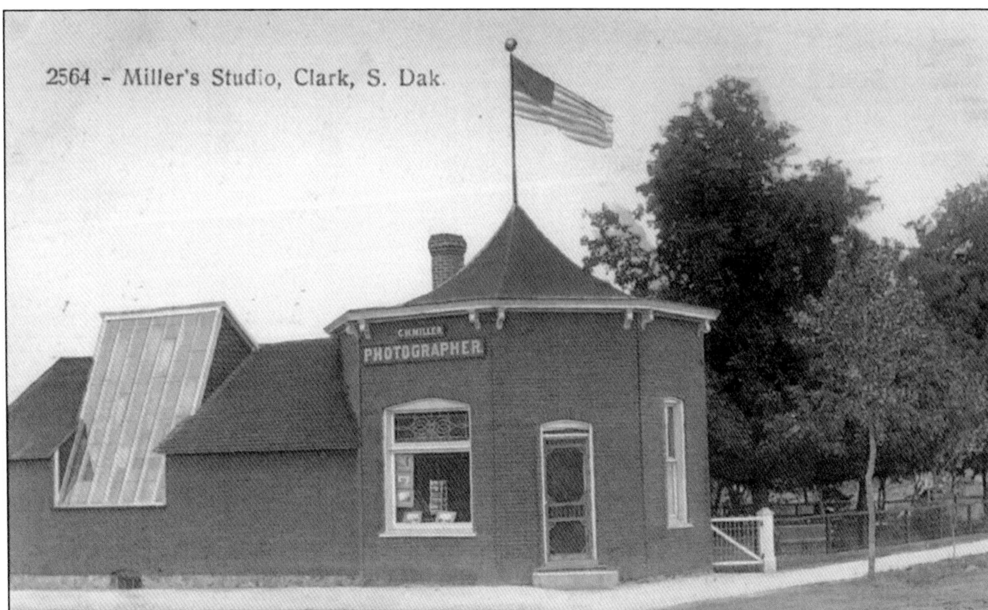

Photographers were an important part of business in early South Dakota history, and the postcards in this book would not exist without them. C.H. Miller took photos in the Clark area for more than 25 years, and his son opened a photo studio in Pierre that is still in operation. Notice the oversized skylight in the back of the studio, and the photos and postcards within view in the front window.

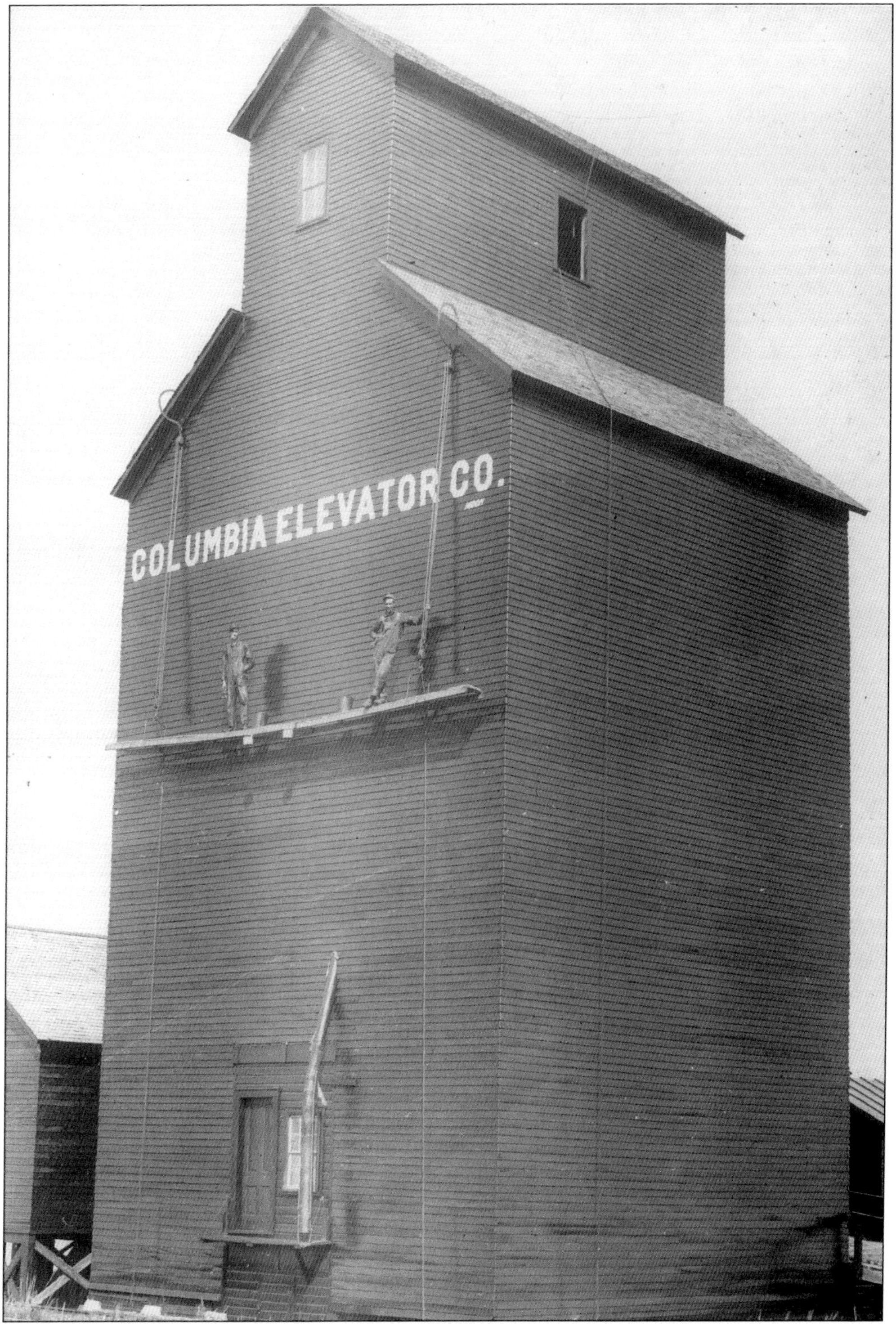

Painters show off their work on a new elevator sign in Thunder Hawk, which could probably be seen for miles around.

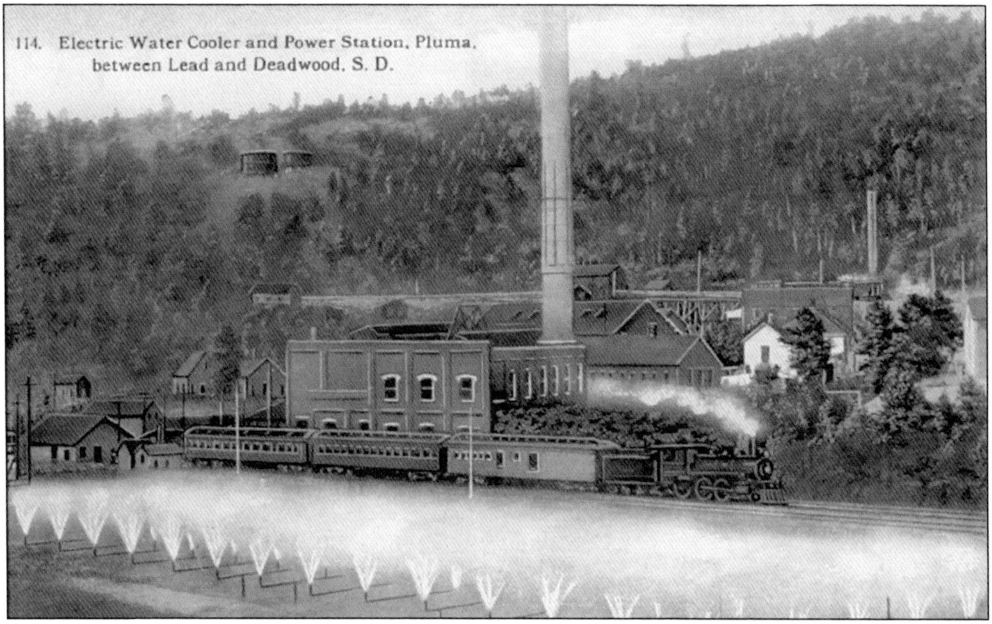

The Belt Light and Power company had an electrical generating plant in Pluma as early as 1895.

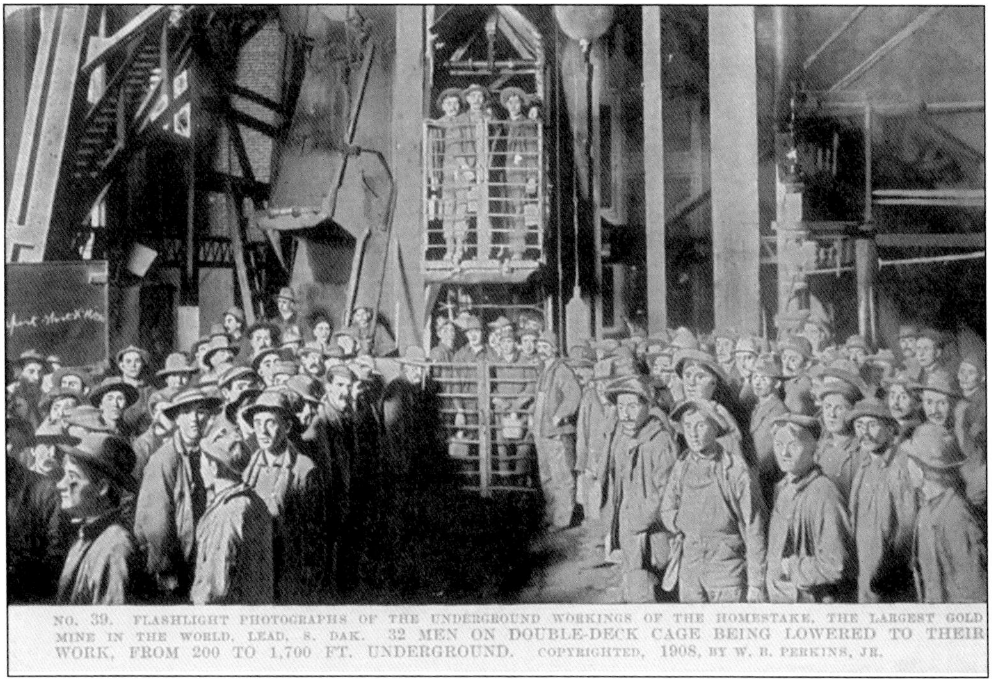

After a brief period of prospecting, gold mining in the Black Hills was taken over by corporations that brought in huge machines necessary for hard-rock mining. The original Homestake mine was sold to a group of California investors in 1877, and by 1878, an 80-stamp mill was hauled by ox team from Sydney, Nebraska, and was put into operation. Homestake became the largest gold mine in the western hemisphere, and it supported the economy of Lead as well as much of the Black Hills.

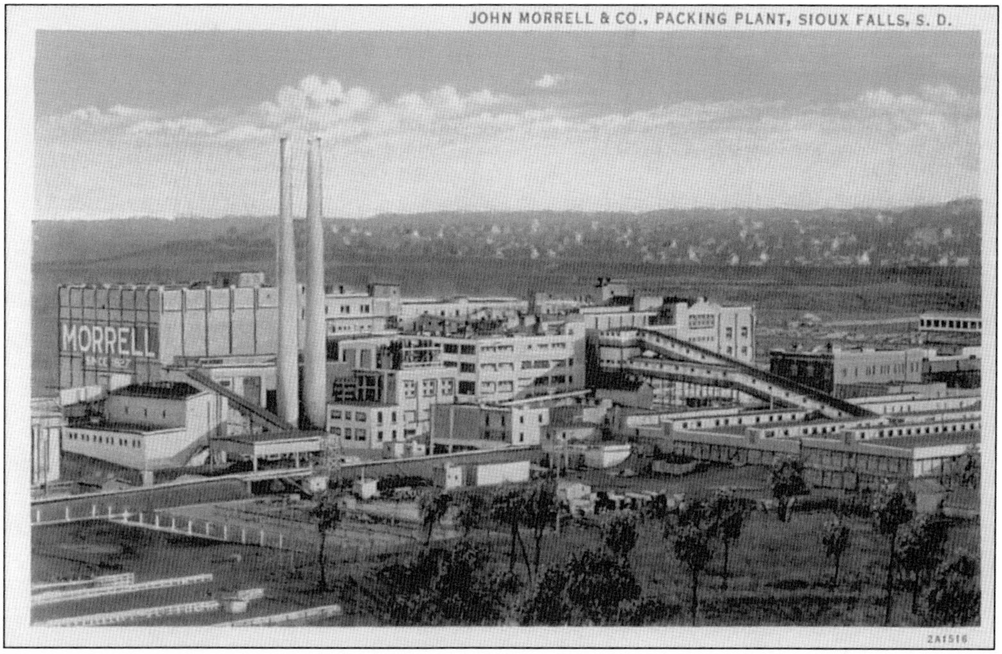

The John Morrell & Co. meatpacking plant in Sioux Falls opened in 1911, and for many years was the largest single industry located in South Dakota.

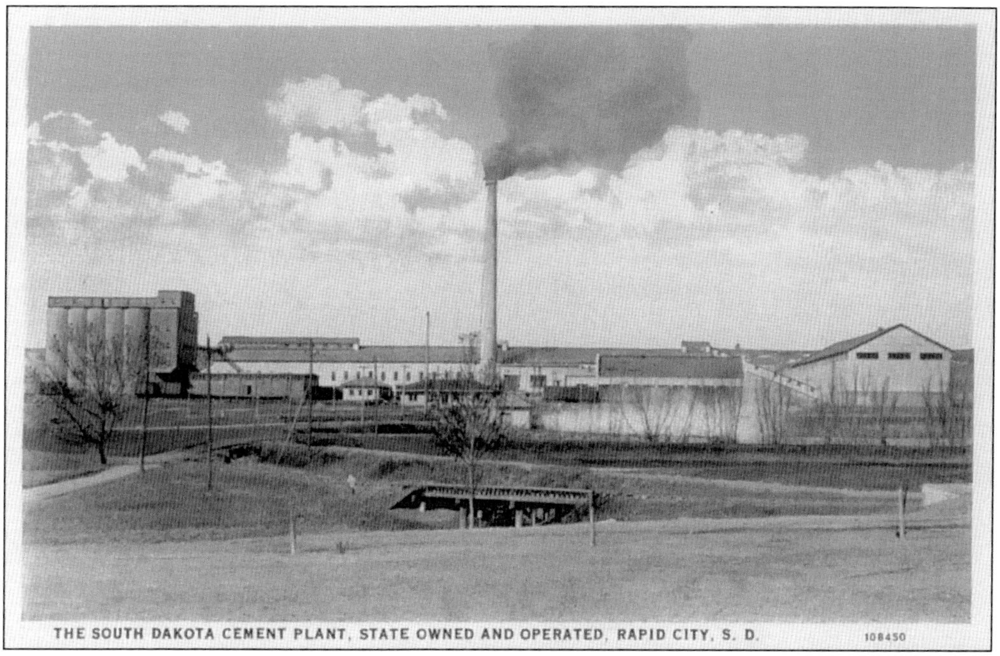

Although state-owned industries were considered to be socialist by many in the early 1900s, the Republican administration of Governor Peter Norbeck initiated plans for a state cement plant, coal mine, and hail insurance program. Production of cement at the Rapid City plant was under way by December 1924.

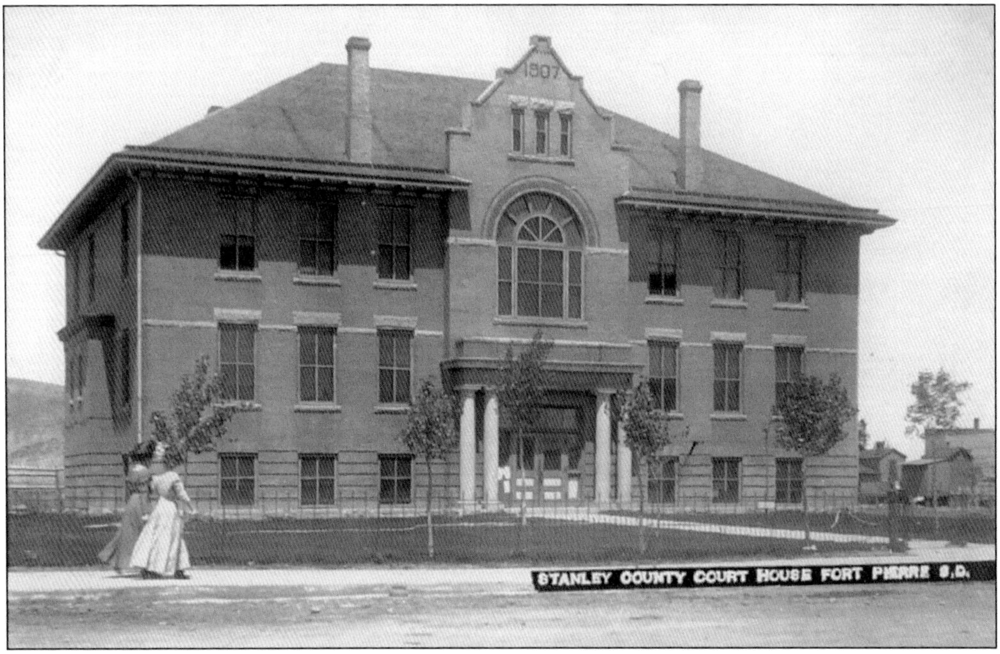

A brick courthouse was completed for Stanley County in 1907, and housed both county and city government offices. The building remained in use until it was replaced in 1971.

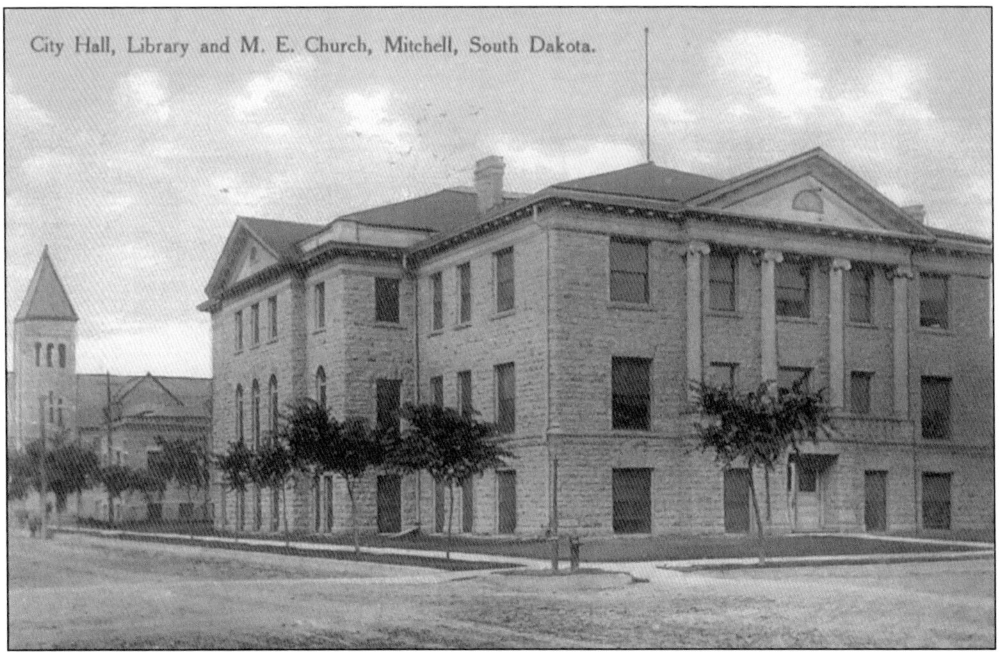

As pioneer settlements developed into towns and cities, both government and private institutions erected new buildings in brick and stone to prove their stability and permanence.

The Butte County Courthouse, completed in 1912, displays elements of "Renaissance Revival" and "Beaux Arts" styles. Even in isolated places such as Belle Fourche, public architecture could reflect the more sophisticated styles of larger cities, but on a smaller scale. The building was added to the National Register of Historic Places in 1998.

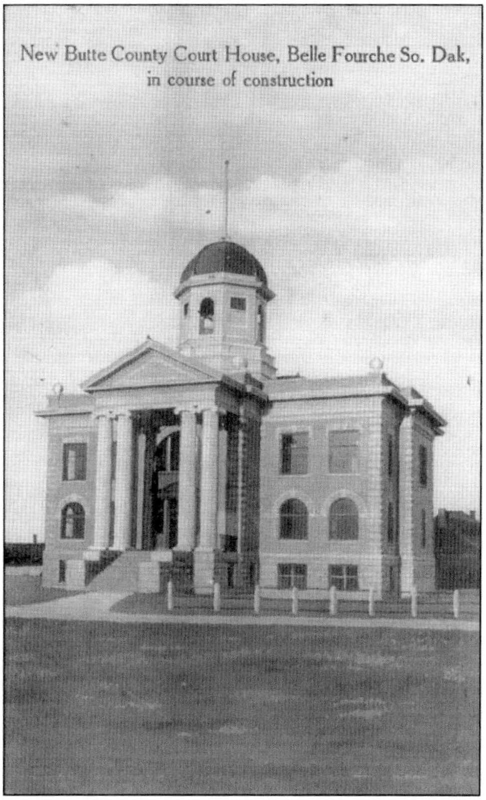

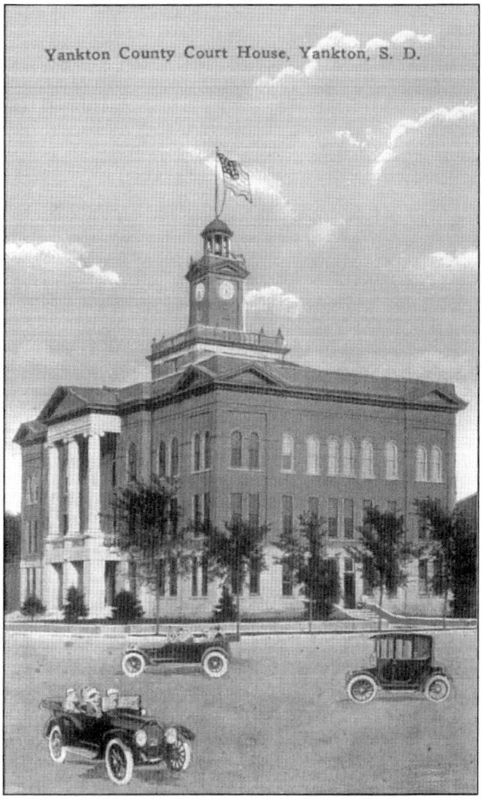

The elegant touring cars pasted into this photograph are not the correct scale, and they make the Yankton County Courthouse appear much larger than it really is.

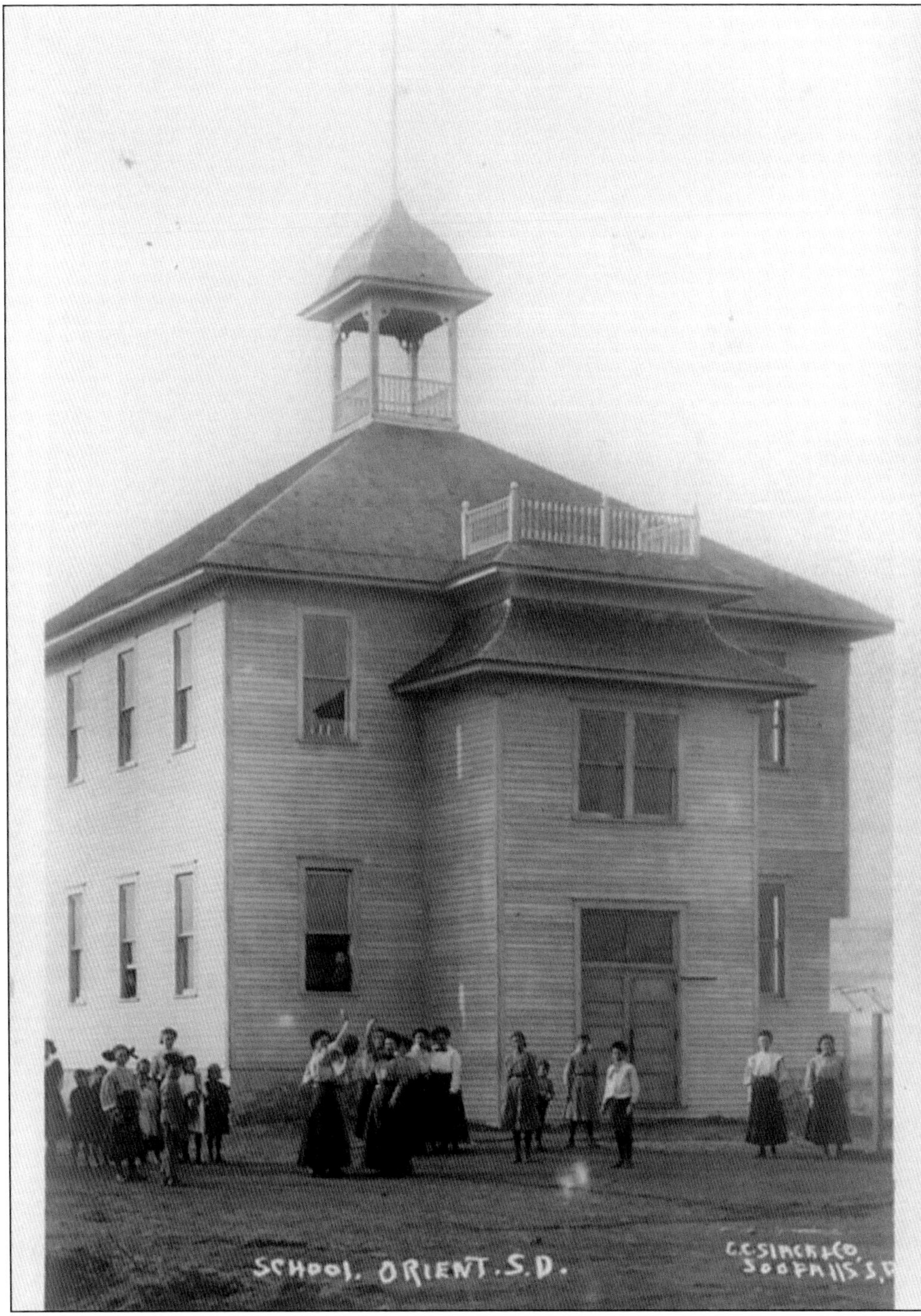

The town of Orient started with a one-room school in 1888, and 20 years later was ready to move into this four-room building, with two classrooms on each floor, plus a full basement. The school offered a full 12-year course from 1912 to 1958, but in 1960, it scaled back to grades 1–4. Orient still had one teacher in 1974, until the school finally closed in 1976.

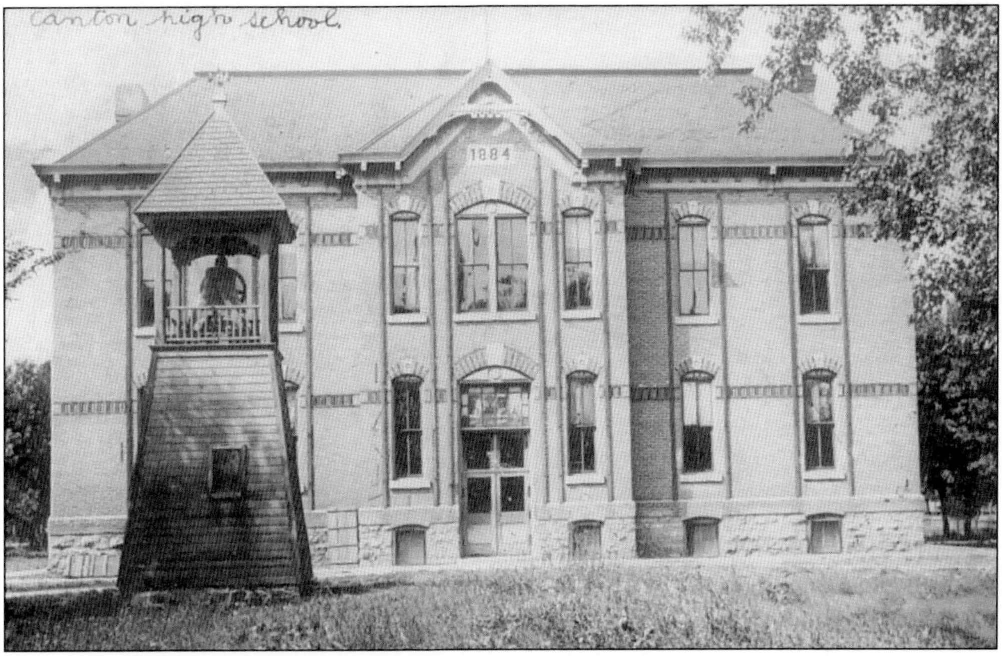

This Canton school replaced a two-room frame building built in 1878, but faced many structural problems as its foundation sank into an old creek bed. The building remained in use until a new high school was built in 1922.

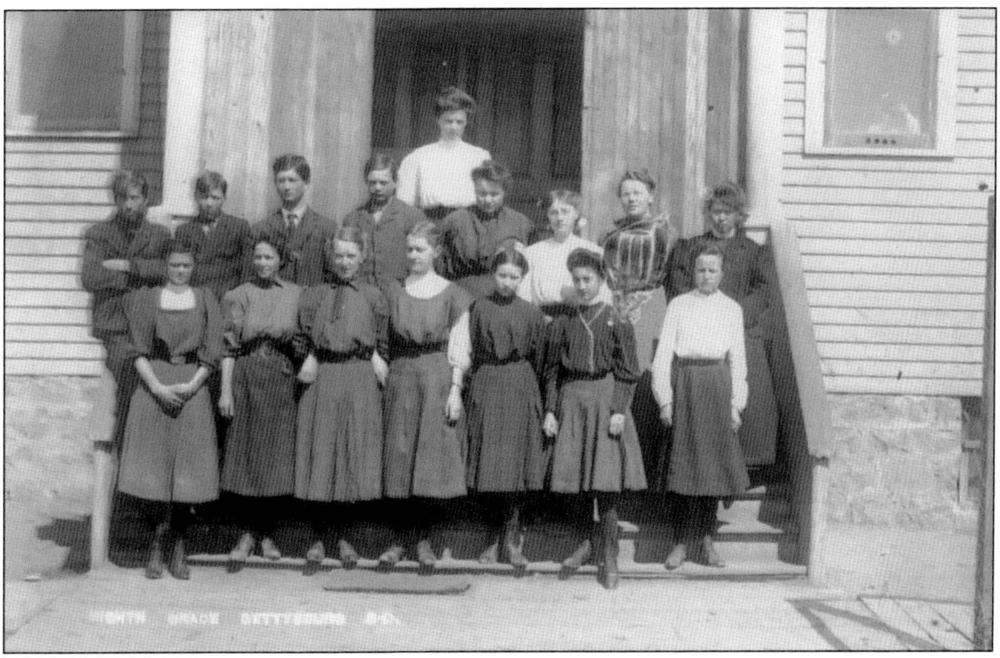

Gettysburg's one-room schoolhouse was replaced in 1893 with a two-story frame structure. It burned shortly after it was completed, but townspeople rebuilt it and used it until 1923.

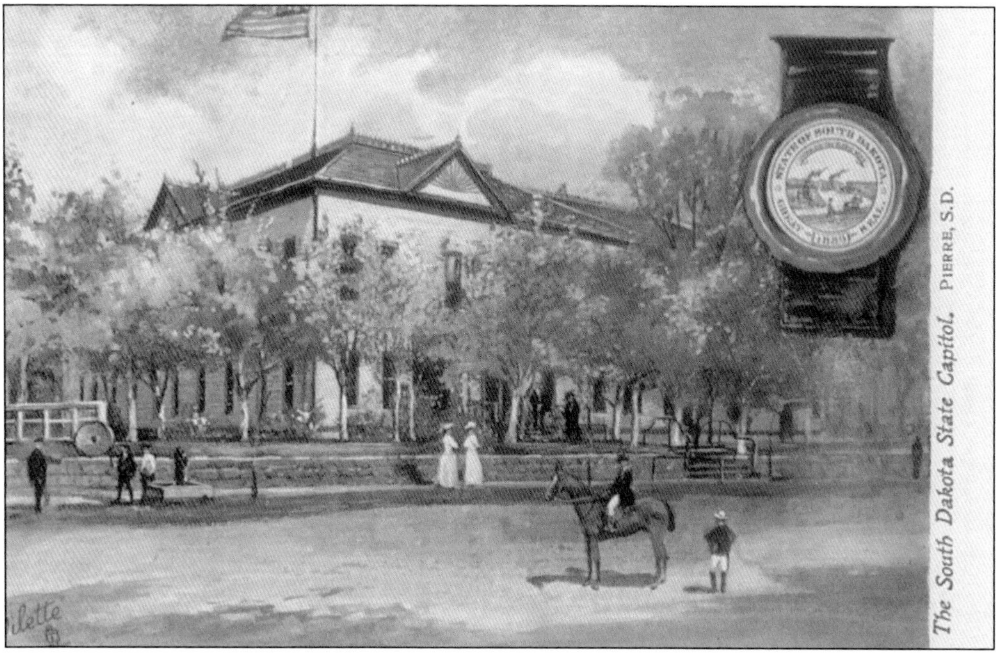

Raphael Tuck & Sons, the premier postcard publisher in England, included this artistic rendering of South Dakota's original wooden capitol building in its "Oilette" state capitol series. This building was used from 1890 to 1910, when the structure now in use was completed.

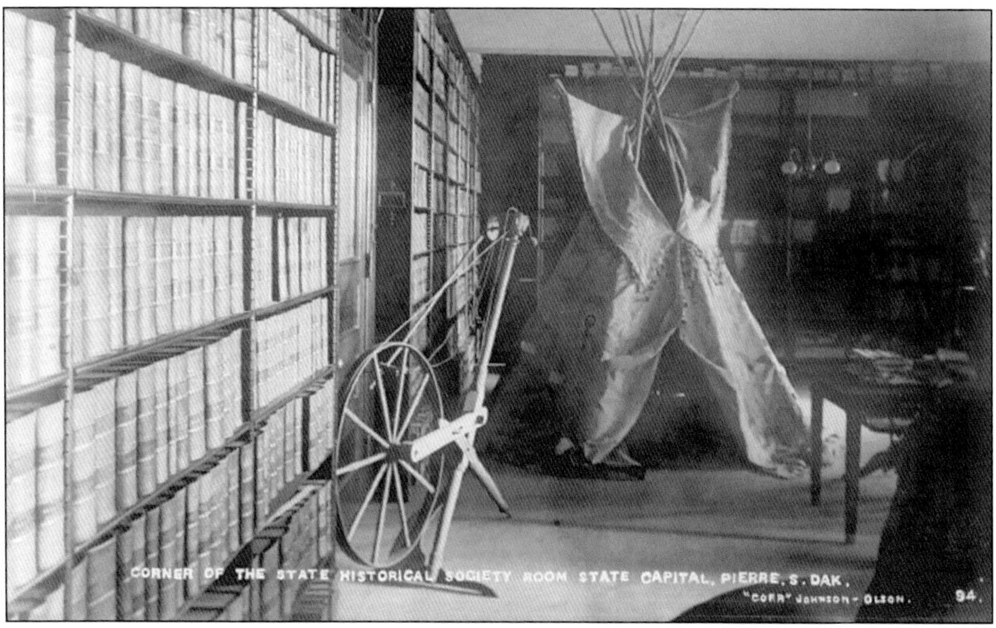

In 1901, the state legislature established the Department of History and provided a room in the capitol building for research collections and exhibits. The first state historian, Doane Robinson, not only compiled and wrote the state's history, but he also created much of it, being directly involved in many projects including Mount Rushmore and the Missouri River dams.

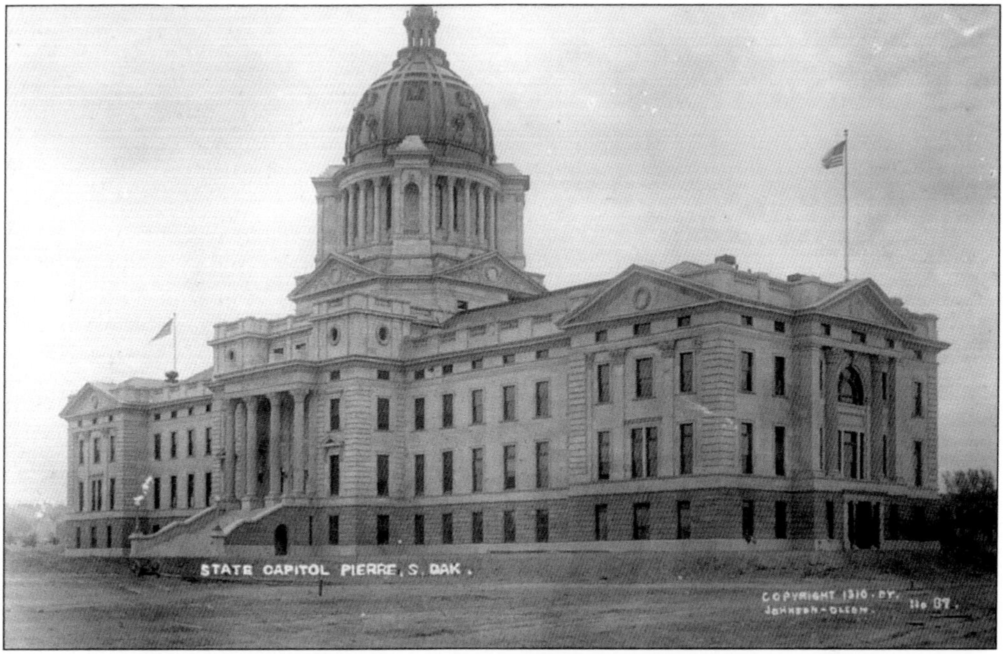

Pierre faced four separate elections to decide which city would become capital of South Dakota. The issue was finally put to rest when a permanent stone building was completed in 1910. South Dakota's capitol was modeled on the new building in Helena, Montana, and was designed by the same architect.

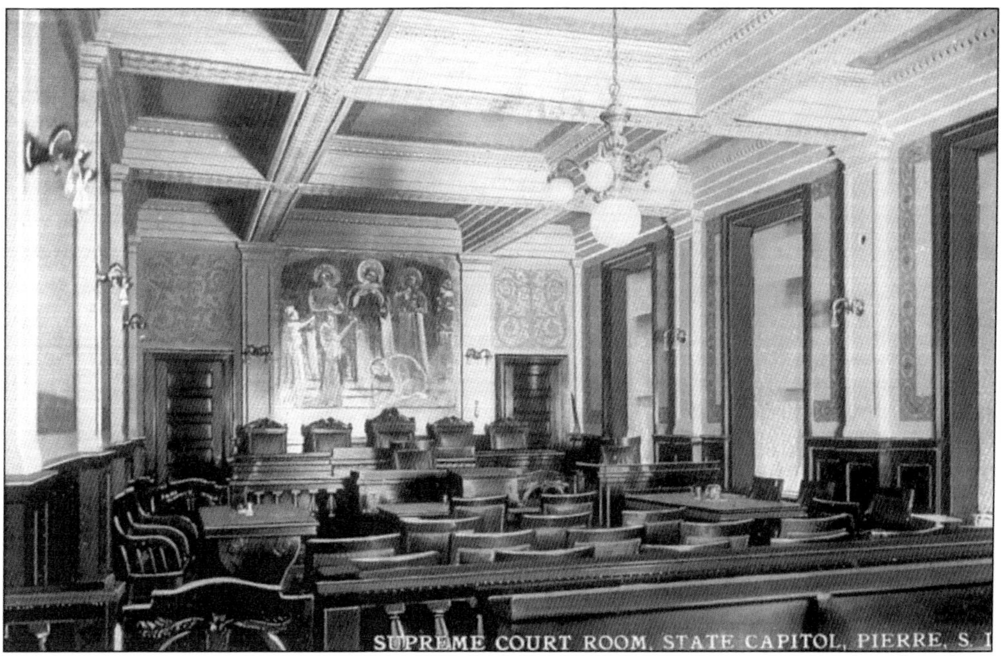

Nine wall-sized murals graced the new capitol in Pierre, including "The Gate of Justice," painted by Charles Holloway, then a rising young artist from Chicago.

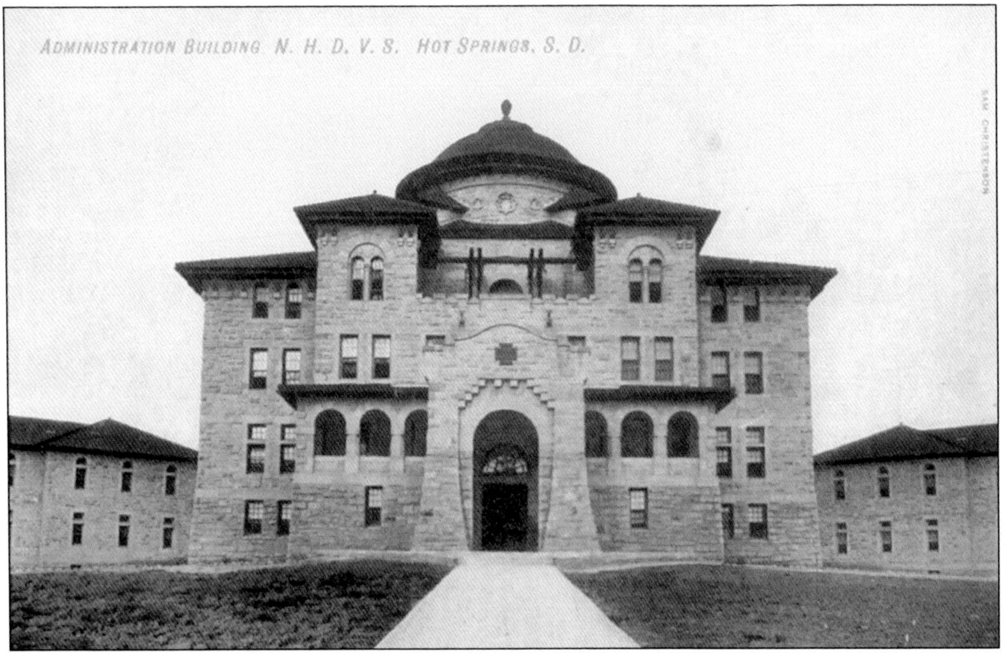

The National Home for Disabled Volunteer Soldiers located a branch in Hot Springs in 1907, to take advantage of "hot mineral waters and climatic conditions," and served veterans with illnesses including tuberculosis, rheumatism, neuritis, nephritis, and various skin conditions.

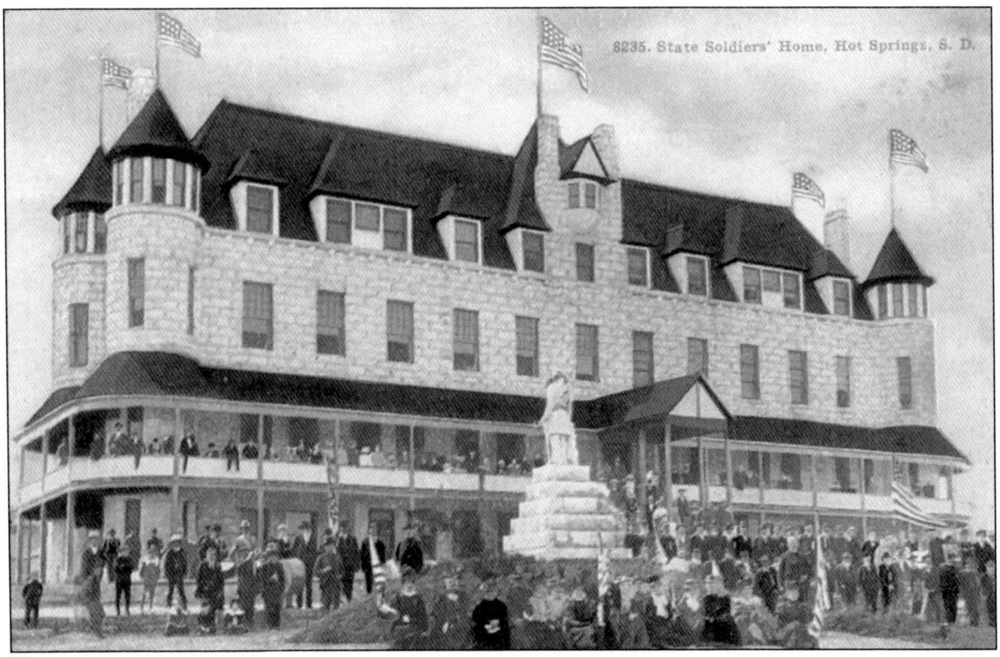

In its last session in 1889, the Dakota territorial legislature funded a home for veterans to be located in Hot Springs. The original building still houses administrative offices and recreational facilities.

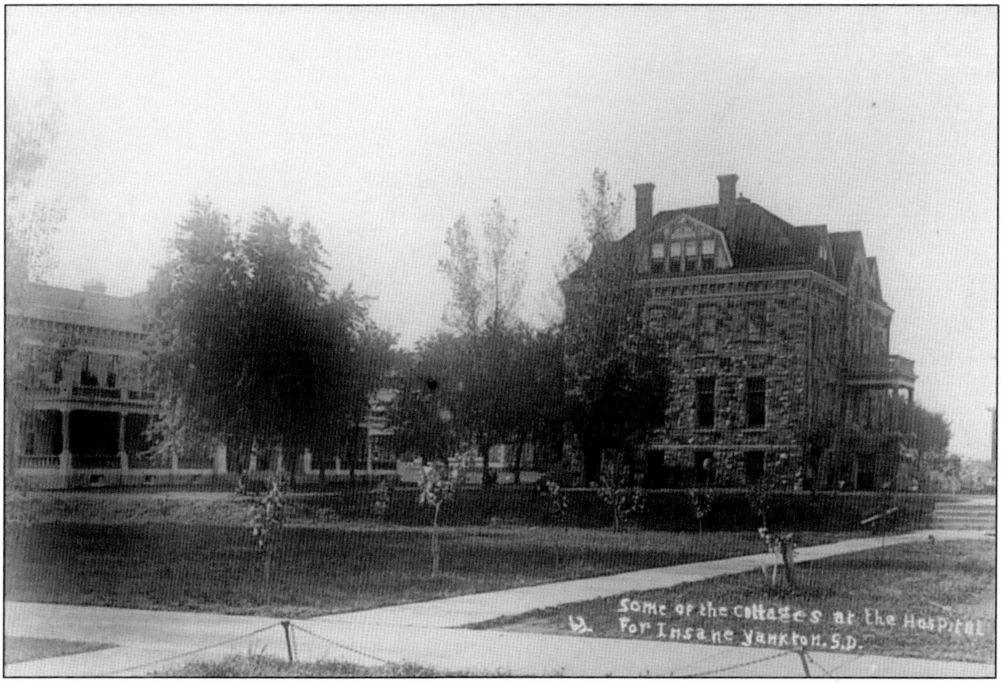

A territorial hospital for the insane opened in Yankton in 1879, after the State of Minnesota declared that it could no longer accommodate patients from Dakota. A hospital for the physically ill was not available in Yankton until 1895.

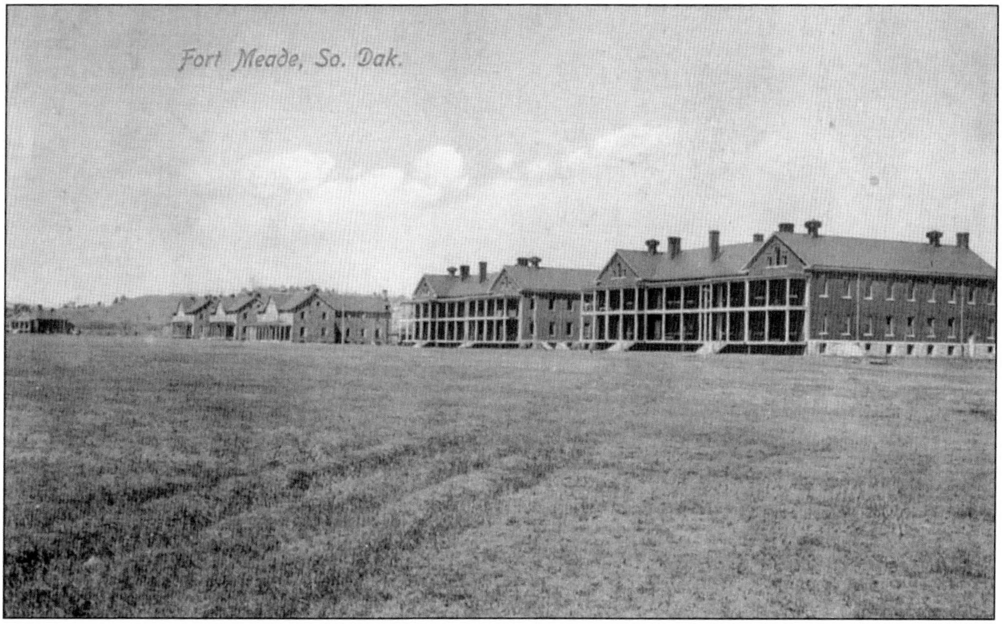

Fort Meade was established in 1878 to provide protection for the new gold camps in the nearby Black Hills. Named in honor of General George G. Meade, commander of the Army of the Potomac at the Battle of Gettysburg, Fort Meade served as the regimental headquarters of the 7th Cavalry from 1879 to 1888.

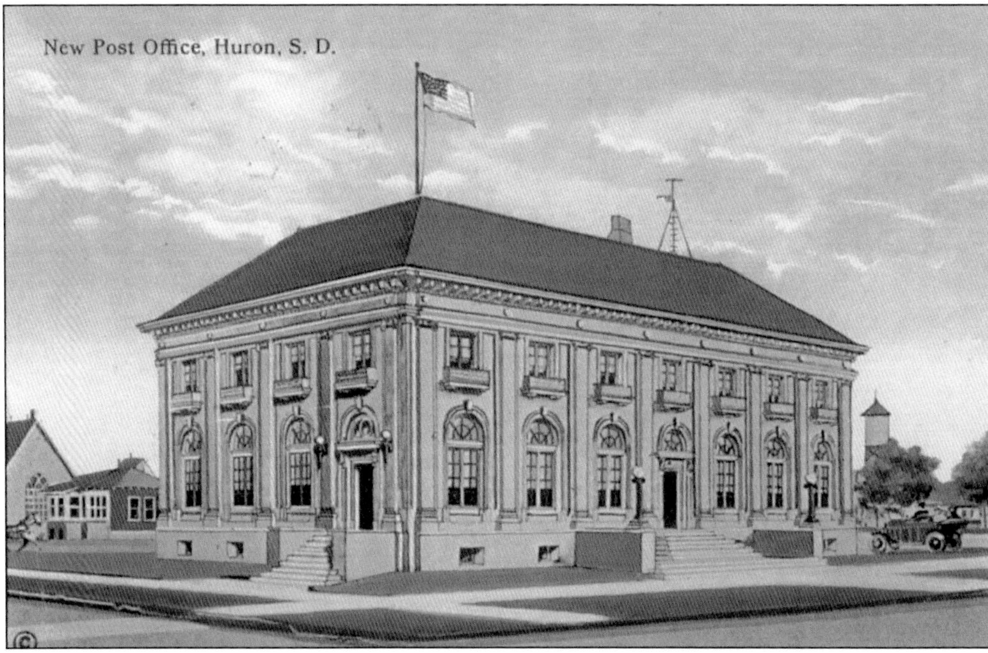

A stately new post office was completed at Fourth and Dakota in Huron in 1914 to meet the demands of growing business and population.

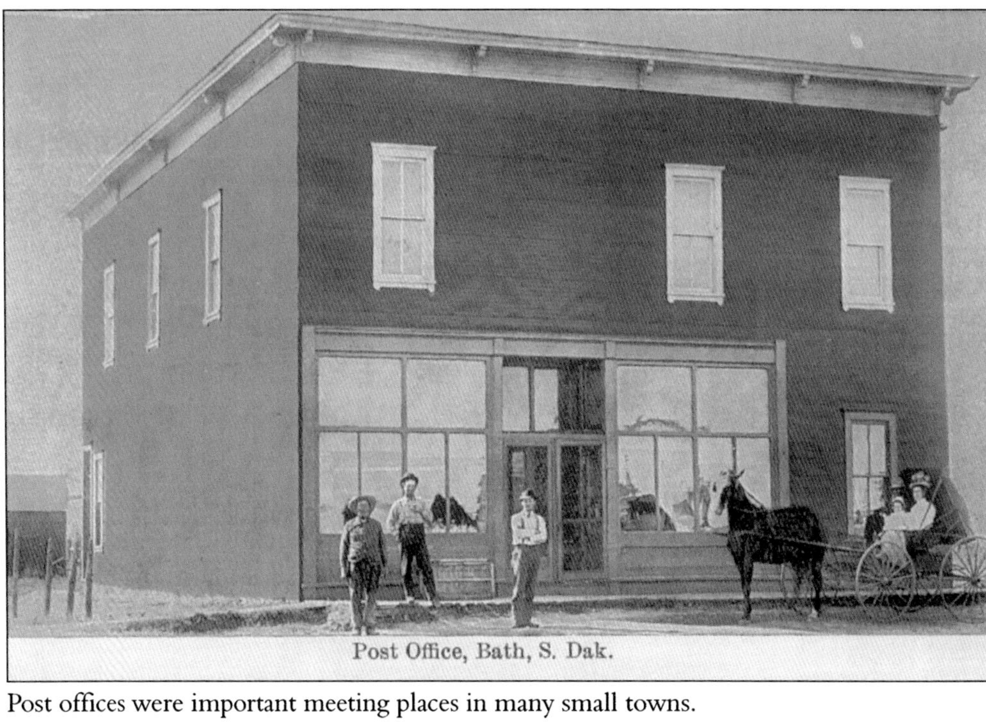

Post offices were important meeting places in many small towns.

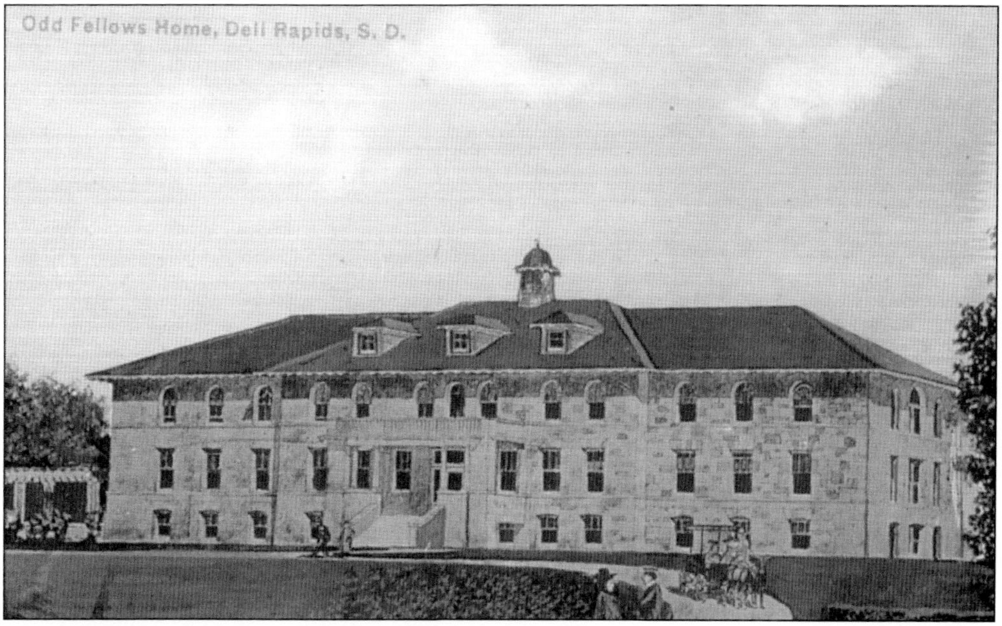

The International Order of Odd Fellows was the first "secret society" to organize in Dell Rapids, holding its first meeting there in 1876. In 1910, the Odd Fellows chose Dell Rapids as the site for a home for aged men and women.

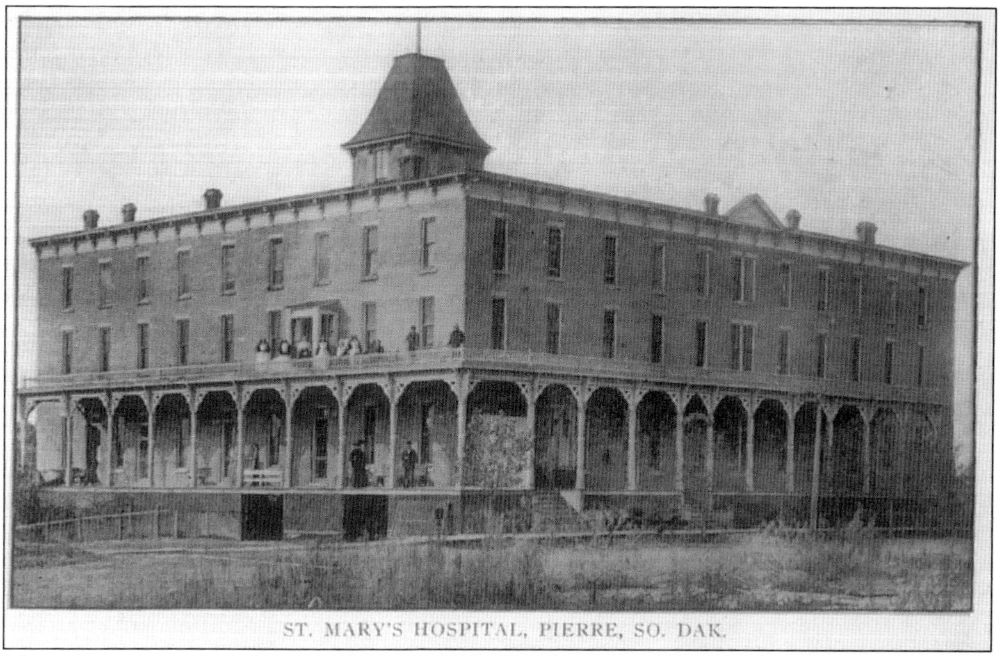

The 102-room Park Hotel drained the pockets of several owners before it closed. It sat empty on the Pierre riverfront for several years, until a group of Benedictine sisters looking for a hospital site realized that it was a ready-made facility. St. Mary's Hospital opened in the hotel building in 1899, and continued to operate here until 1952, when it was torn down to make room for Maryhouse, a home for the elderly.

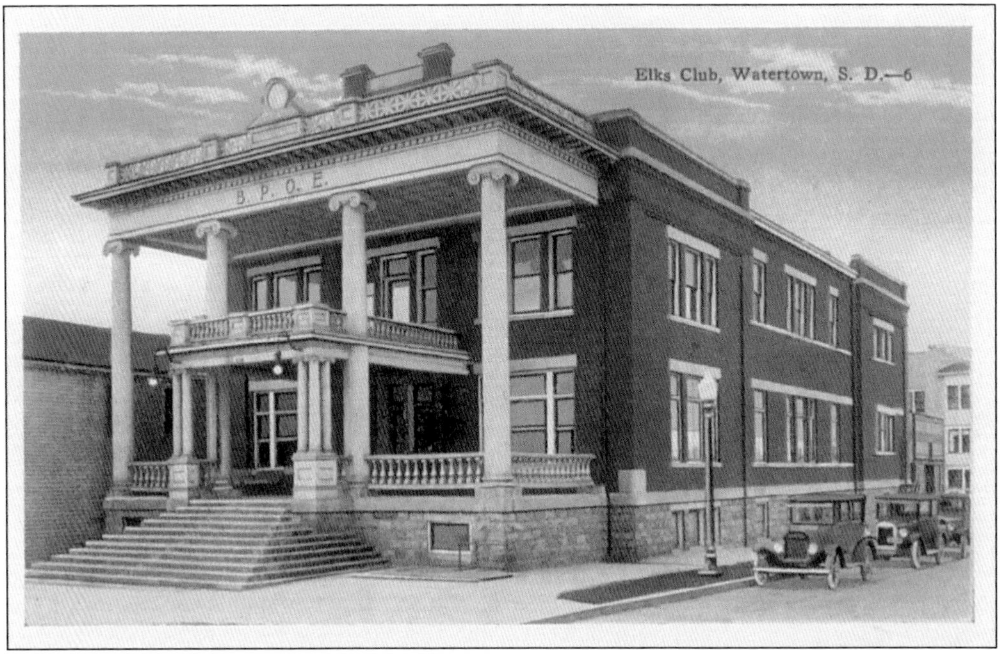

Many private organizations built solid buildings, both to serve their members and to show their stature and stability in the community.

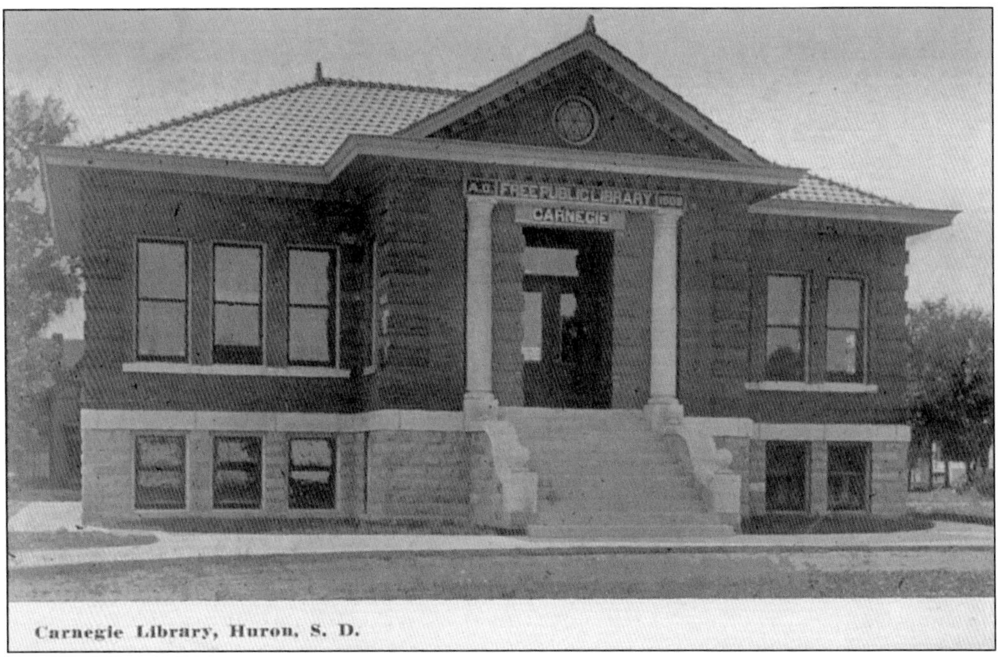

After making millions in the steel industry, Andrew Carnegie gave back some of his wealth by constructing 2,519 public libraries in the United States and other English-speaking countries. Twenty-five Carnegie libraries were built in South Dakota between 1901 and 1917, costing $254,000. Eighteen of the buildings were still in use in 1996, including seven still being used as libraries. The Carnegie library in Huron was replaced by a new structure on the same site in 1966.

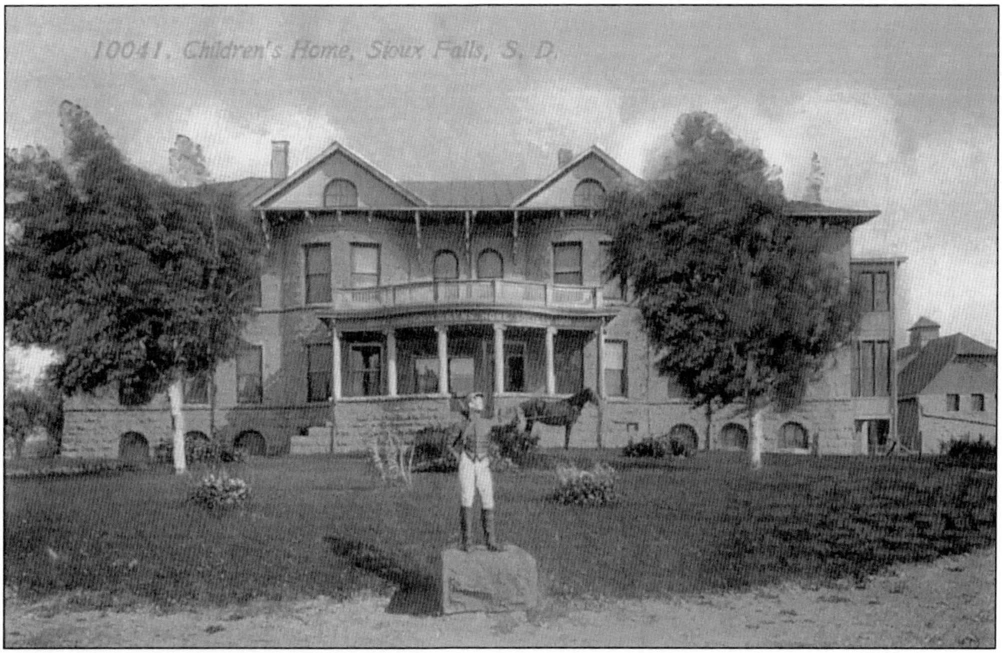

The Children's Home Society opened a new 33-room orphanage in Sioux Falls in 1902, constructed with stone provided by convict labor at the state penitentiary.

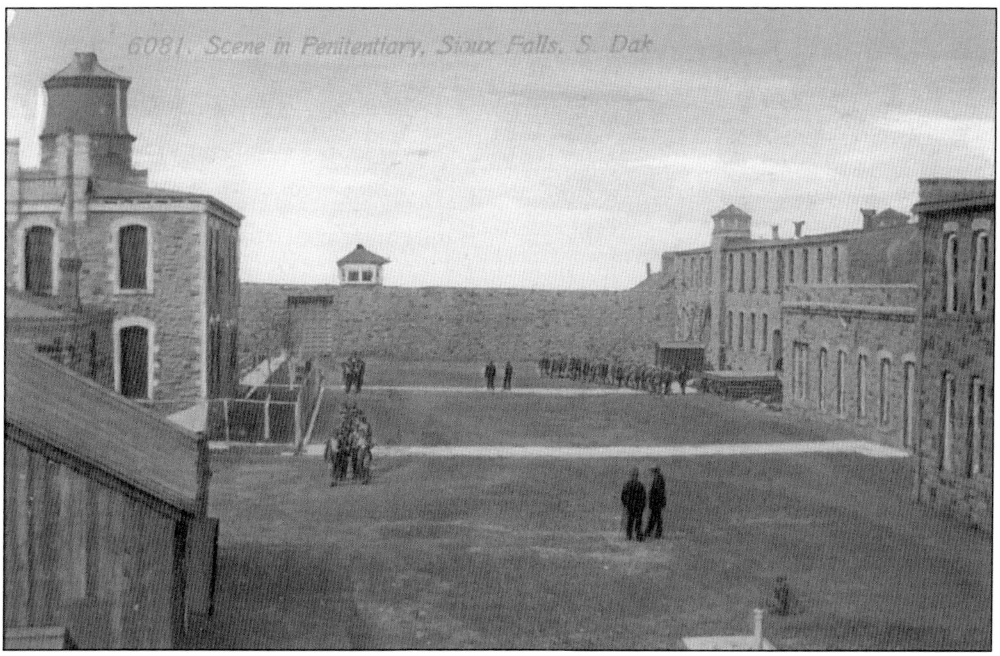

A territorial penitentiary was built in Sioux Falls in 1881. Although the facility has seen many changes over the years, the original structure is still used and remains a distinctive landmark on a bluff above the Big Sioux River.

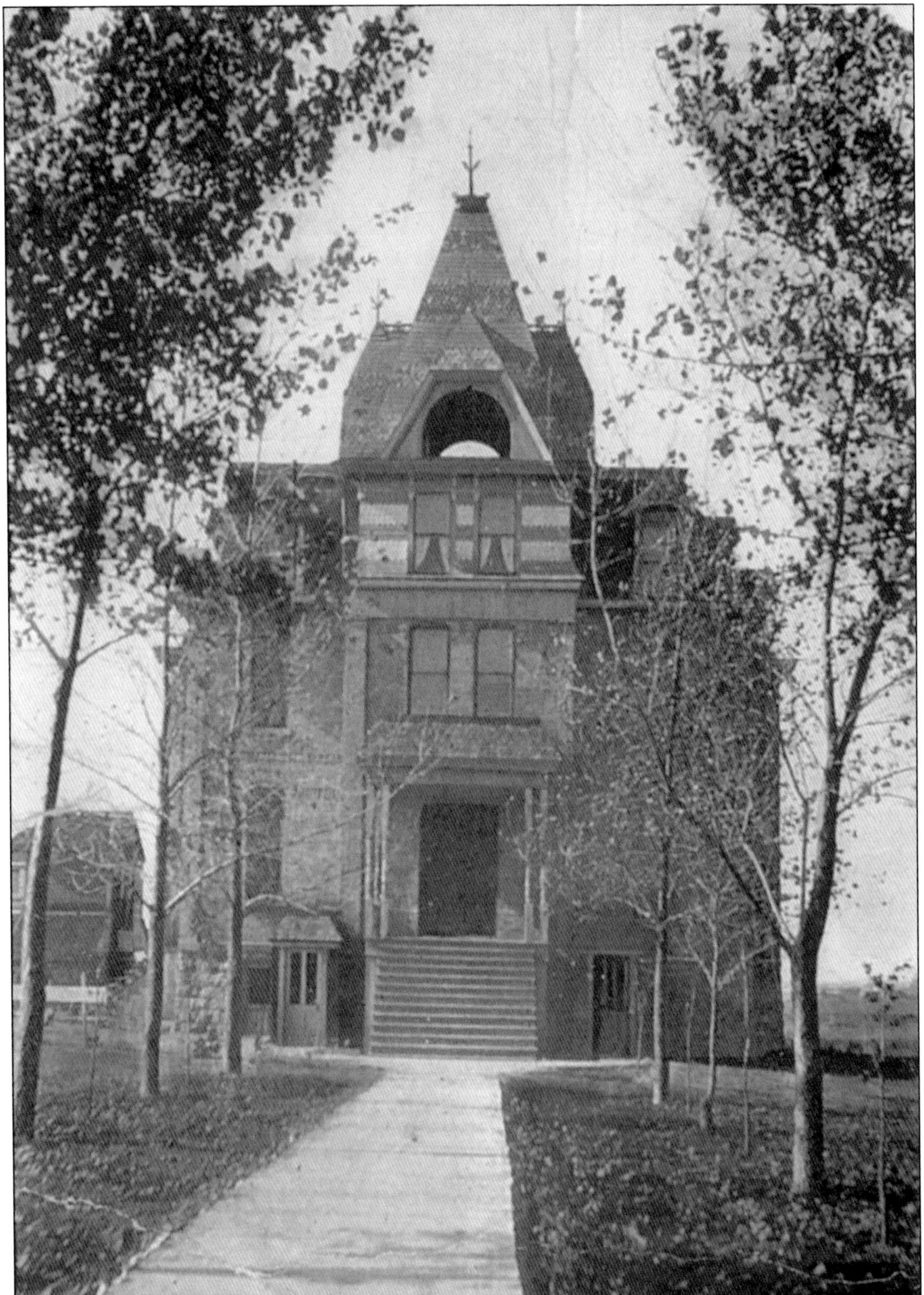

Redfield College opened in 1887, under the sponsorship of the Midland (later Northern) Association of Congregational Churches. In 1932 it merged with Yankton College, and the building was used as a home for elderly members of the Order of the Eastern Star until 1975.

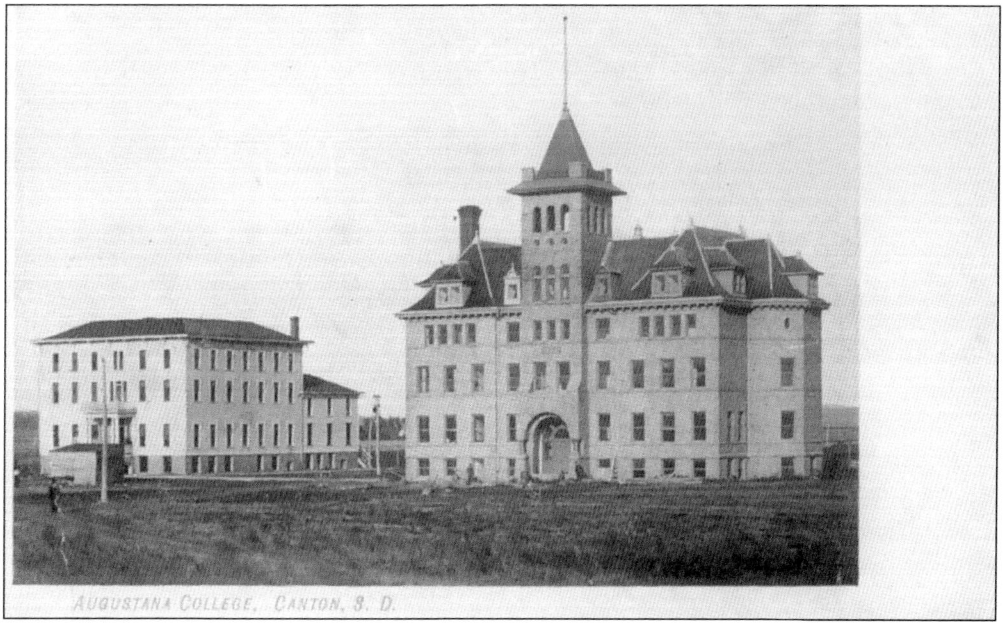

Augustana College was founded by Lutherans in Chicago in 1860, and moved to Canton in 1884. The picture shows a new building completed in 1903, and the older college building that was moved to this location in 1901. After a merger of three Norwegian synods in 1917, the college joined the Lutheran Normal School and moved to its present location in Sioux Falls.

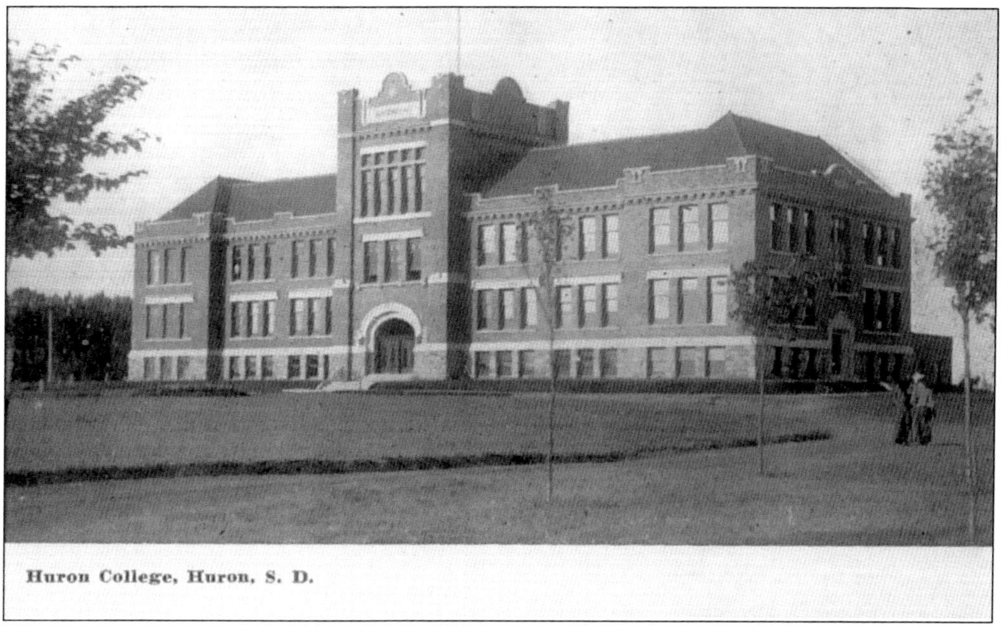

Presbyterians chose Pierre as the site of their school in South Dakota and operated Pierre University from 1883 to 1898. After struggling to obtain funds and students, the school moved to Huron and became Huron College. Located in the old Huron Hotel building for eight years, the college moved into this permanent structure in 1907, with 342 students—40 of those in college-level classes.

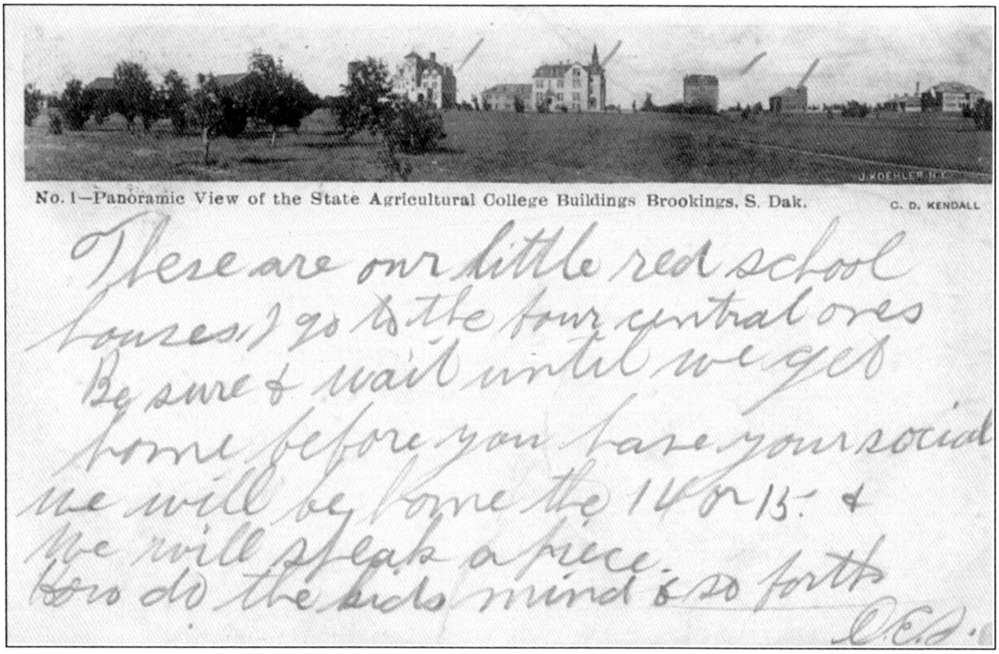

Government "plums," such as the penitentiary and mental hospital, had already been handed out by the territorial legislature to important cities such as Sioux Falls and Yankton, so Brookings settled for what some called the "cow college," which eventually became South Dakota State University. The campus had already grown to a considerable size by the time this picture was taken, around 1907.

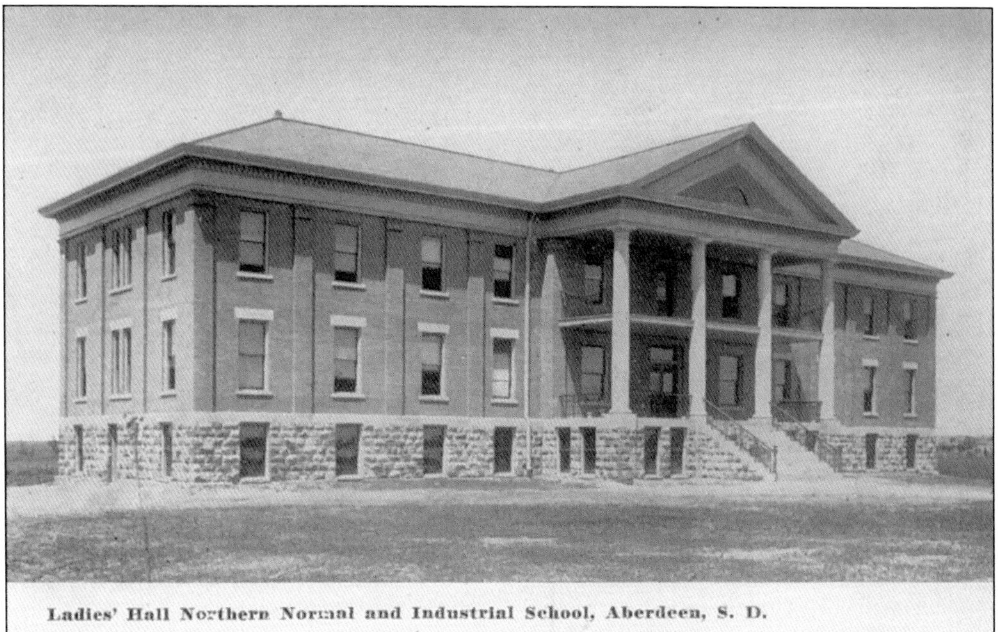

Northern Normal and Industrial School was established in Aberdeen by the state legislature in 1901, with separate programs in teacher training and industrial trades.

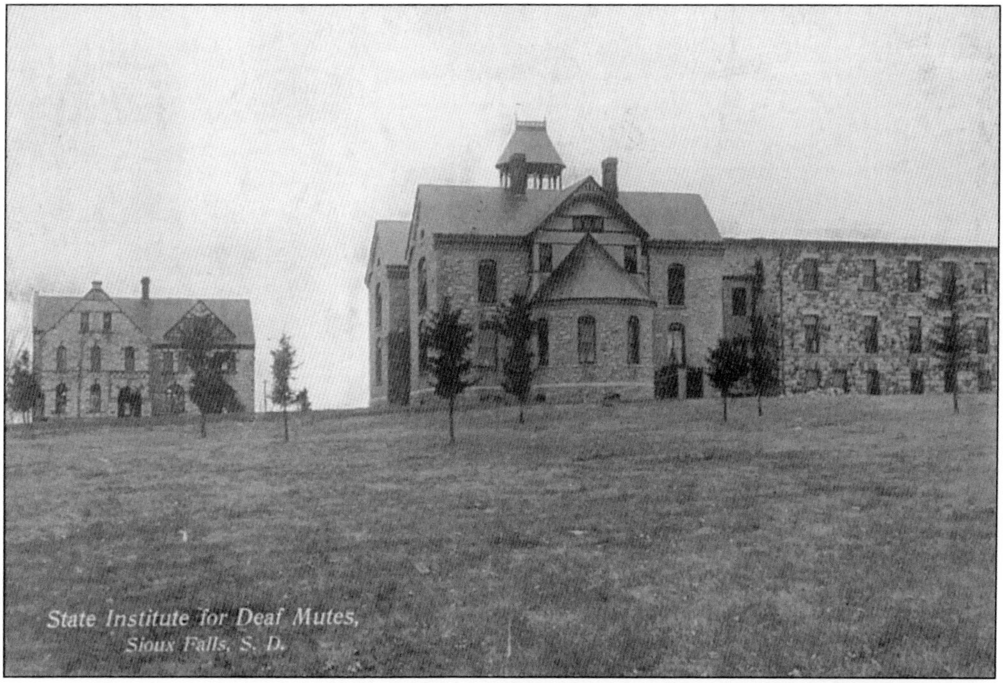

A school for the deaf opened in Sioux Falls in 1880. Blind and visually impaired students had to attend school in Iowa until 1900, when South Dakota created a school for them in Gary. Both schools are now operated by the State Board of Regents.

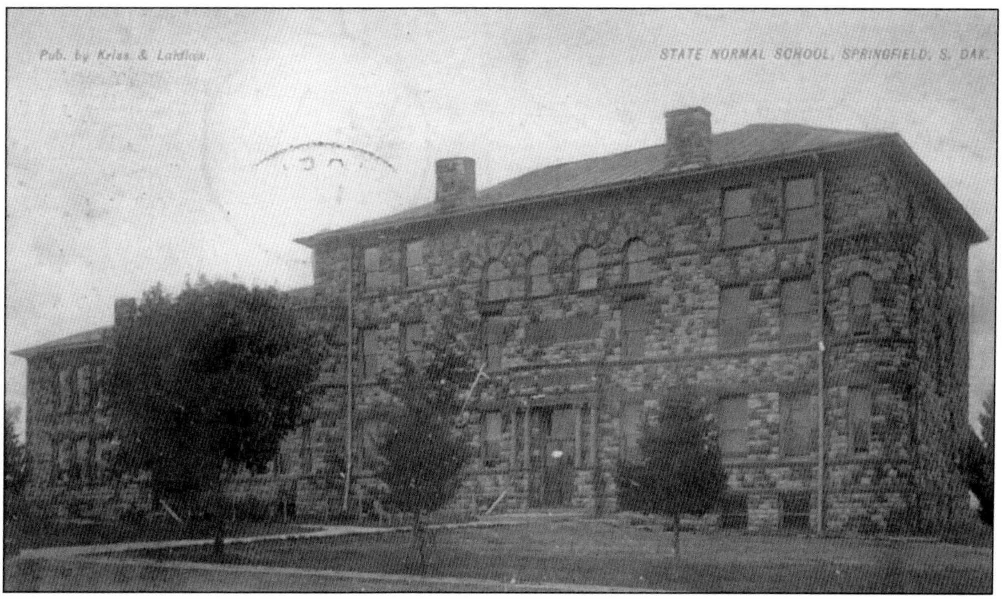

A normal school was authorized for Springfield in 1881, but did not open until 1897. The school operated until 1984, when it was decided that the state had too many colleges and not enough prisons. A double chain-link fence topped with razor wire now surrounds the campus, recently renamed the Mike Durfee State Prison. The original main building, erected in 1901, houses the prison commissary, laundry, and uniform storage.

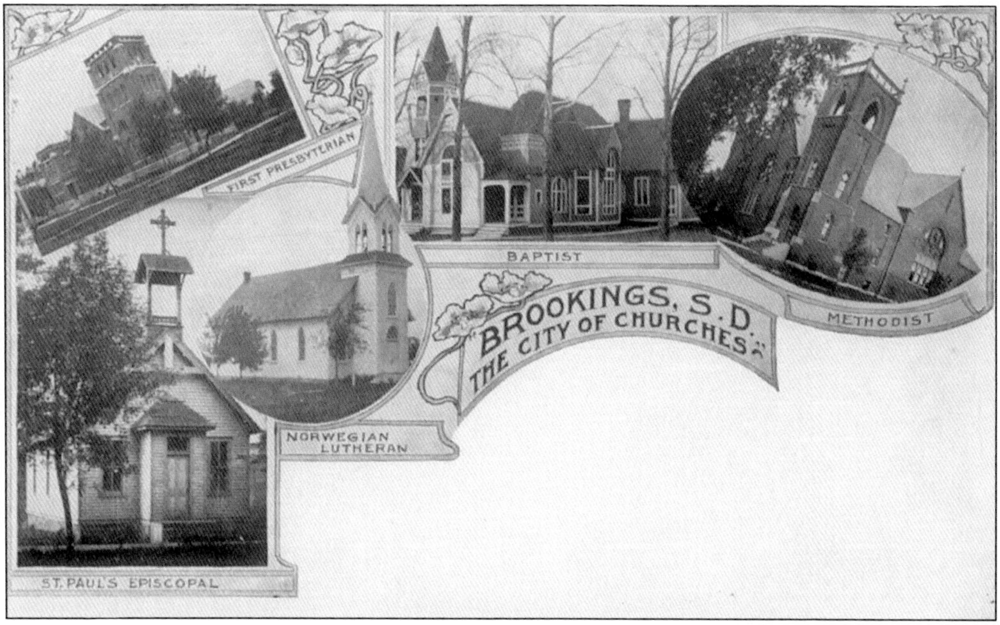

Many communities produced postcards with composite pictures of churches, schools, businesses, and other institutions to indicate their level of development.

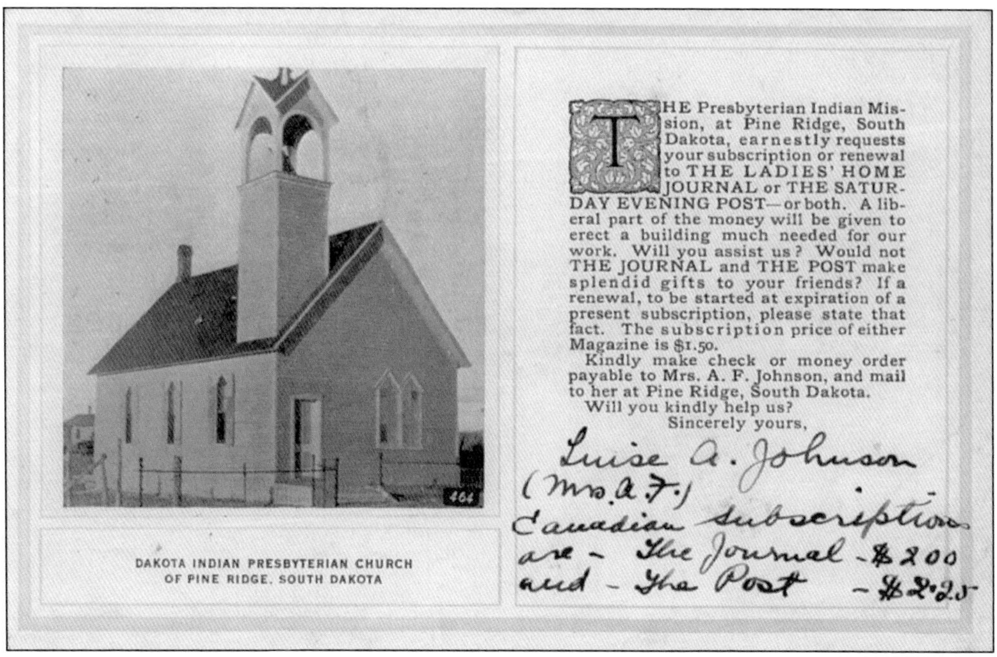

THE Presbyterian Indian Mission, at Pine Ridge, South Dakota, earnestly requests your subscription or renewal to THE LADIES' HOME JOURNAL or THE SATURDAY EVENING POST—or both. A liberal part of the money will be given to erect a building much needed for our work. Will you assist us? Would not THE JOURNAL and THE POST make splendid gifts to your friends? If a renewal, to be started at expiration of a present subscription, please state that fact. The subscription price of either Magazine is $1.50.

Kindly make check or money order payable to Mrs. A. F. Johnson, and mail to her at Pine Ridge, South Dakota.

Will you kindly help us?

Sincerely yours,

Luise A. Johnson
(Mrs. A. F.)
Canadian subscriptions
are - The Journal - $200
and - The Post - $2.25

A Presbyterian missionary sent this notice to a minister's daughter in Montreal, Canada, asking for subscriptions to *The Ladies Home Journal* and *The Saturday Evening Post* as a way to raise money for a new building in Pine Ridge, and provided her with the Canadian rates.

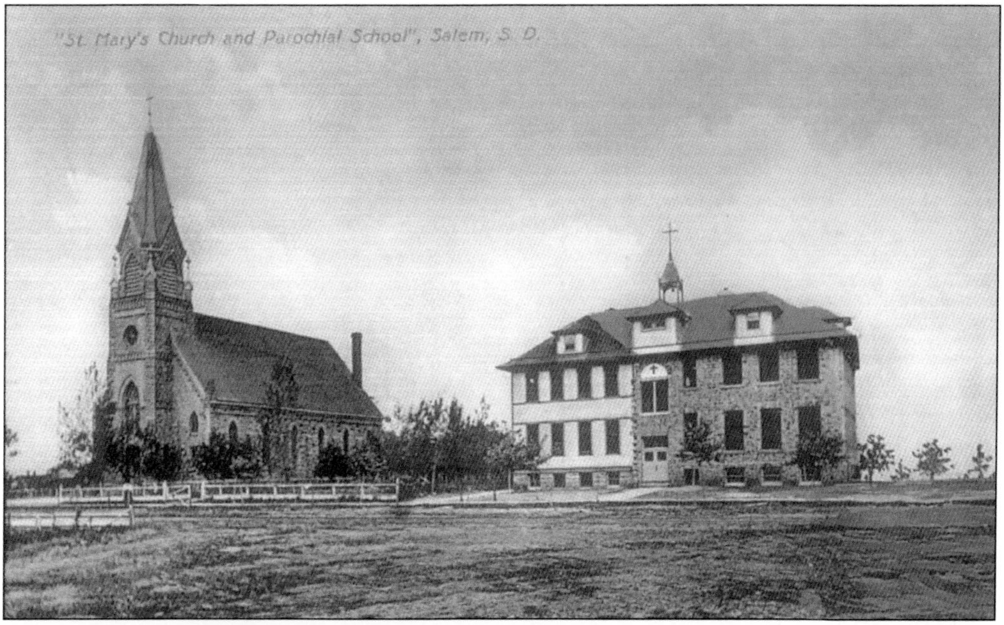

Within six years after the railroad platted the town of Salem in McCook County, Catholics built a church on this site. The church in the picture replaced the original wood structure in 1898, and the school building was completed in 1902.

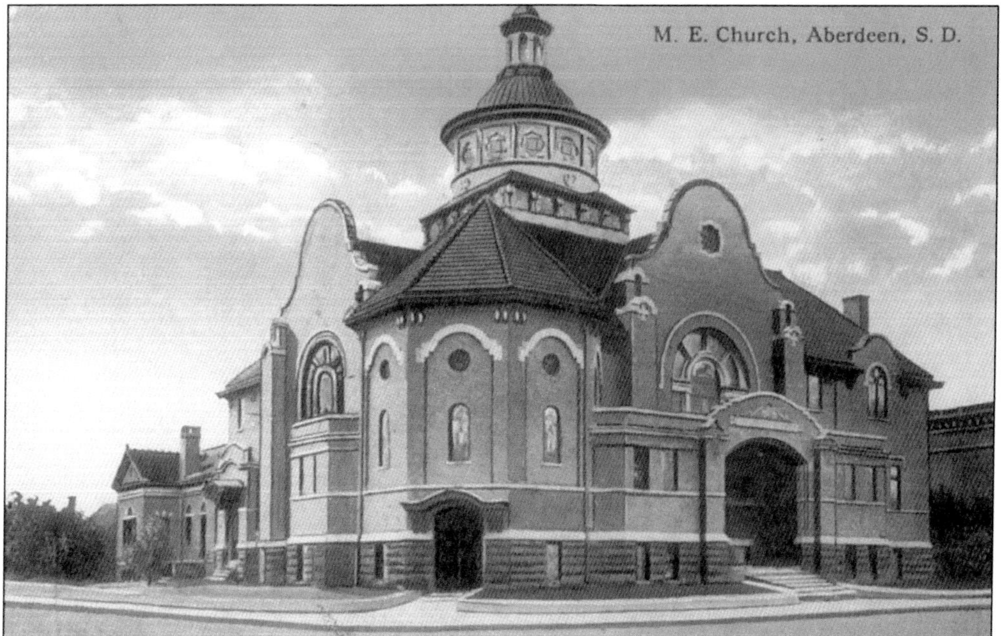

Methodists in Aberdeen completed a church edifice in 1909, with all the amenities, including a sanctuary, parlor with fireplace, reading room, offices, kitchen, dining room with seating for 250, a large plunge pool, showers, restrooms, lockers, and a gymnasium. Designed in an "Eclectic Revival adaptation of the Byzantine style of architecture," the building is still a unique landmark in downtown Aberdeen.

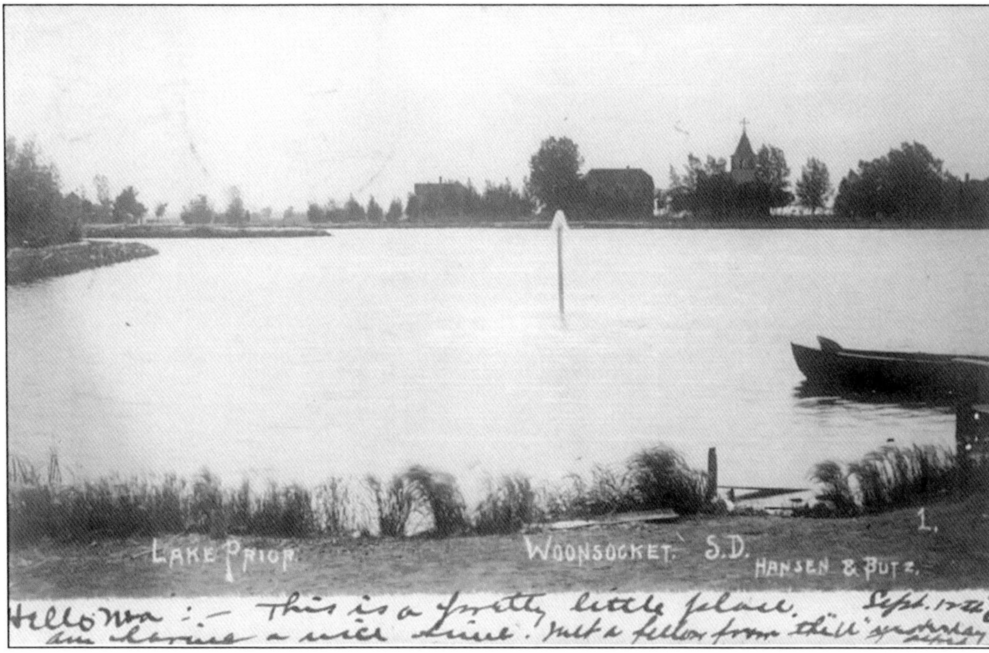

C.H. Prior, a railroad agent for the Chicago, Milwaukee, & St. Paul Railway, named the siding of Woonsocket after his hometown in Rhode Island. Settlers returned the favor by placing his name on Lake Prior. After a well was drilled in 1890, the swampy area was deepened and turned into a shimmering lake, 3 to 10 feet deep. In 1912, the first water carnival was held, complete with canoes, launches, rowboats, a baseball park with grandstand, an auditorium/dance hall, a bandstand on the island, and a 40-foot-high "Shoot the Chutes" tower.

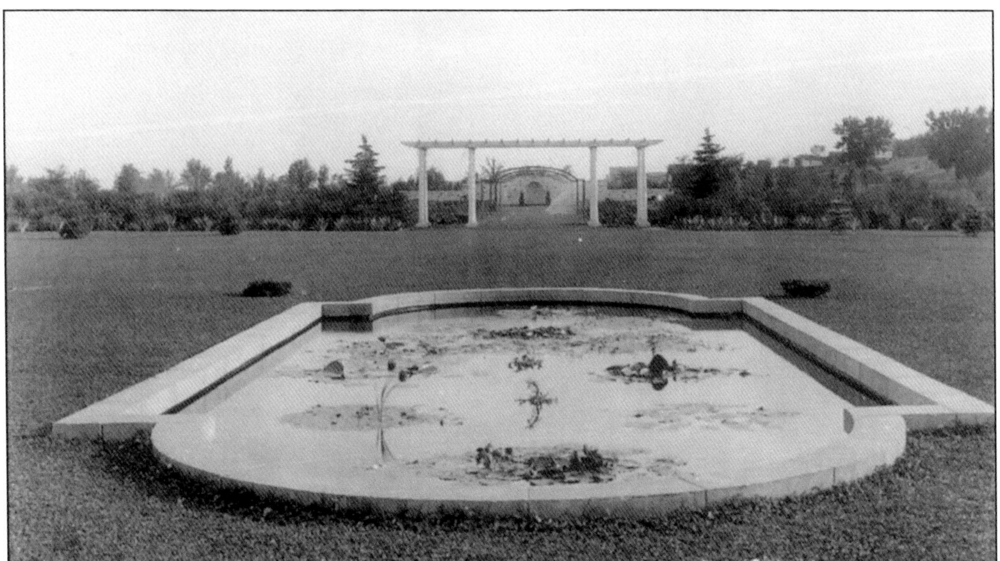

Open space was not an issue in South Dakota as it was in congested eastern cities, but town planners recognized the need to create parks to beautify their communities and to provide space for recreation.

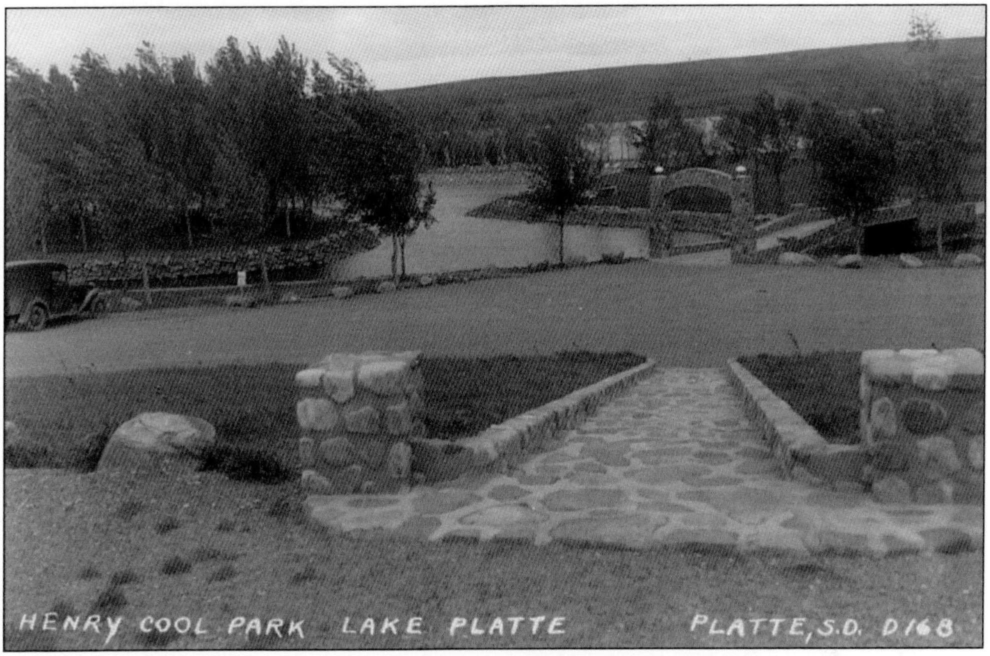

Citizens of Platte built a dam and spillway in 1931, to create Lake Platte 2 miles west of town. An island in the lake was landscaped to form Henry Cool Park, named for one of the project's organizers.

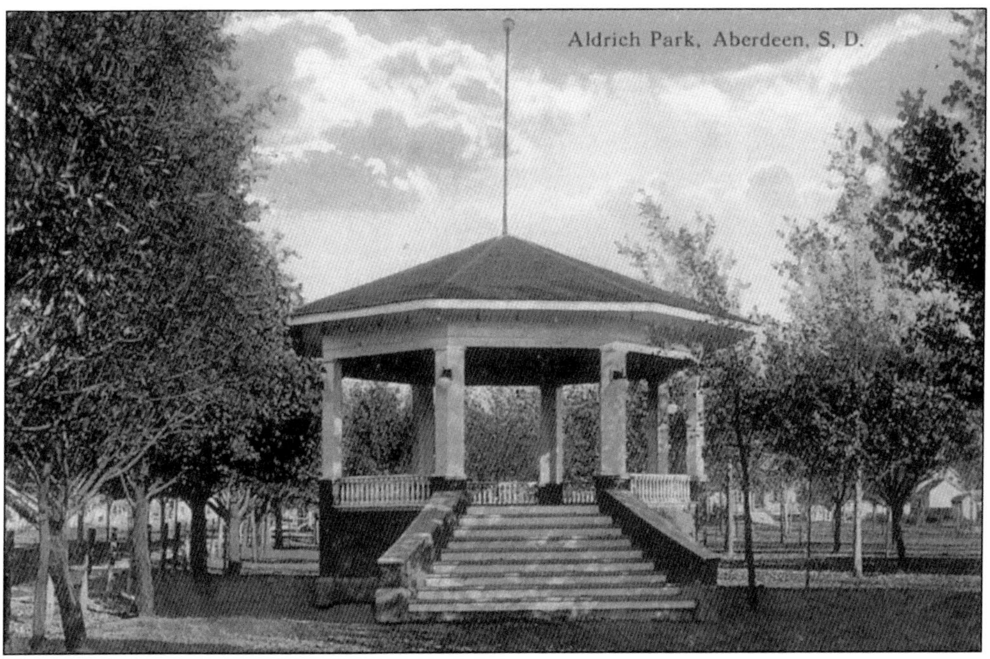

The site of the first Brown County Courthouse was turned into a park in 1909, and this bandstand was built there in 1910.

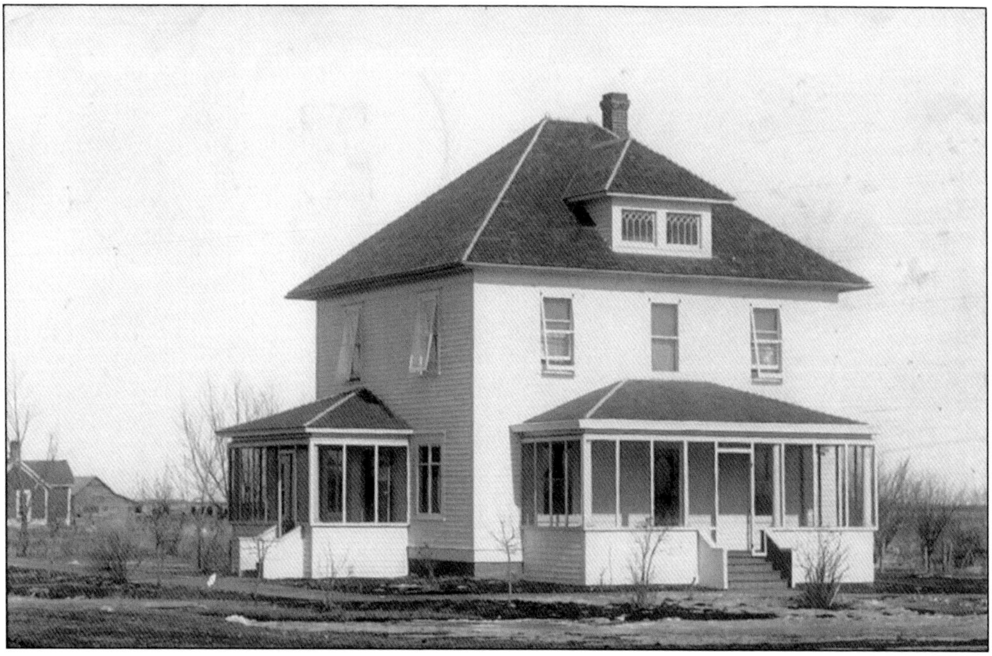

Mila wrote to her friend Blanche Vandever in Ballard, Washington, in 1909, "How does this compare with that new house of yours? My room is the N.W. one upstairs [far left]. Come and make us a visit and we will show you the inside." C.H. Miller of Clark, whose photo studio is pictured earlier in this chapter, took this photograph.

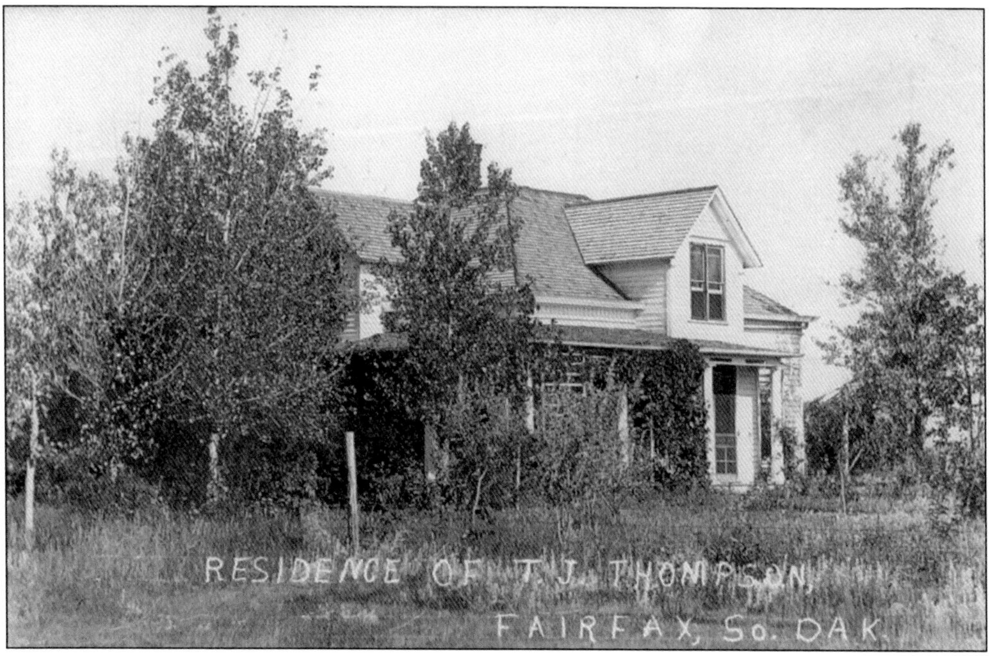

T.J. Thompson was a merchant in the town of Fairfax, and came to South Dakota with his wife May about 1901.

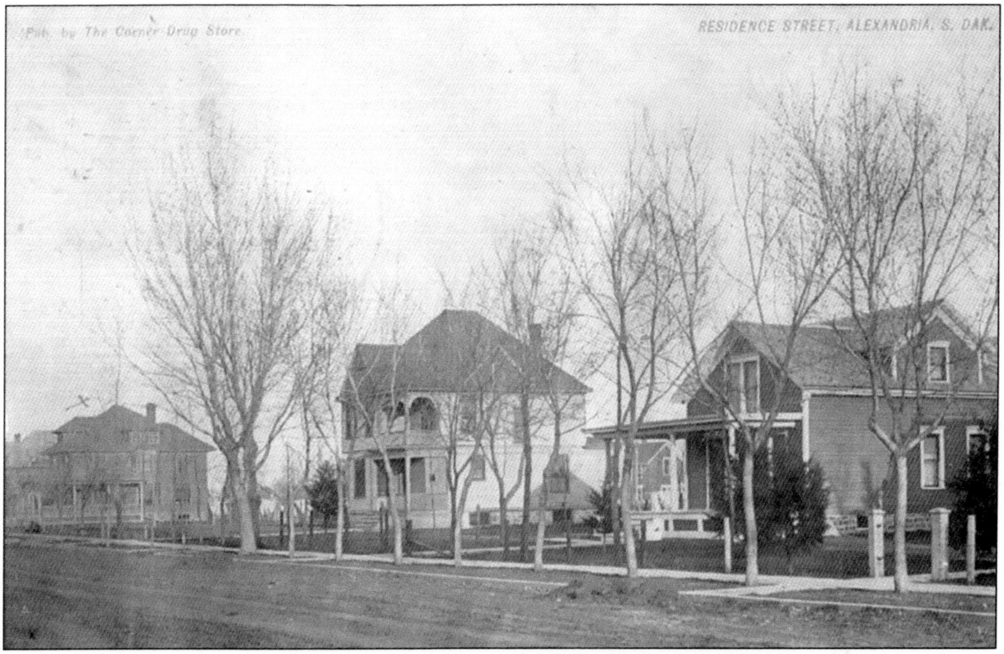

Alexandria, founded in 1880, was a well-established town by the time this picture was taken around 1909. A promotional booklet for Hanson County published in 1901 described Alexandria this way: "It is a city of homes, many of them beautiful and artistic, all of them neat and tasty. The city and its additions are well bunched, not scattered over all creation, as is the case in many western places."

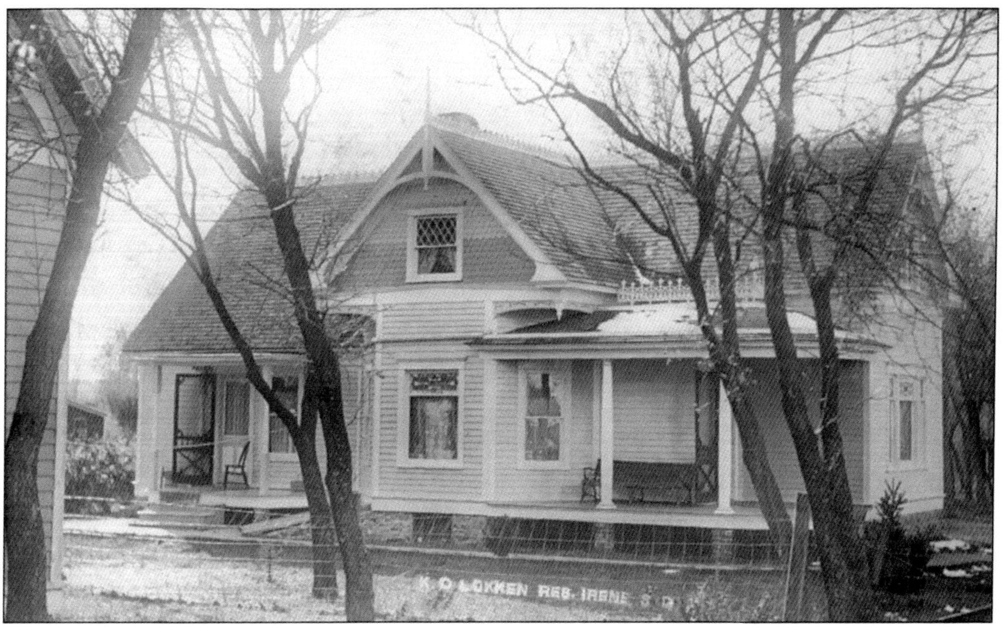

State census records from 1915 show that K.O. Lokken was a 42-year-old Norwegian immigrant who lived in Irene with his wife, Ida Bjorke, and children, Olin, Chester, Inga, Myrtle, and Elisabet.

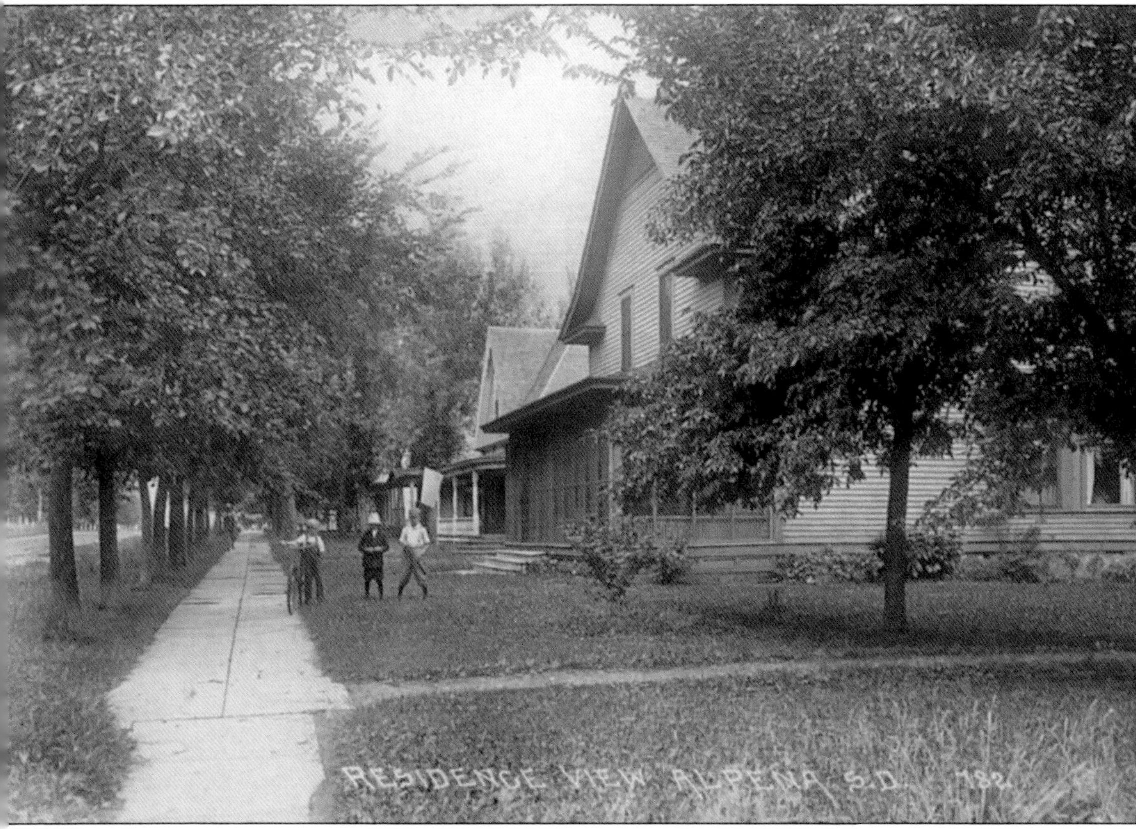

Founded in 1883, the town of Alpena was more than 25 years old when this picture was taken—old enough to have mature trees, lawns, and sidewalks for children to play on.

Five

TRANSPORTATION

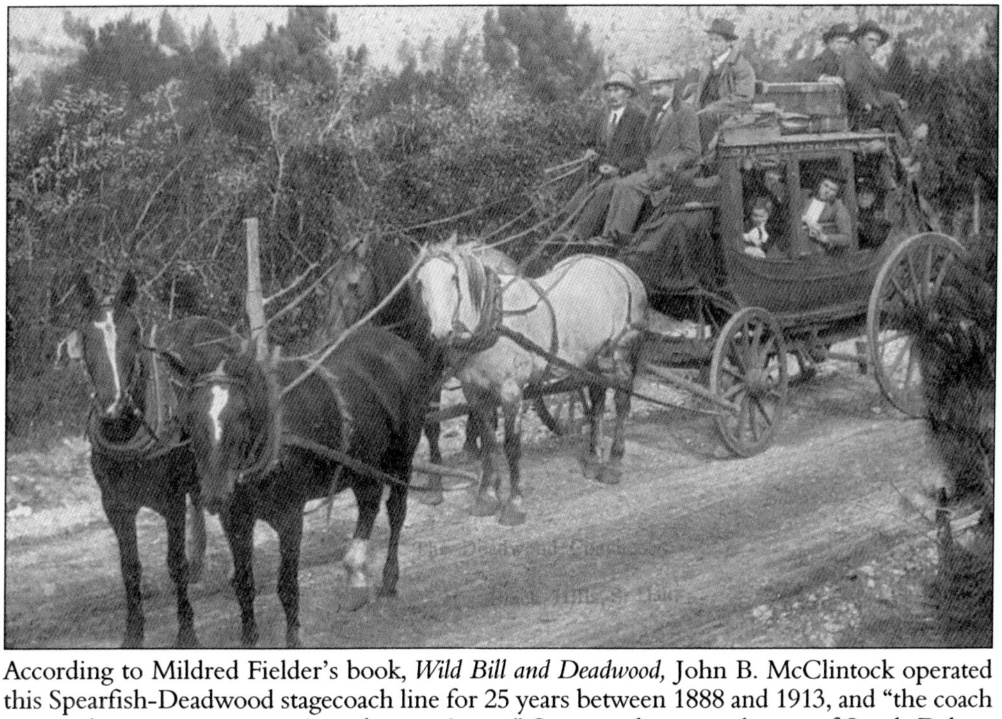

According to Mildred Fielder's book, *Wild Bill and Deadwood,* John B. McClintock operated this Spearfish-Deadwood stagecoach line for 25 years between 1888 and 1913, and "the coach averaged ten passengers a trip as long as it ran." Stagecoaches served parts of South Dakota well into the 1900s, until train lines and roads for automobiles became available.

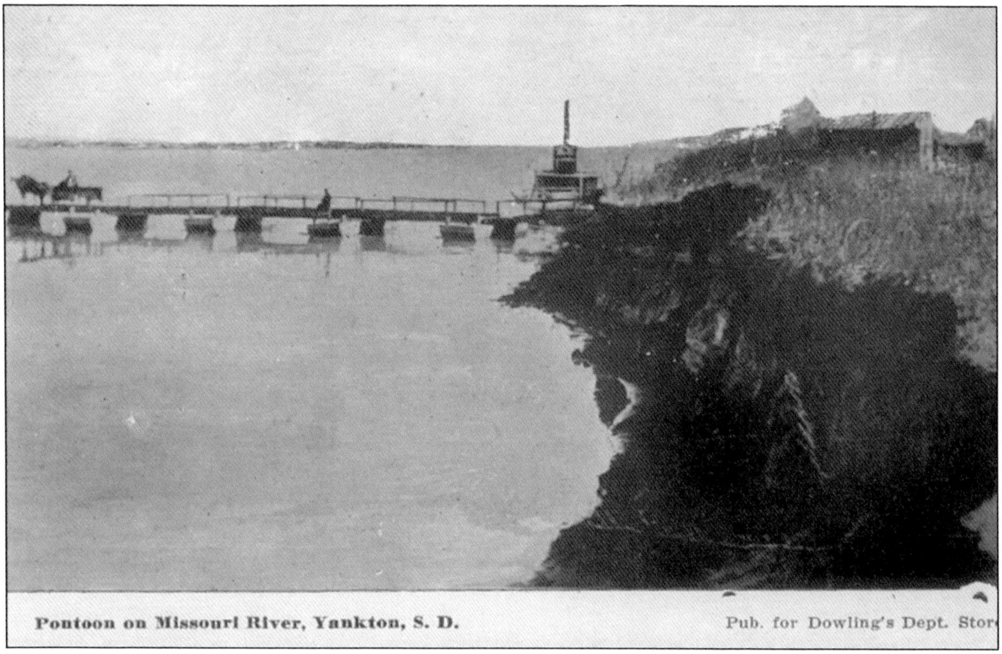

Pontoon bridges were used to cross the Missouri River at several points before permanent bridges were constructed, but they were expensive and difficult to maintain. The width and speed of the river changed rapidly throughout the year, and the floating bridges had to be dismantled quickly when ice buildups threatened to break them up.

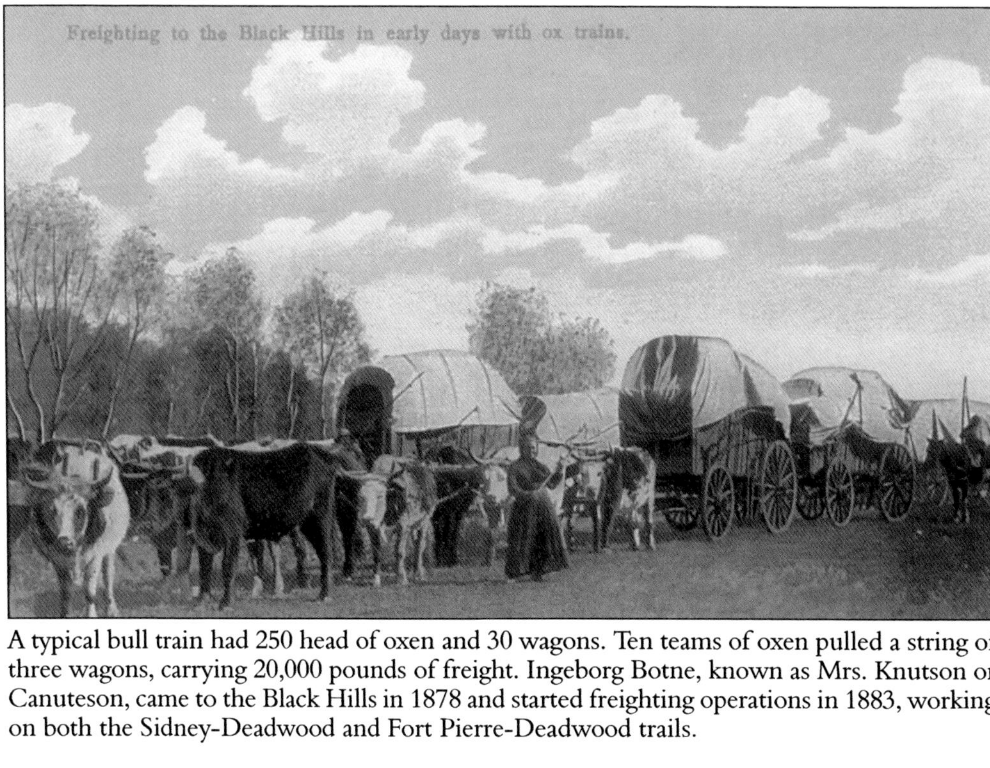

A typical bull train had 250 head of oxen and 30 wagons. Ten teams of oxen pulled a string of three wagons, carrying 20,000 pounds of freight. Ingeborg Botne, known as Mrs. Knutson or Canuteson, came to the Black Hills in 1878 and started freighting operations in 1883, working on both the Sidney-Deadwood and Fort Pierre-Deadwood trails.

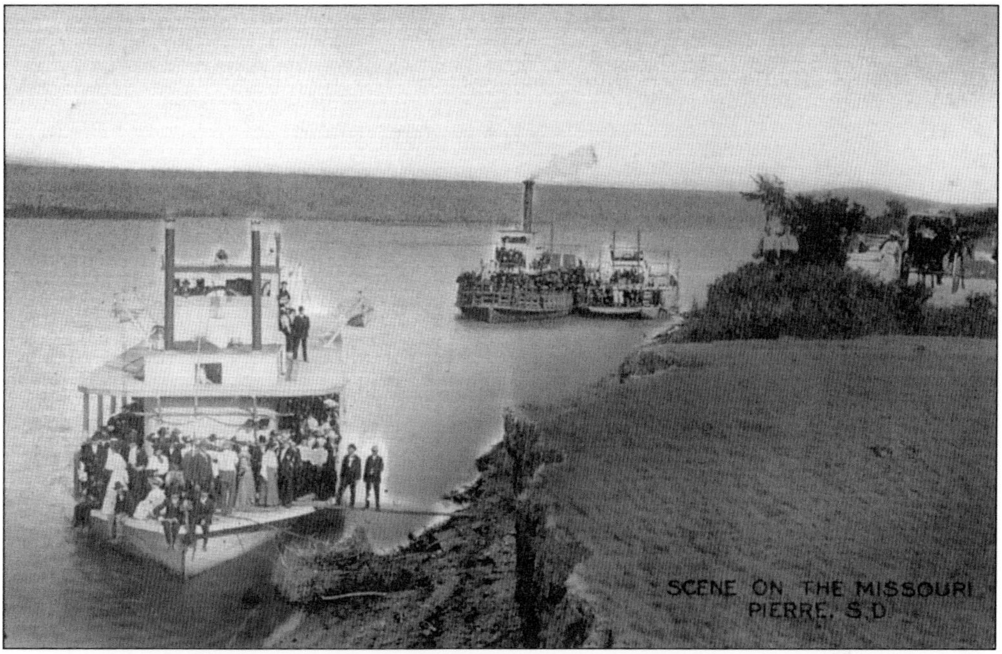

Steamboats provided important transportation on the Missouri River, beginning in 1831, when Pierre Chouteau brought his steamboat, the *Yellow Stone*, from St. Louis to the fur trading station that became Fort Pierre. People crossed the river from Pierre to Fort Pierre in a variety of ways. They used steam ferries like the ones pictured when the water was deep enough. At other times, they could use pontoon bridges or go by foot when the river froze over.

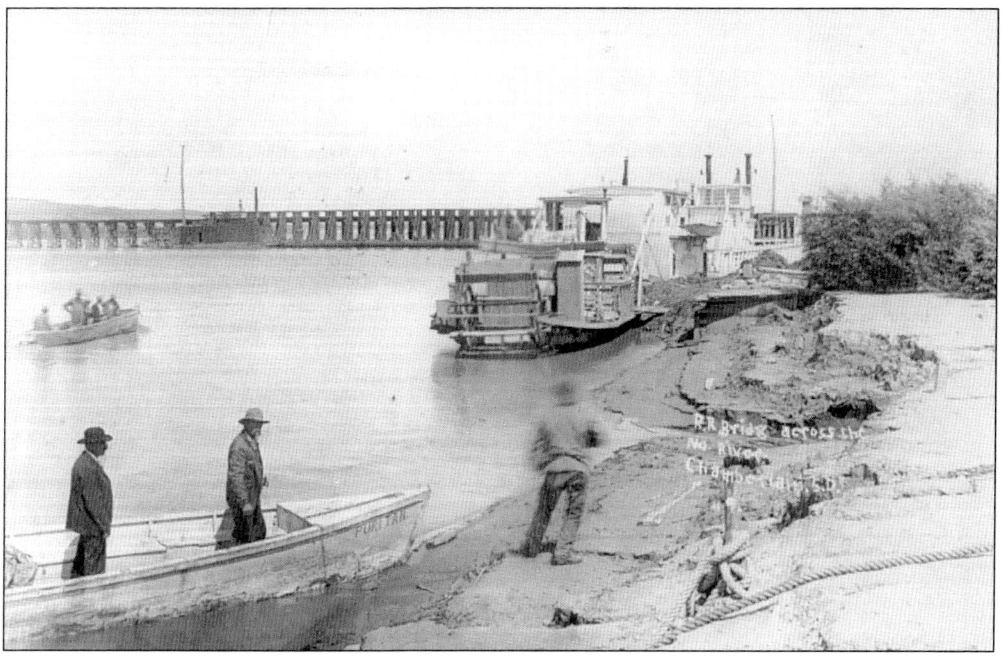

The first bridge of the Chicago, Milwaukee, & St. Paul Railway to cross the Missouri River was completed at Chamberlain in 1905.

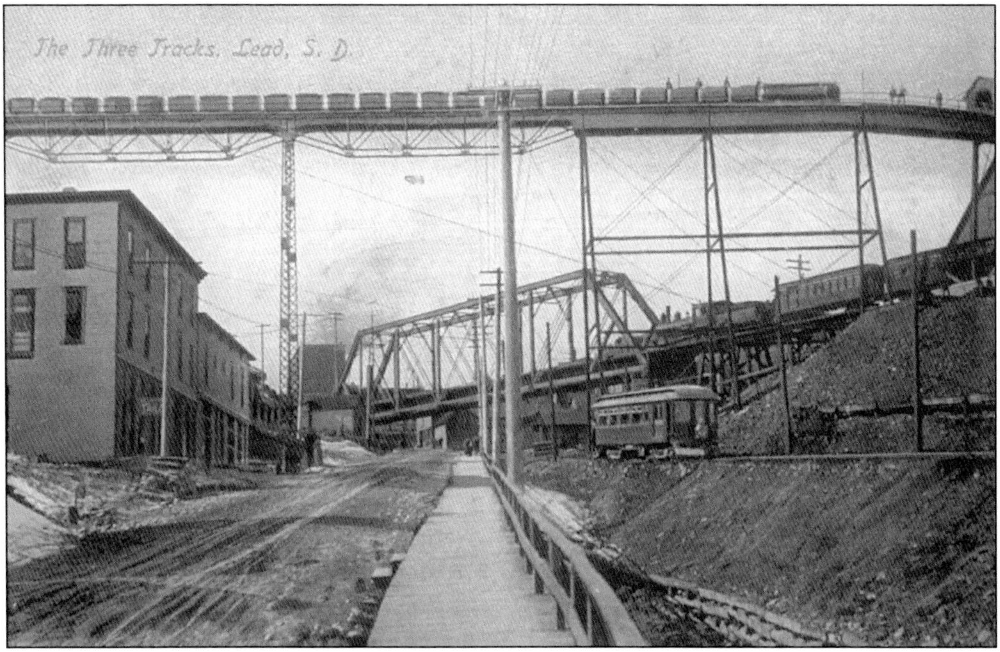

This famous spot in Lead featured the crossing of three different railroad lines, including the Homestake ore train on the top trestle.

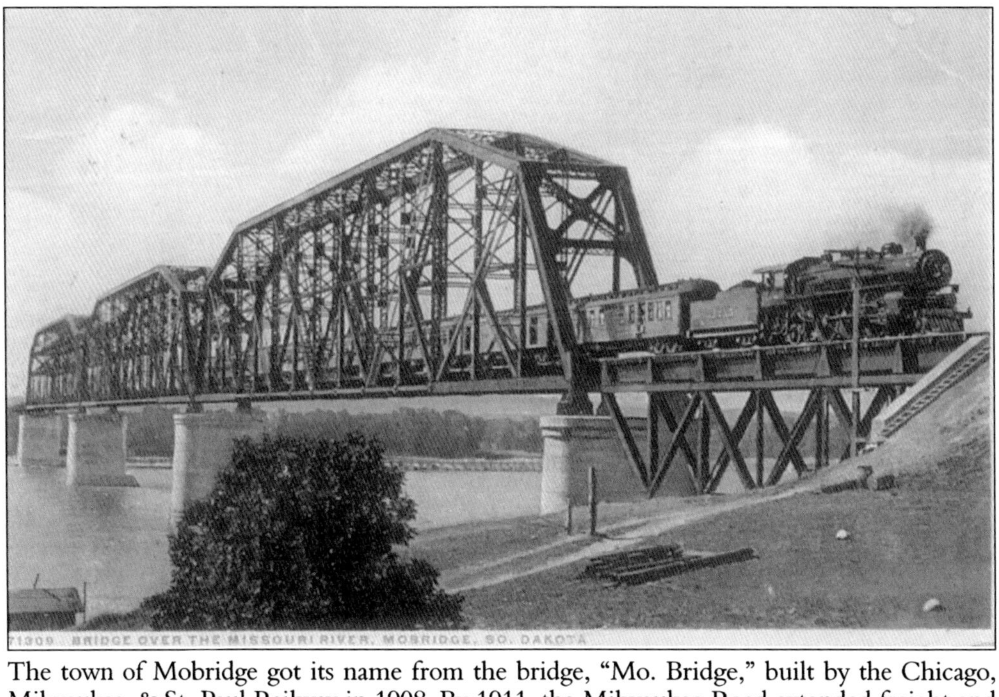

The town of Mobridge got its name from the bridge, "Mo. Bridge," built by the Chicago, Milwaukee, & St. Paul Railway in 1908. By 1911, the Milwaukee Road extended freight and passenger service on this line all the way to the west coast.

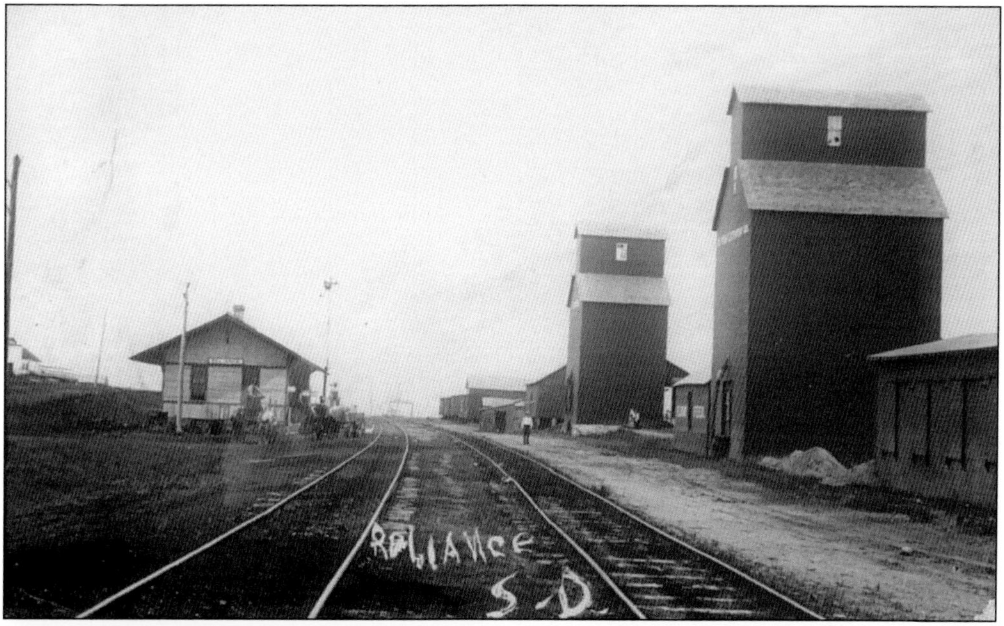

Many small towns boomed or died depending on where the railroads decided to place their lines. Railroad companies platted and named many town sites themselves, and laid out streets and business areas either parallel or perpendicular to the tracks. Typical of many South Dakota towns, Reliance had its train depot, grain elevators, and warehouses arranged along the tracks.

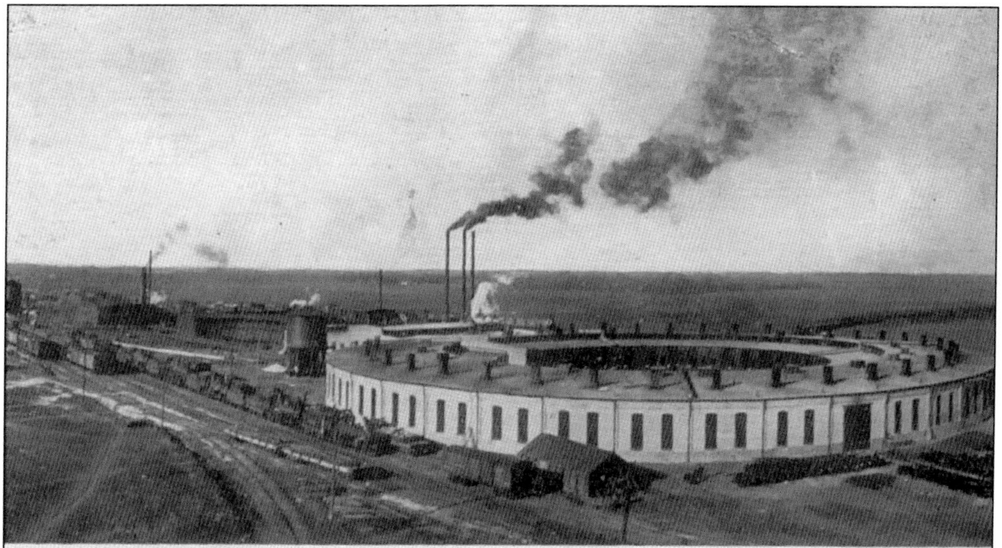

C. & N. W. Roundhouse, Huron, S. D.

Huron became a division station for the Chicago and North Western railroad on its main line between Chicago and Rapid City, and served as a junction with the C&NW north-south line from Omaha to Oakes, North Dakota. Huron was also a terminal for the Great Northern line from Duluth and the Twin Cities, and joined these railroad lines with the Milwaukee Road at Wolsey, 16 miles to the west.

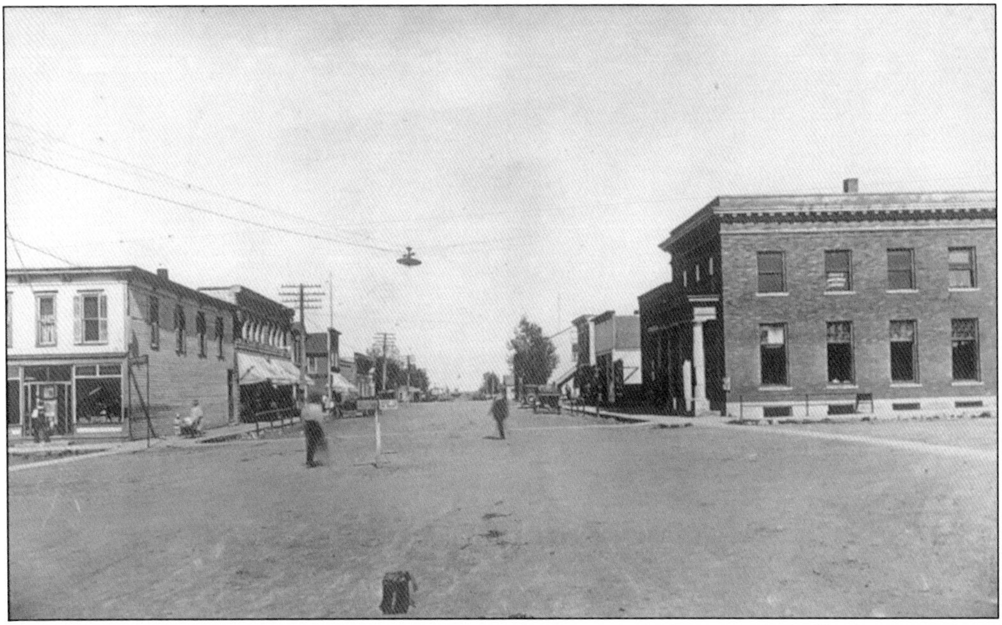

By 1922, busy intersections in Highmore were lit by streetlights, single bulbs hanging from wires. The intersection of Second and Iowa Streets also had a post in the middle of the street with a sign that read, "Keep to the Right."

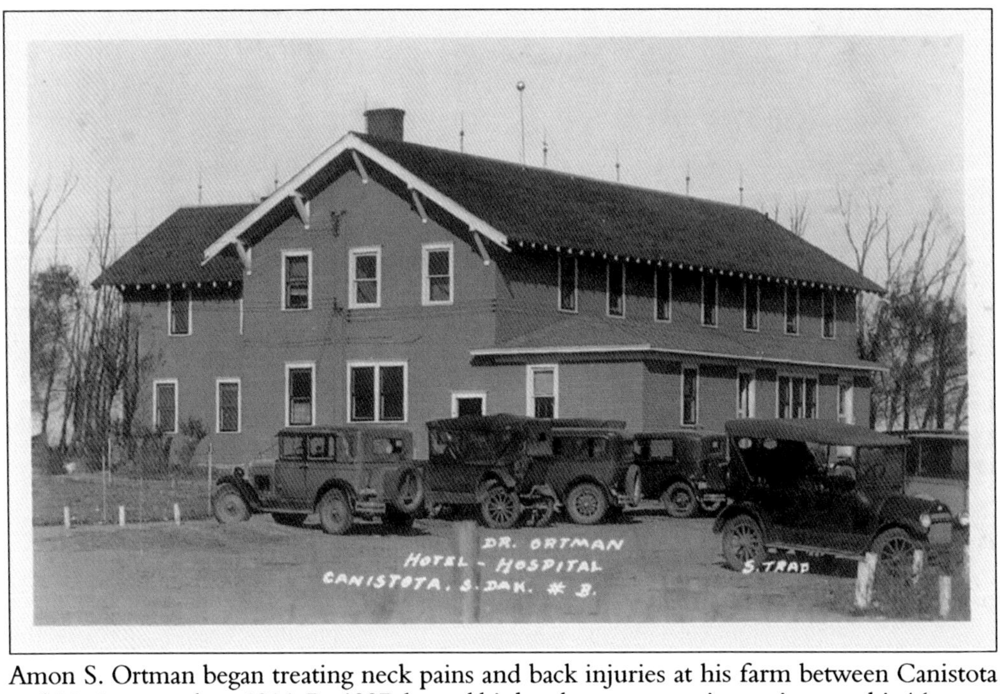

Amon S. Ortman began treating neck pains and back injuries at his farm between Canistota and Marion as early as 1914. By 1927, he and his brother were treating patients at this 16-room hotel and hospital. Their brother Albert managed the hotel and cafe, and another brother, Emil, operated a taxi service to bring people from the train stations in Canistota, Marion, and Monroe.

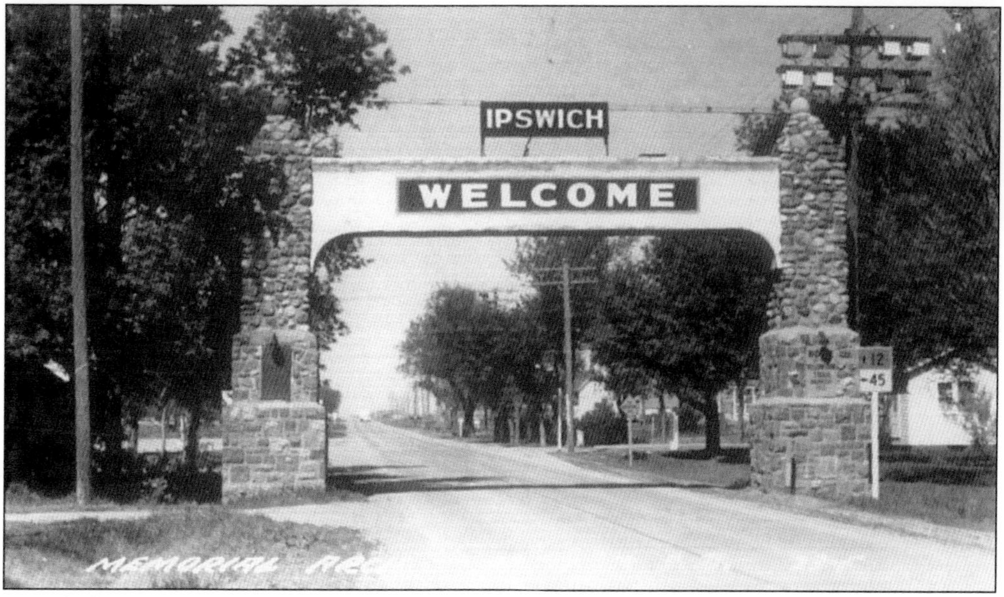

Long before the start of federal and state highway programs, J.W. Parmley of Ipswich helped to initiate a plan to create and mark an automobile route from Plymouth Rock to Puget Sound. The Yellowstone Trail, marked with stones painted yellow with a black arrow, later became U.S. Highway 12. A wooden arch, built as a memorial for soldiers in World War I, was replaced in 1928, by a stone and steel arch to mark the origin of the Yellowstone Trail in Ipswich.

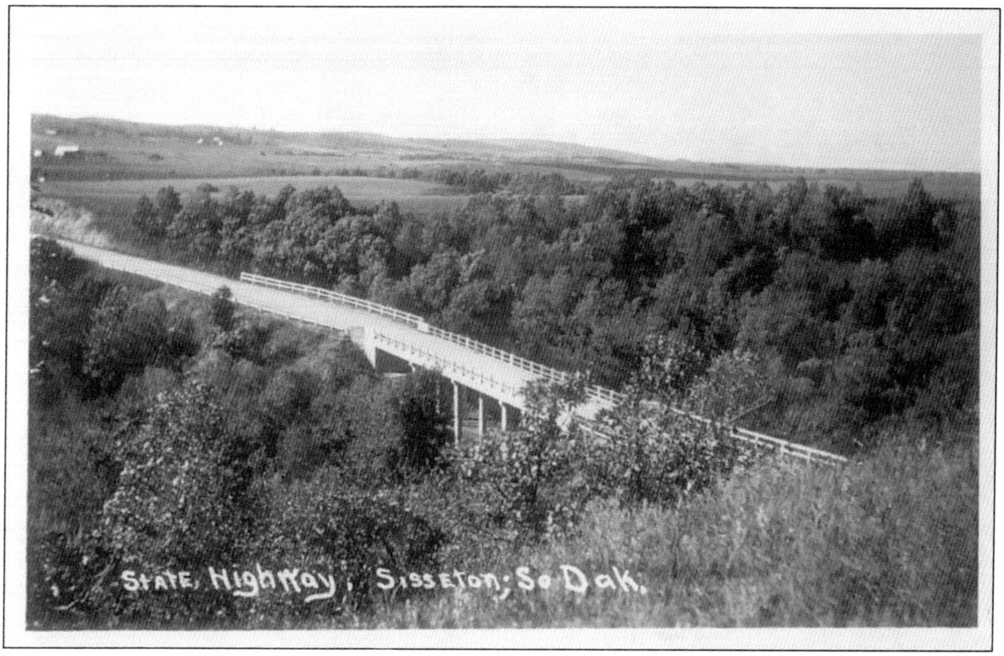

Automobiles arrived in South Dakota in the early 1900s, but it took another 20 years before a highway program was developed. Old horse and wagon trails were used until the state began planning a grid of east-west and north-south routes with a standard numbering system. Some highways still take unusual jogs at points where old trails were connected together.

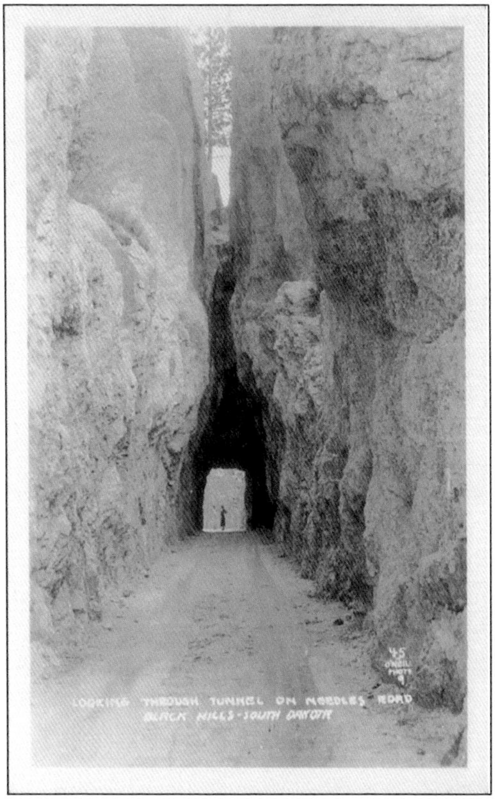

While in the State Senate in 1912, Peter Norbeck initiated plans for a forest and game preserve that led to the creation of Custer State Park. In the 1920s, he helped develop plans for a highway to make the Needles and Harney Peak accessible to tourists. The 14-mile route from the Game Lodge to Sylvan Lake included two tunnels. The Iron Mountain Road with three tunnels and three pigtail bridges was completed in 1933.

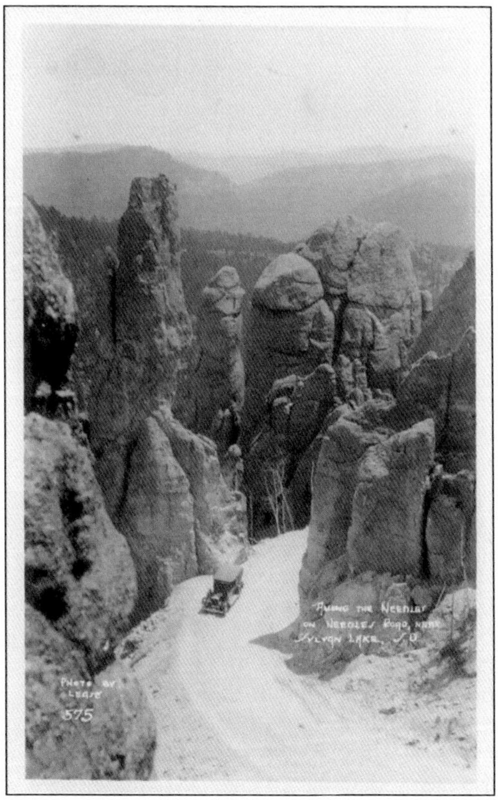

The road through the Needles was designed purposely with loops and inclines to slow cars down to 20-miles-per-hour, to encourage people to enjoy the scenery.

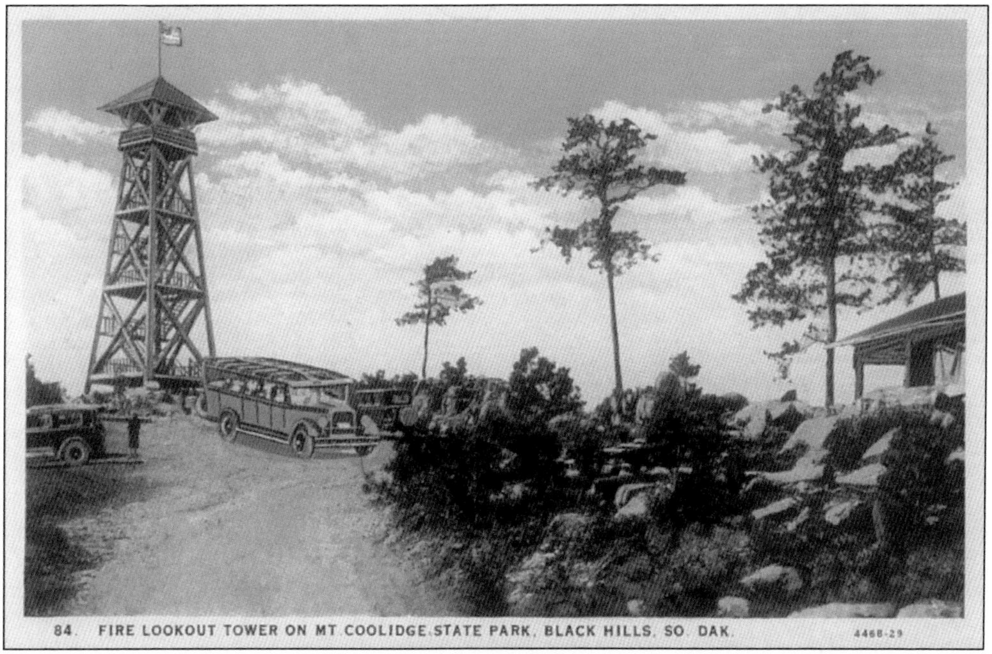

An open-air tour bus uses a newly-constructed highway to reach Mount Coolidge, renamed in 1927, when President Calvin Coolidge spent the summer at the State Game Lodge not far away.

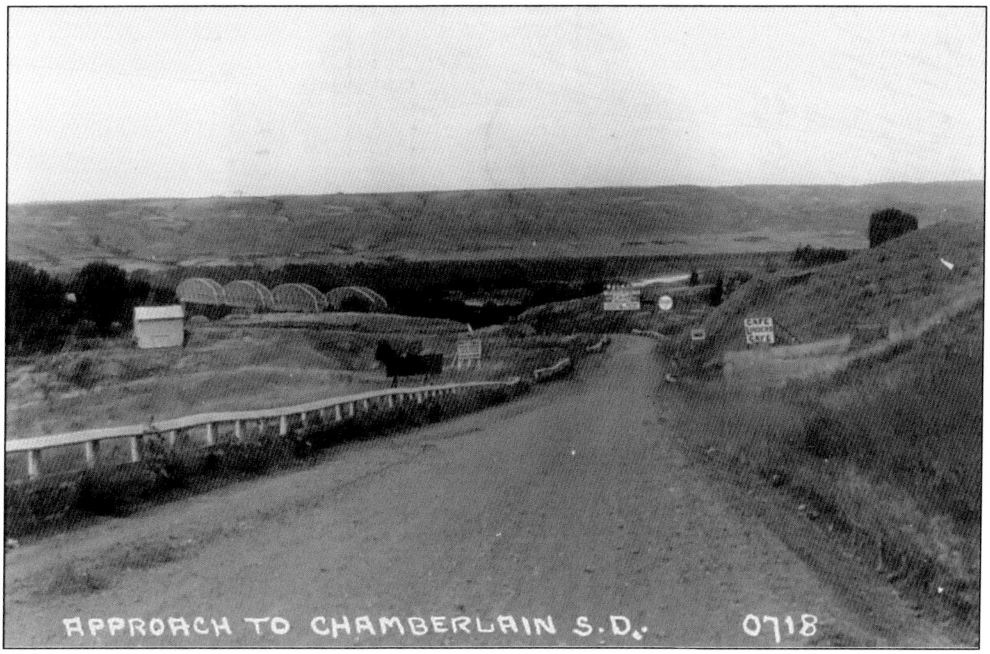

The State of South Dakota completed five highway bridges between 1924 and 1927, crossing the Missouri River at Mobridge, Forest City, Pierre, Chamberlain, and Wheeler. The Chamberlain bridge, still in use next to the newer interstate route, was completed in 1925.

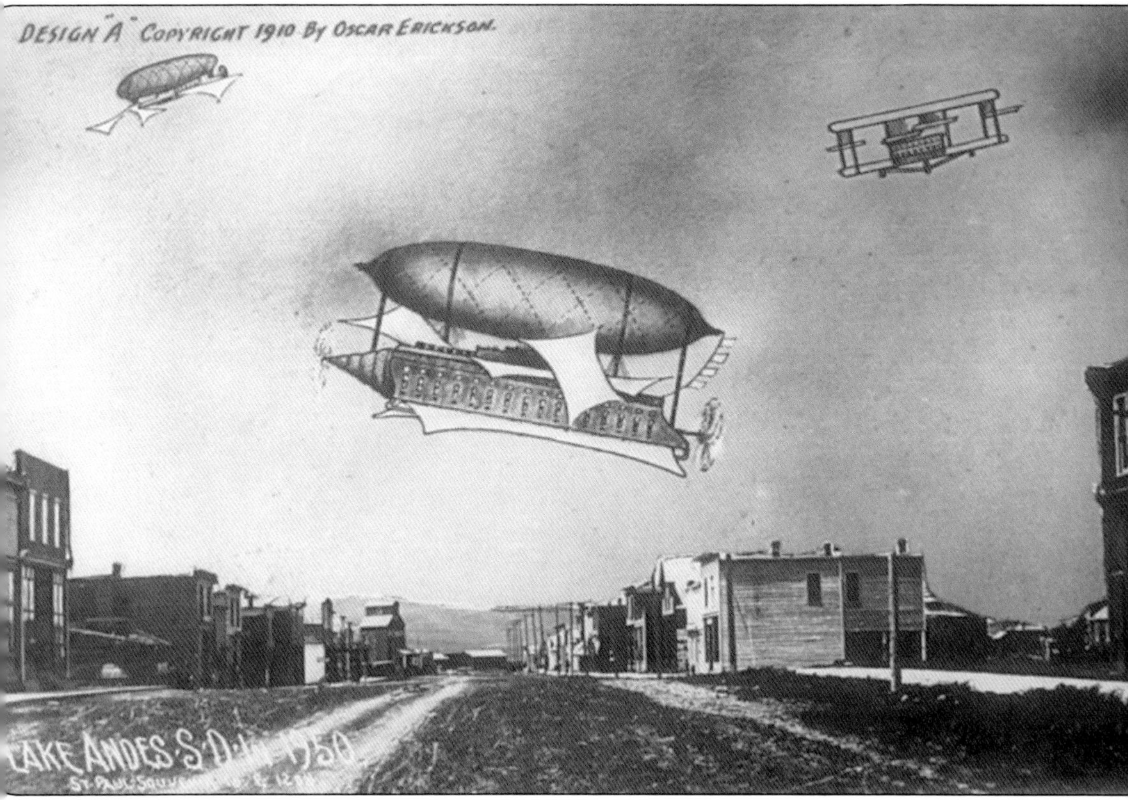

Air travel was still a curiosity when this postcard was printed in 1910, offering a fanciful view of what Lake Andes would look like in 40 more years, when the skies filled with aeroplanes and dirigibles.

Six

Special Events

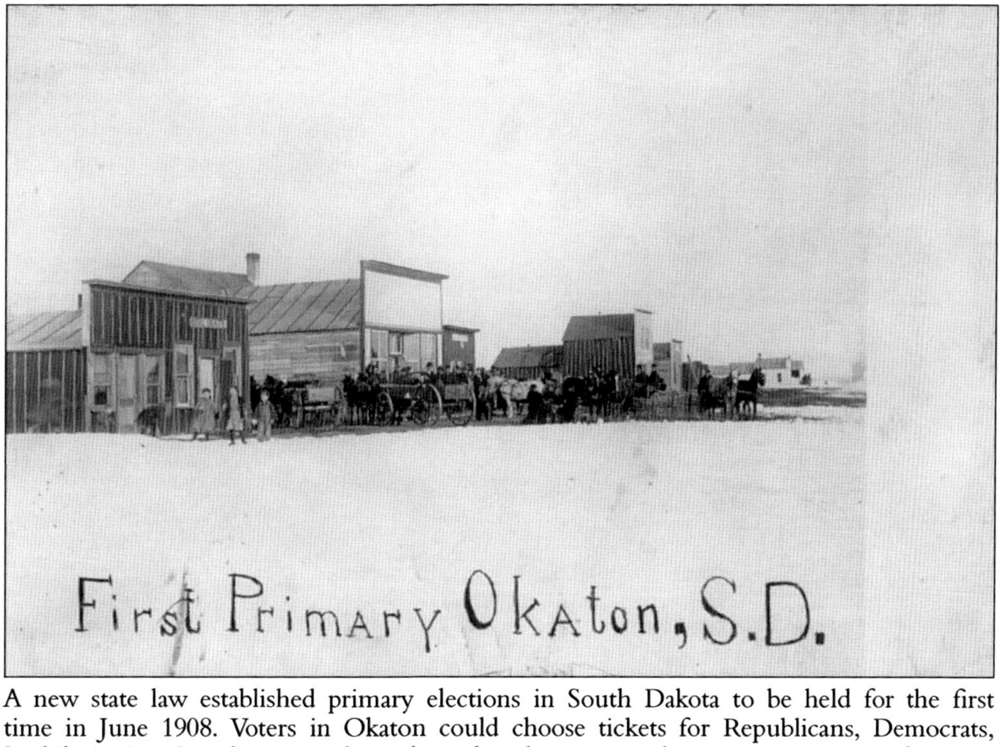

A new state law established primary elections in South Dakota to be held for the first time in June 1908. Voters in Okaton could choose tickets for Republicans, Democrats, Prohibitionists, Socialists, or Independents, but then as now the main contests were between Republican candidates.

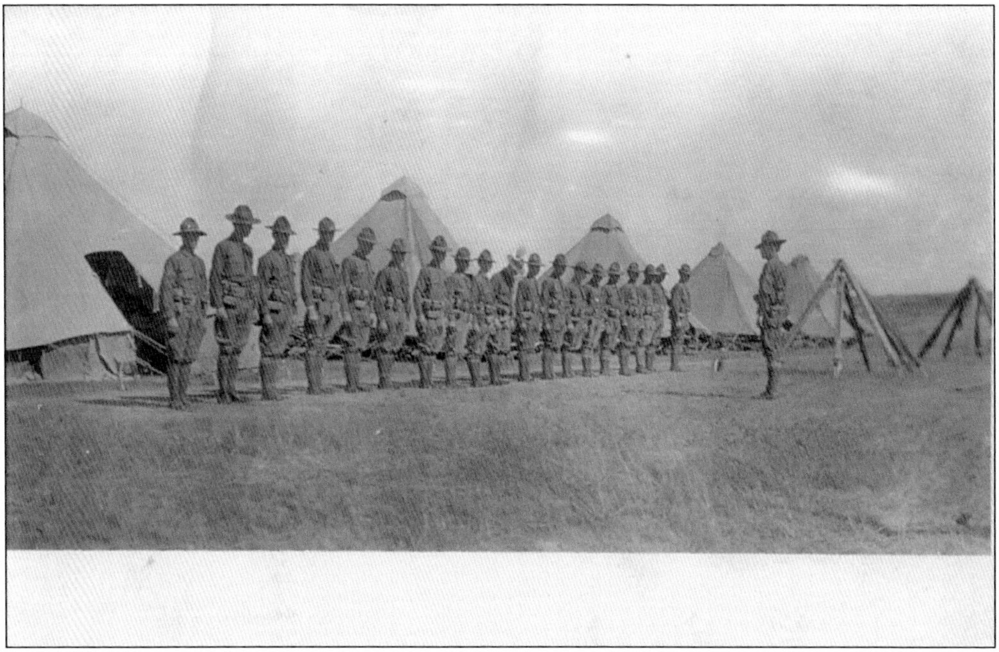

World War I affected South Dakota both by sending many farm boys to France and by increasing prices for farm crops. This postcard shows an ambulance corps of the South Dakota National Guard training at Camp Pierre.

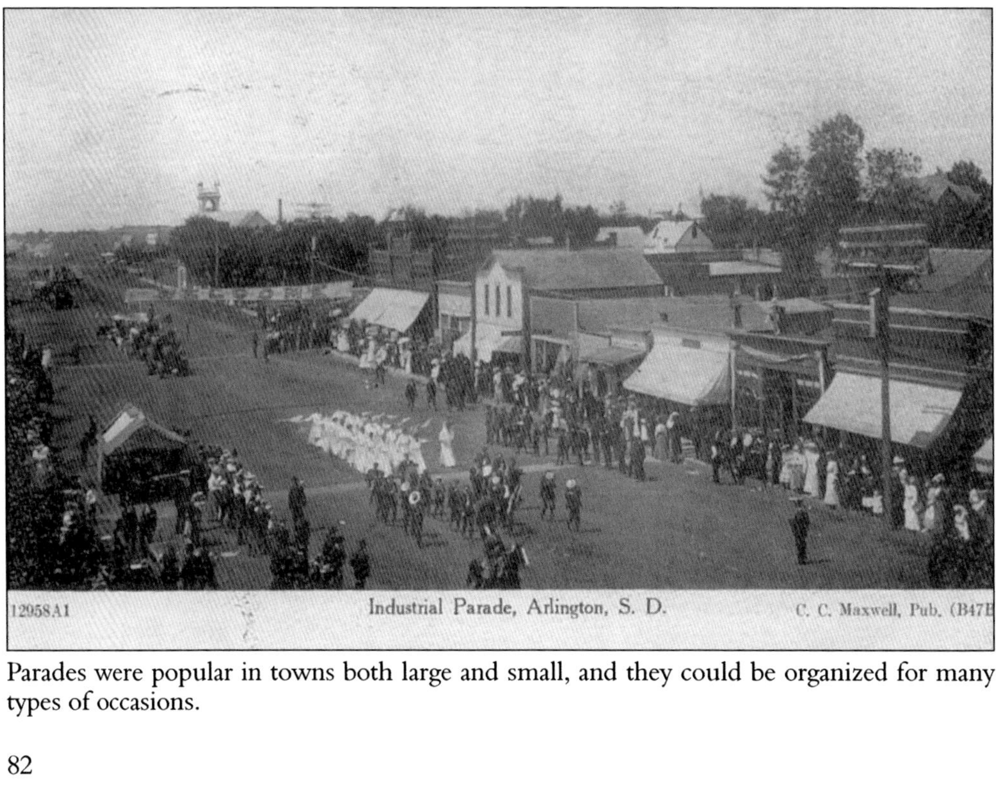

Parades were popular in towns both large and small, and they could be organized for many types of occasions.

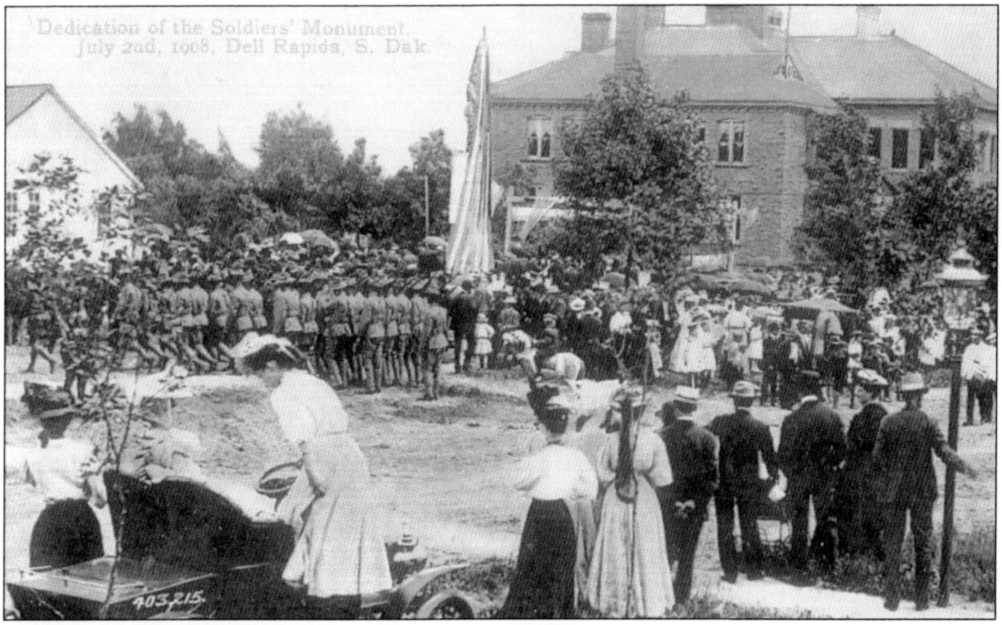

Everyone in Dell Rapids turned out for the unveiling of a new soldiers' monument, shown here still wrapped in a huge American flag.

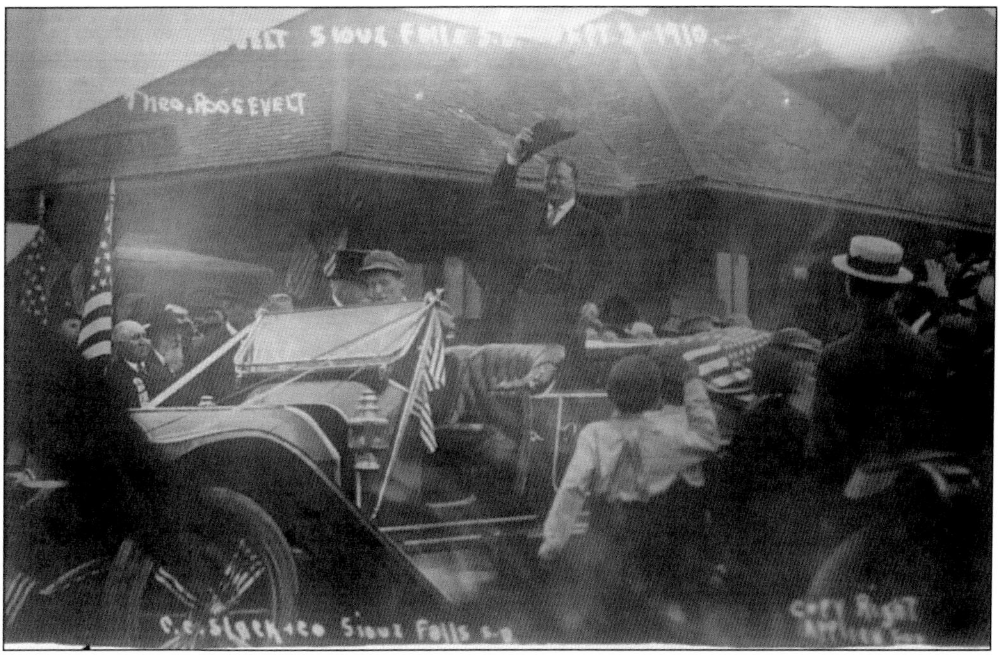

Twenty-five thousand people welcomed former president Theodore Roosevelt to Sioux Falls on September 3, 1910, in the afternoon after speaking in Sioux City that morning. The audience jammed a huge tent set up at Ninth Street and Minnesota Avenue, as he spoke about tariffs and other issues of the day.

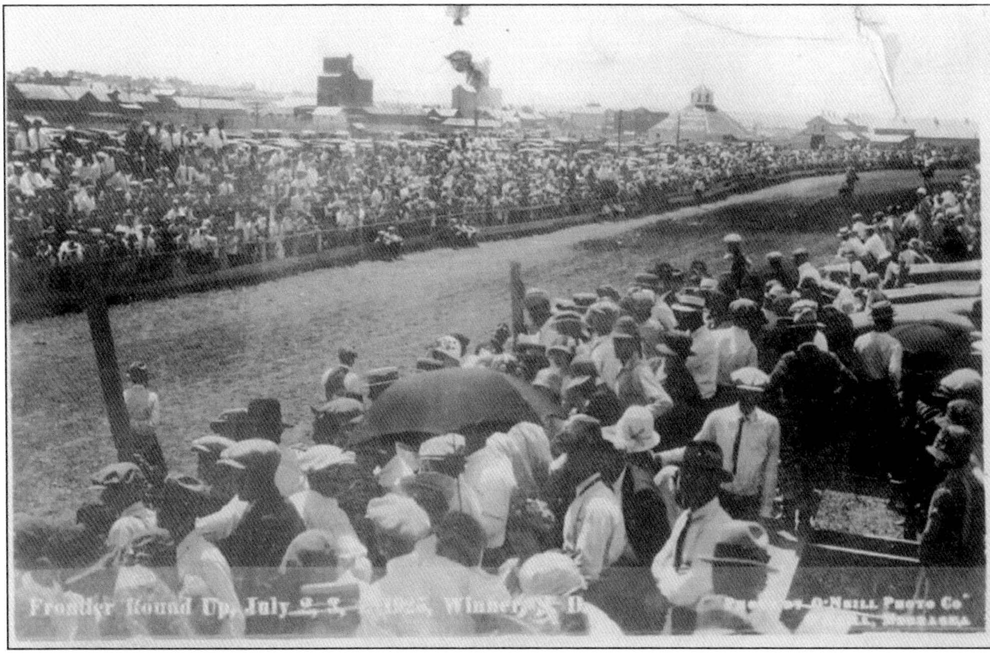

People must have come from miles around to fill the stands for a horse race on the Fourth of July in Winner in 1925.

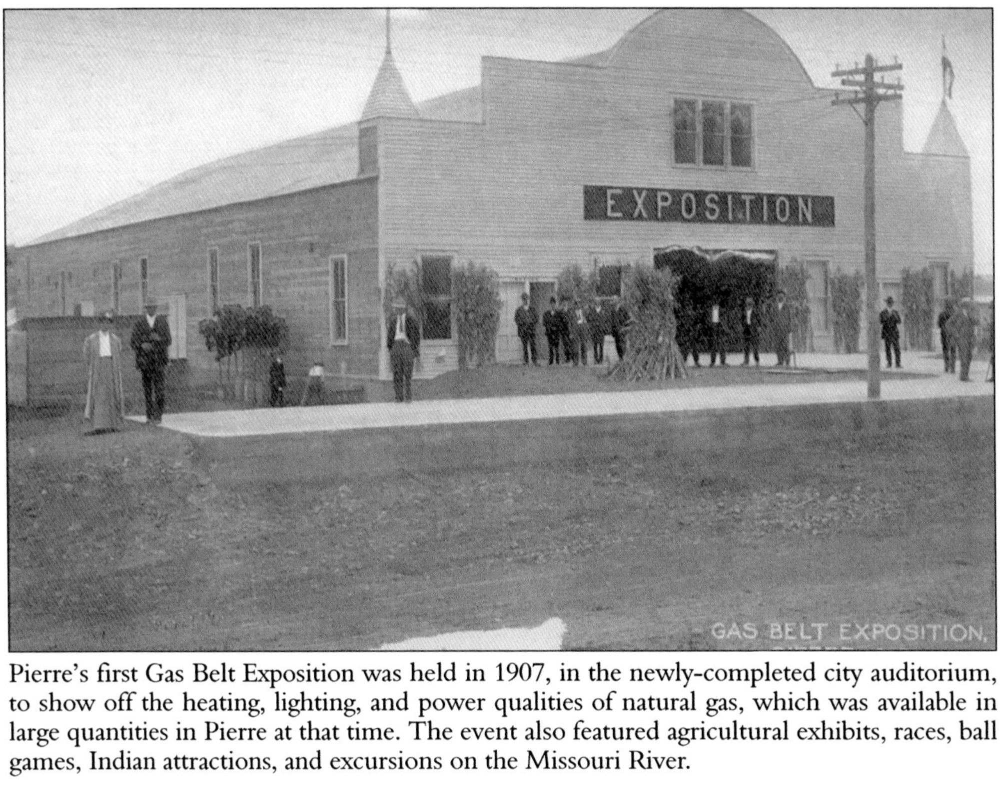

Pierre's first Gas Belt Exposition was held in 1907, in the newly-completed city auditorium, to show off the heating, lighting, and power qualities of natural gas, which was available in large quantities in Pierre at that time. The event also featured agricultural exhibits, races, ball games, Indian attractions, and excursions on the Missouri River.

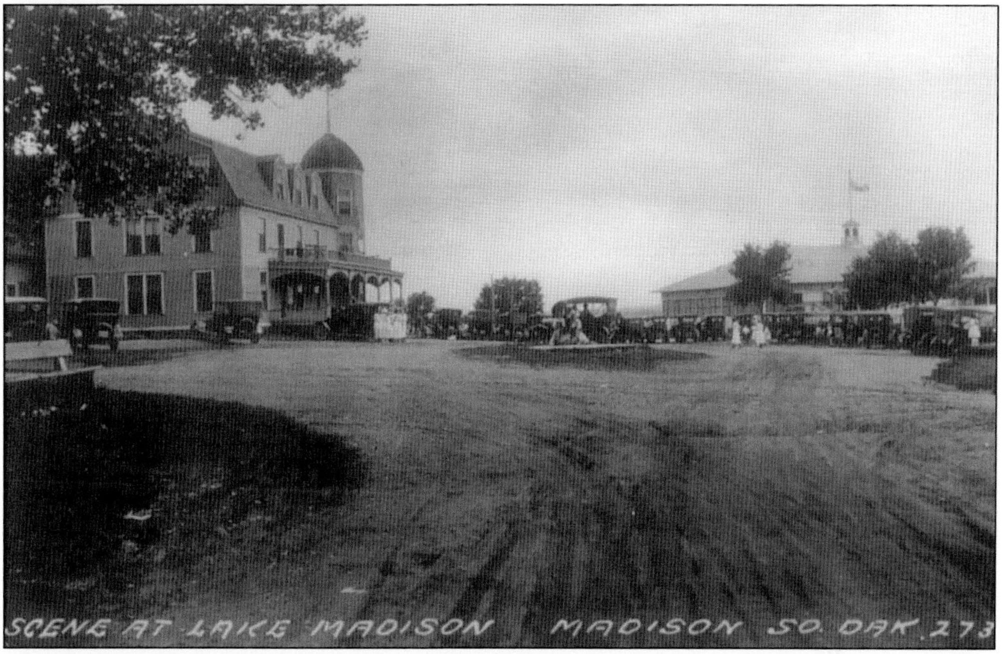

The Chautauqua movement brought entertainment and education to small towns throughout America beginning in 1874. Permanent Chautauqua grounds at Lake Madison opened in 1891, including the Grand View Hotel (shown at left), an auditorium, boat and bath house, dining hall operated by the Woman's Christian Temperance Union, and sites for 300 tents. During 42 years of Chautauqua events at Lake Madison, 360 different speakers delivered 757 formal lectures.

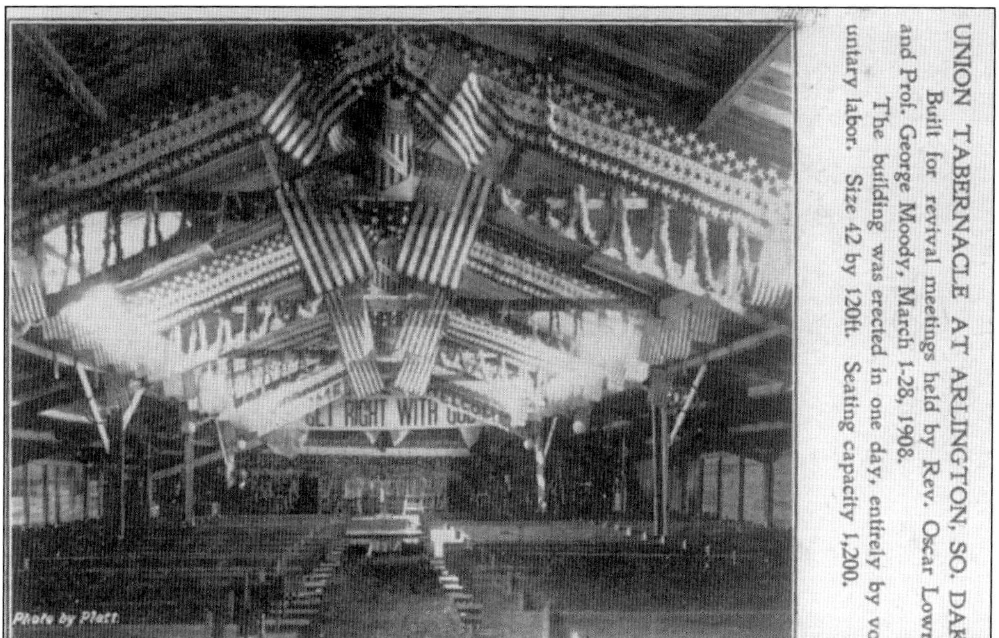

Special facilities were needed for a revival meeting in Arlington in 1908, and volunteers erected a tabernacle in one day. The theme for the revival was, "Get Right with God."

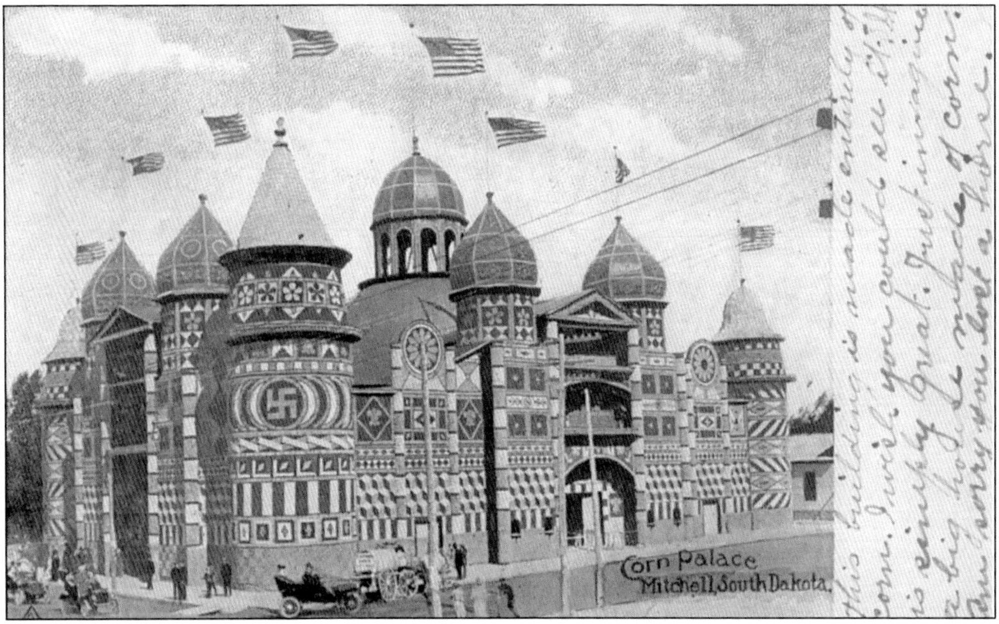

Mitchell's first Corn Palace was built in 1892, and later its decoration became part of an annual fall festival. This picture shows the ninth Corn Palace as it looked in 1907. The swastika was a popular design not yet associated with the Nazi Party. The sender was at a loss for words to describe the sight to her niece in Garrison, North Dakota: "This building is made entirely of corn. I wish you could see it. It is simply great. Just imagine a big house made of corn."

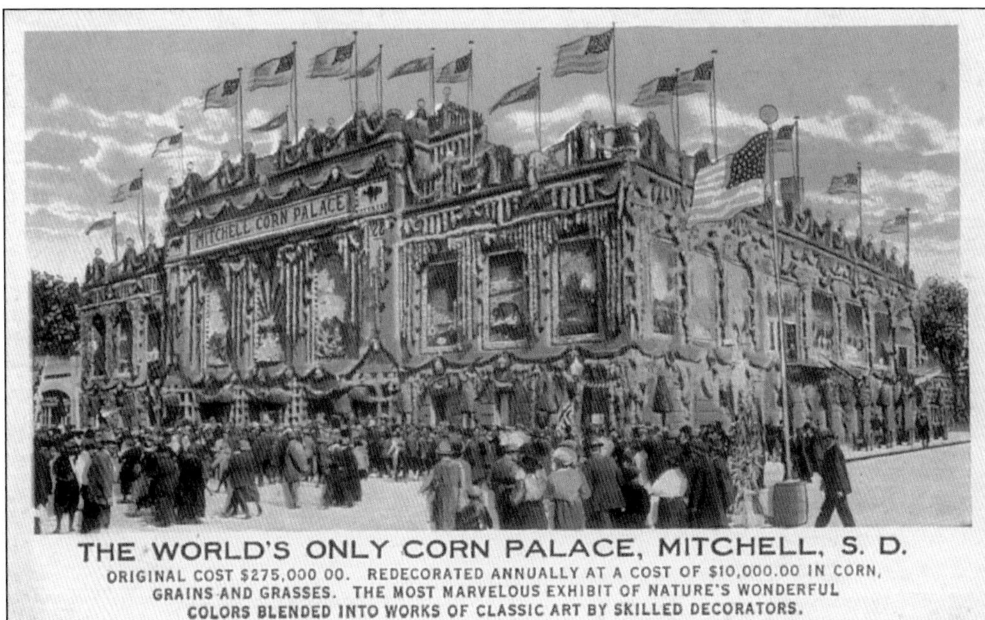

A new Corn Palace auditorium was constructed in 1921, and this building is the one still in use today. Pictured is the design for 1922.

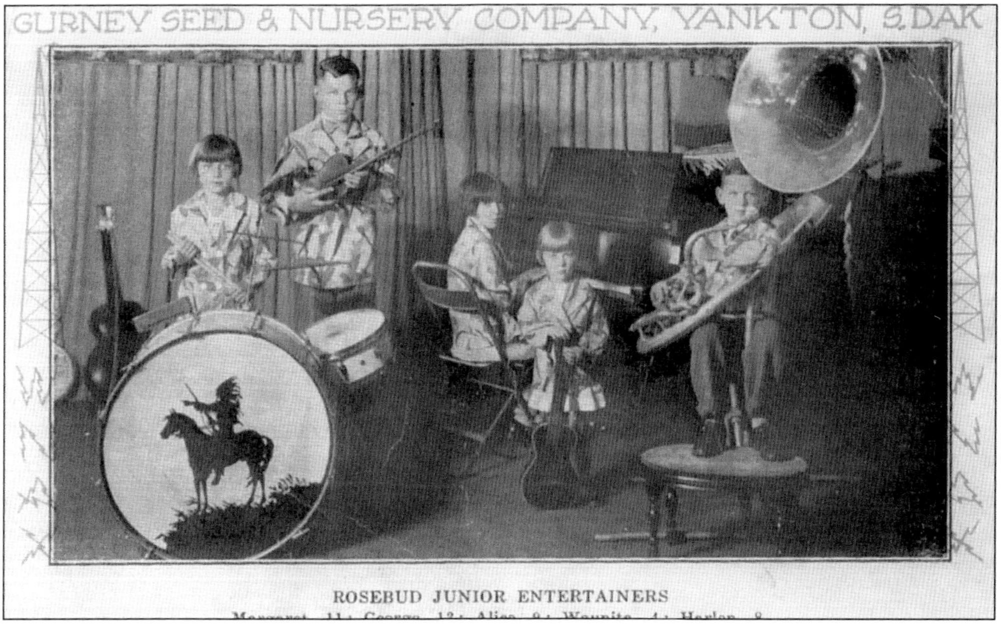

The Gurney family in Yankton owned not only the nationally known seed and nursery company, but also one of South Dakota's early radio stations and a string of oil and tire stores. WNAX radio used many local talents to fill airtime, including the "Rosebud Junior Entertainers."

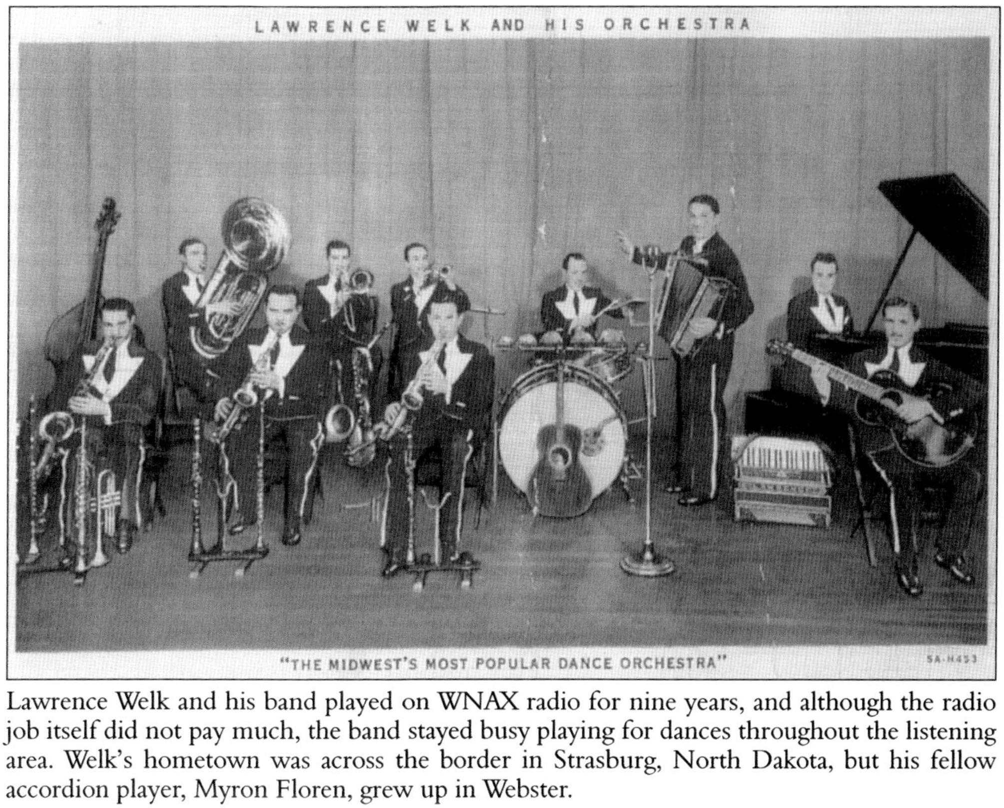

Lawrence Welk and his band played on WNAX radio for nine years, and although the radio job itself did not pay much, the band stayed busy playing for dances throughout the listening area. Welk's hometown was across the border in Strasburg, North Dakota, but his fellow accordion player, Myron Floren, grew up in Webster.

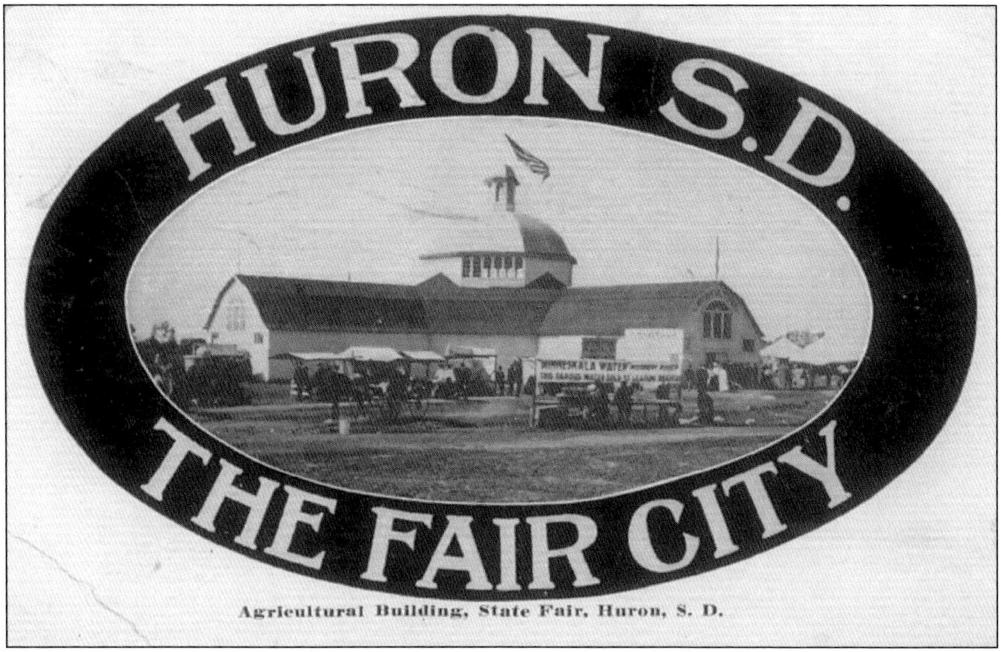

Huron hosted the first two Dakota territorial fairs in 1885 and 1886. After that, the fair rotated to other cities until the state legislature authorized a permanent location for the state fair in Huron in 1905. A visitor to the fair in 1919 wrote home to Hawarden, Iowa, "I am all tired out sure some mob of people here every day. . . . If you lose track of a guy here, he sure is gone for the day."

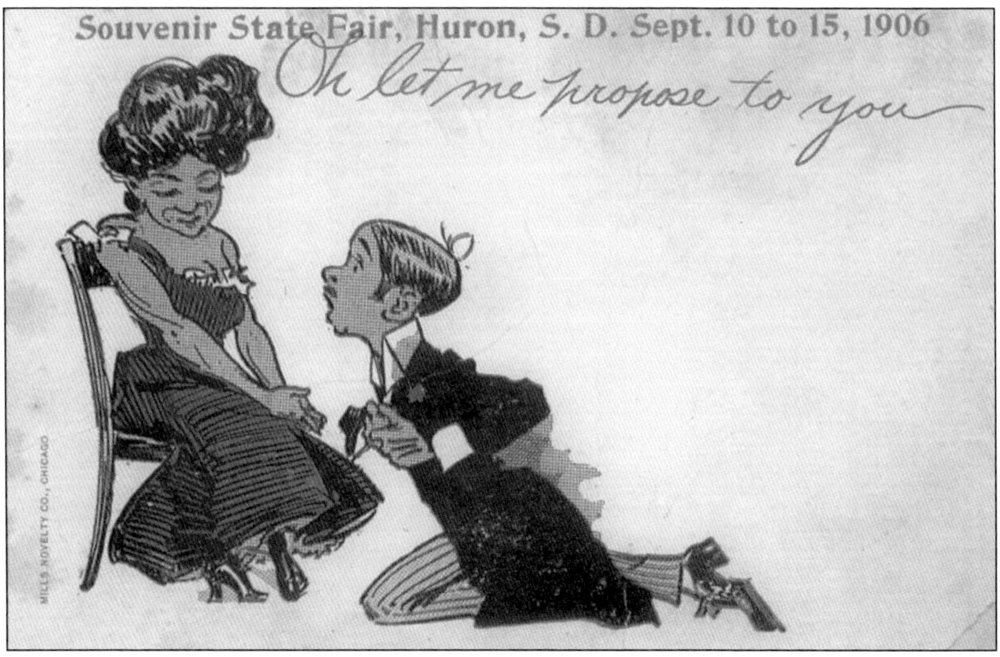

This souvenir from the state fair was sent to Miss Florence Parker in Lebanon.

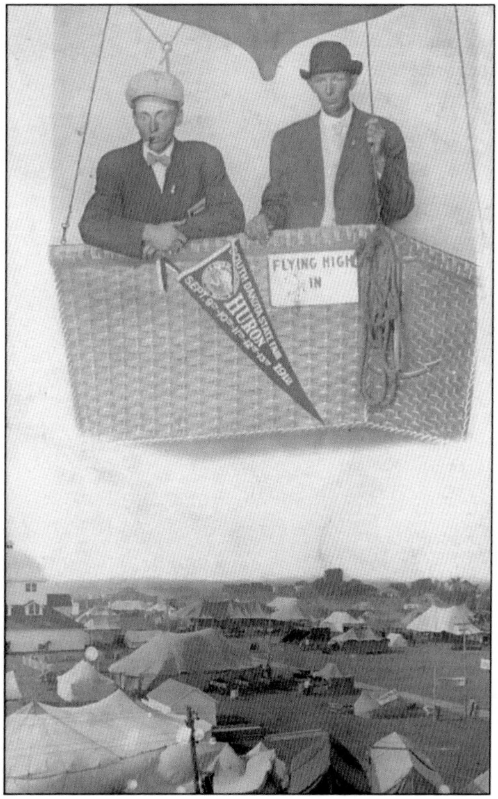

The 1912 state fair featured an "air show, striking mechanical exhibits, and automobiles." Visitors could have their pictures taken in some of the newfangled contraptions.

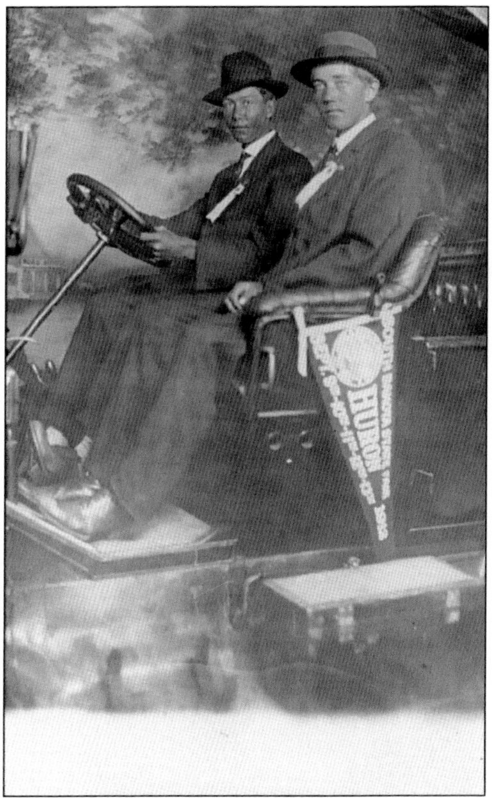

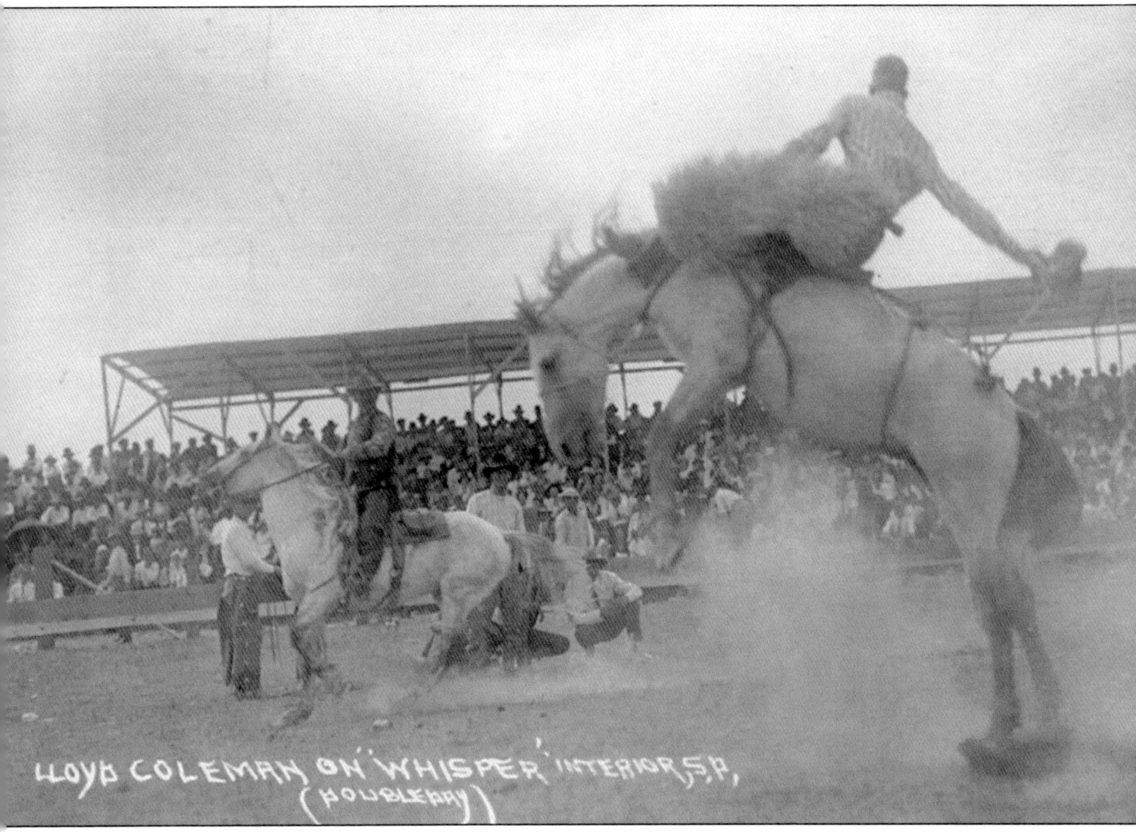

Rodeos have a long history in South Dakota, and they continue to draw large crowds.

Seven

The Grim Reality

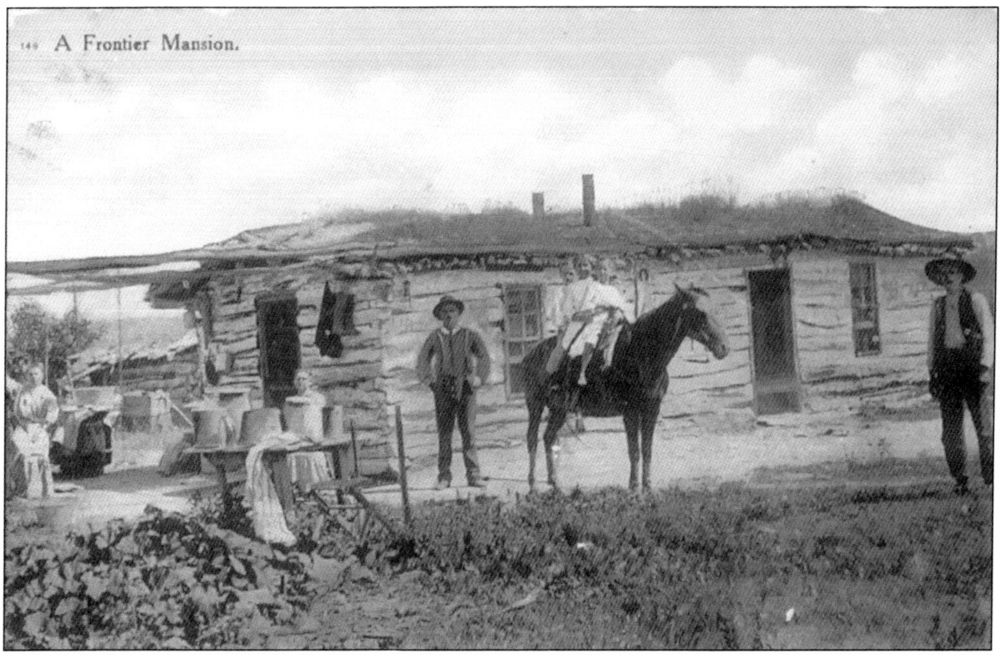

A solid log home like this really would be a mansion for many early South Dakota homesteaders. Settlers braved droughts, tornadoes, blizzards, insects, and many other hazards, and for all those who survived, many others kept moving. Those who stayed on needed a sense of humor to make it through the difficult times.

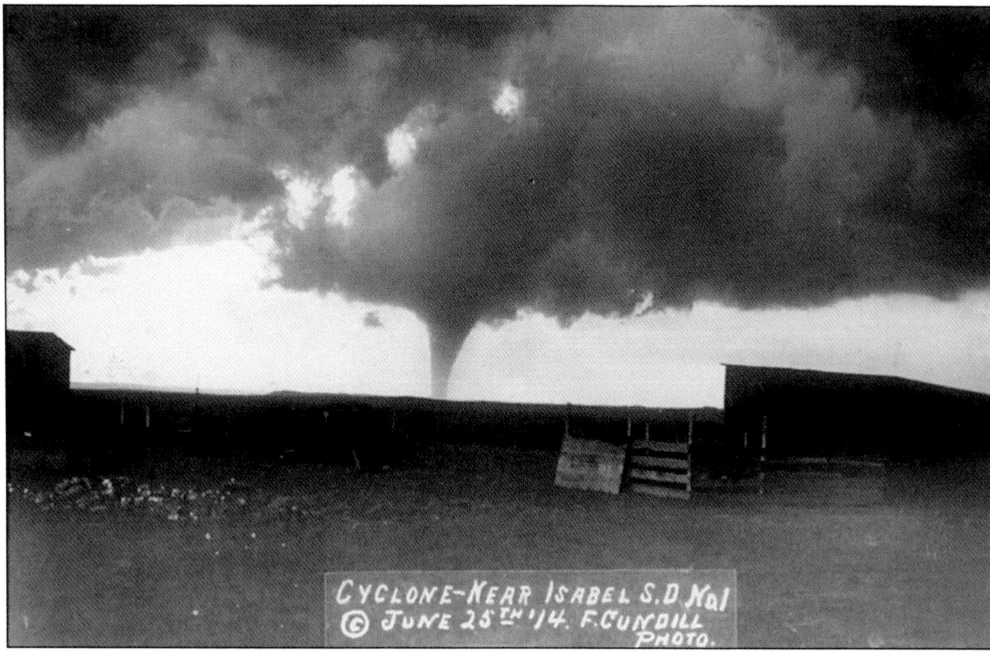

Frank Cundill, who advertised himself as "the honyocker photographer," captured this tornado on film. Cundill moved from Iowa to a homestead near Firesteel in 1911, and lived there for 46 years. He learned photography from his father and sent his glass negatives back home to process, since he did not have his own darkroom equipment.

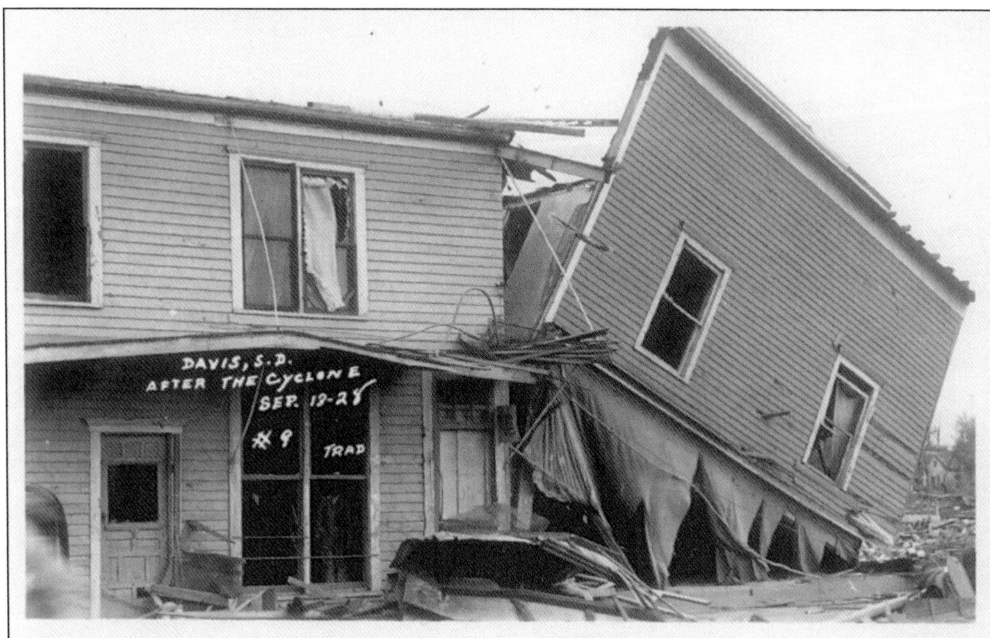

A 1928 tornado in Davis killed one woman and injured many others, and destroyed the brick post office, a bank, and three general stores. The newspaper reported that "household articles and merchandise were flying about the air like straw."

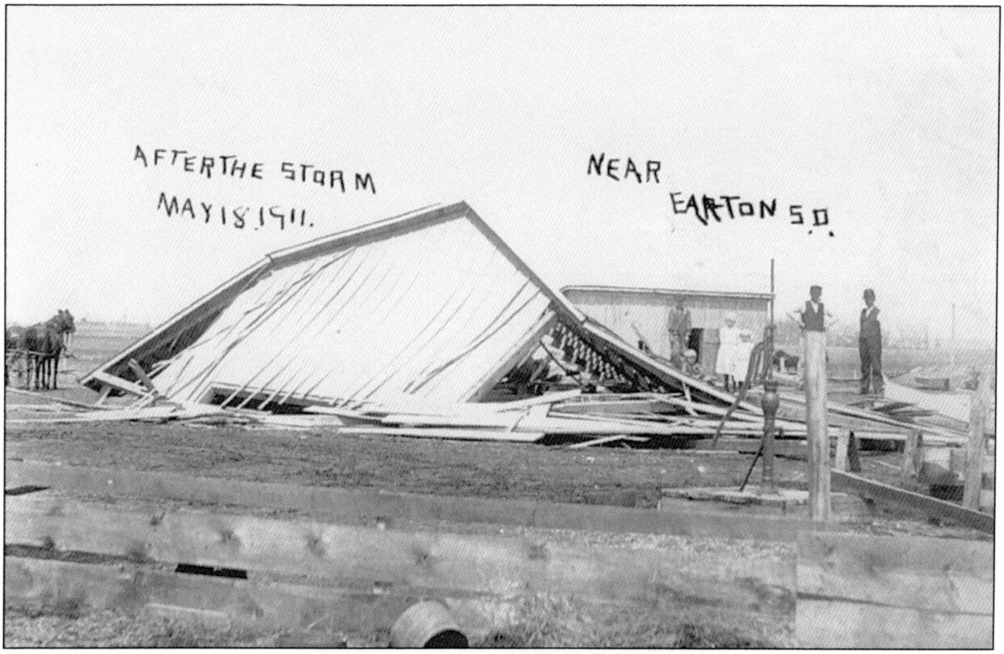

Onlookers survey the damage after a storm hit Elkton in May 1911.

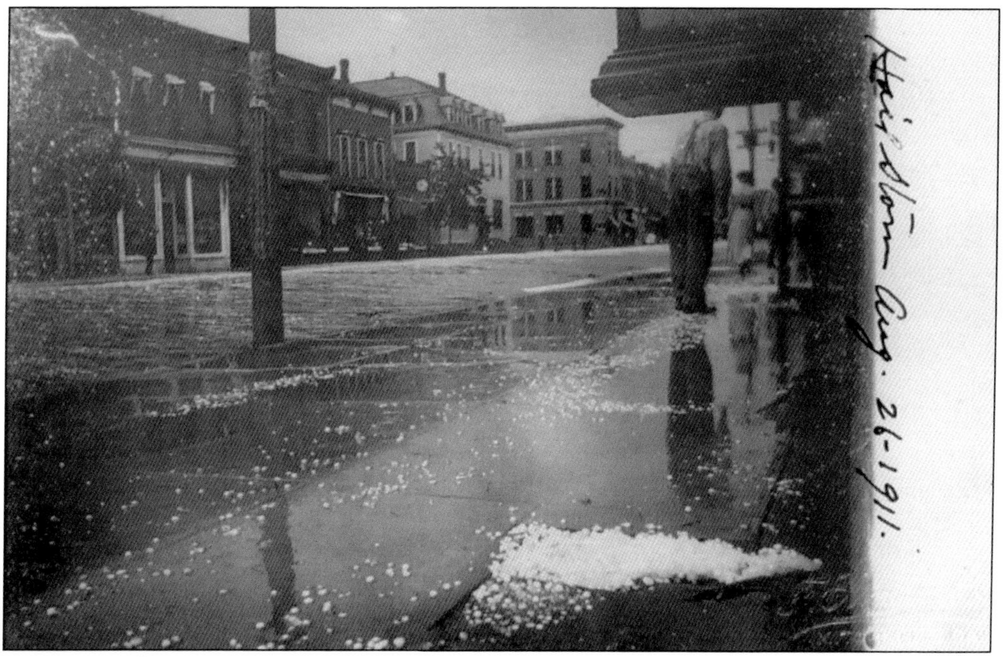

Remnants of a hailstorm make an interesting picture in downtown Mitchell, but the storm ruined gardens throughout town, then continued north where it stripped corn to the ground and destroyed a flax crop just as it was being harvested. The same storm left piles of hail 3 to 4 feet high in Emery, and stopped a train near Spencer.

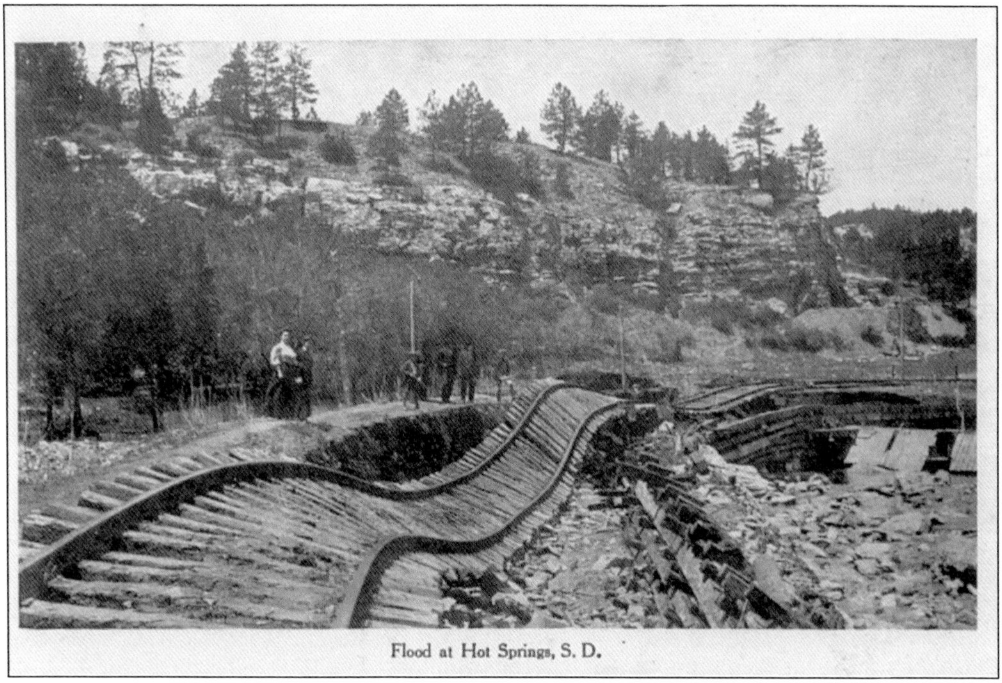

Flooding of the Fall River near Hot Springs destroyed railroad tracks in June 1908.

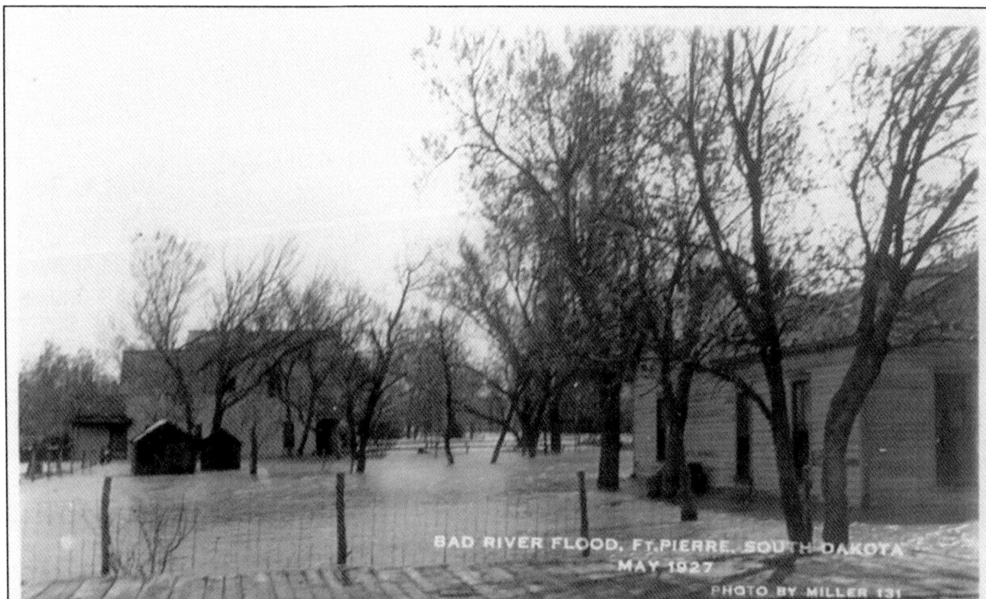

The *Fort Pierre Times* reported damage as the Bad River crested in May 1927: "In less than thirty minutes after the overflow of the dike the street leading to the fairgrounds was a raging torrent and the entire south side of town was submerged. . . . A part of the Mason house, in the west end of town and north of the river, broke away and parked against the Robson garage, while the Hans Johnson house drifted down to the Creager property on Main Street."

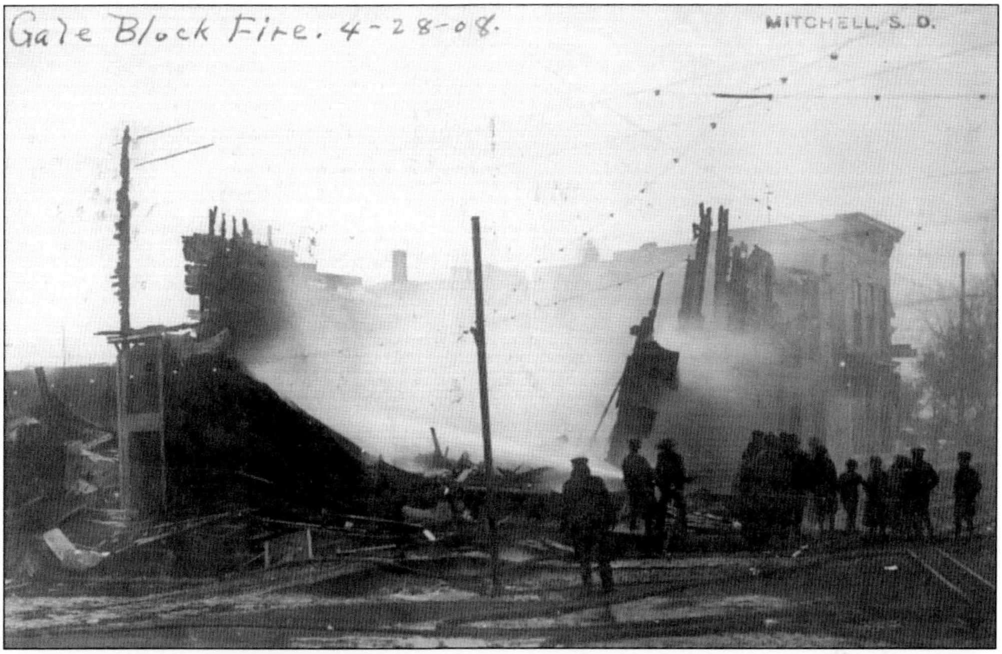

A visitor from Iowa sent this card from Mitchell only three days after a disastrous fire in 1908, with the message, "They had a hot time in Mitchell the other night." A grocery store and a millinery shop started burning at 3 a.m., and five families living behind and above the stores escaped with nothing but their nightclothes.

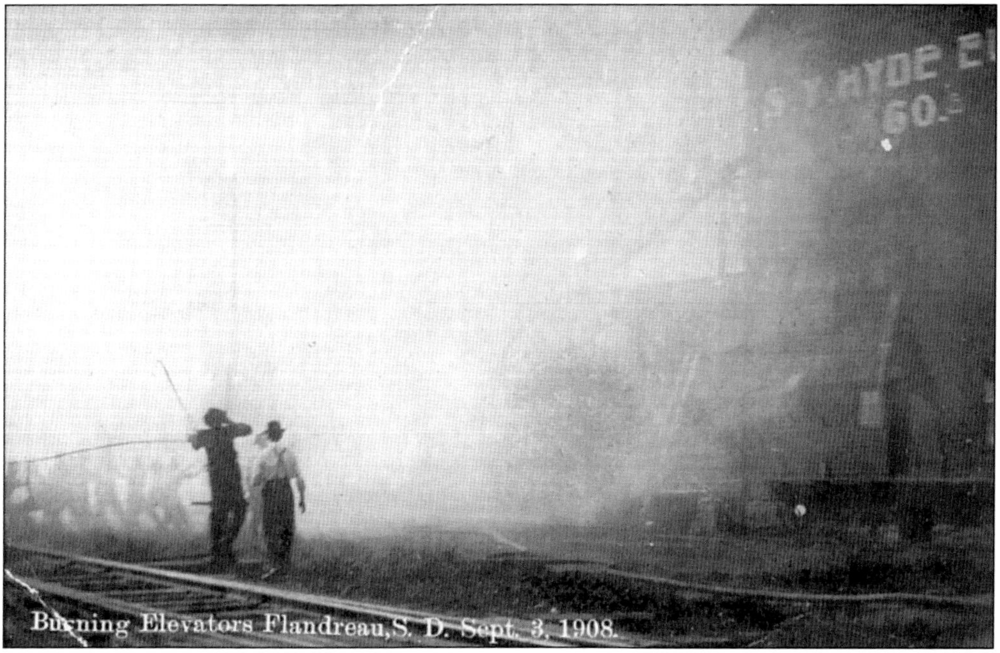

Wheat dust was highly combustible, and grain elevators could virtually explode if conditions were right. Dry weather, a hot day, a high prevailing wind, and a spark from a train leaving the station started a fire in Flandreau that quickly destroyed two elevators in 1908.

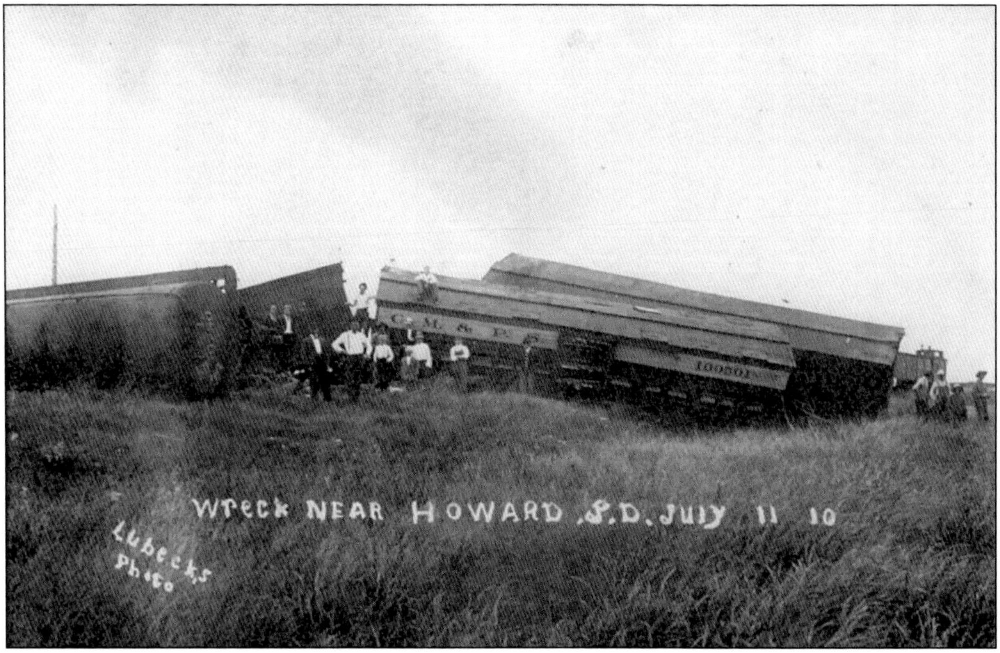

After a freight train jumped the track 2 miles outside of Howard in July 1910, word quickly spread that a tanker car was leaking, and people brought cans, buckets, and barrels to collect the spilling gasoline. The train master told people to carry away as much as they could, since it would otherwise go to waste. Disaster turned into good fortune for some, as farmers and automobile owners collected enough gasoline to last them most of the summer.

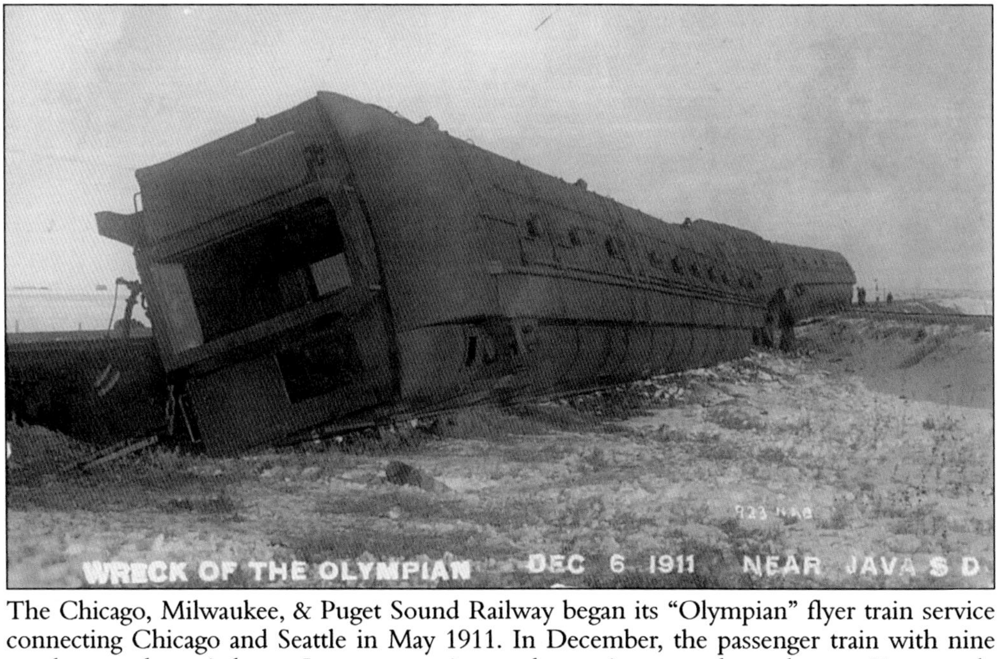

The Chicago, Milwaukee, & Puget Sound Railway began its "Olympian" flyer train service connecting Chicago and Seattle in May 1911. In December, the passenger train with nine coaches struck a switch near Java, overturning an observation car and two sleepers. Fortunately the only injury reported was conductor William Foster, who bruised an arm.

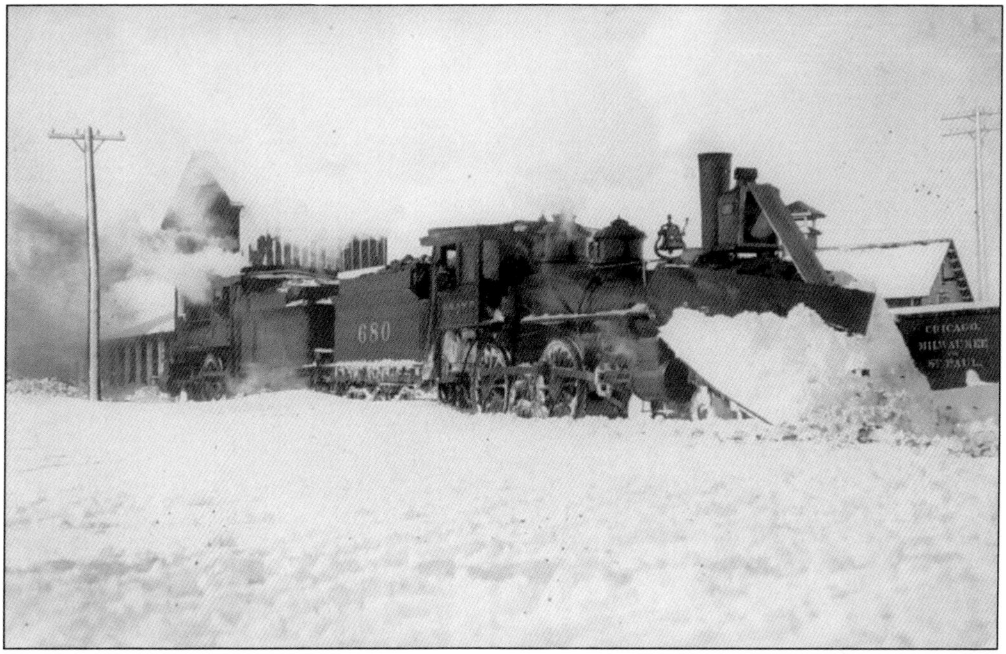

A Milwaukee Road snowplow clears tracks near Scotland. Railroads were the lifelines for many South Dakota communities, and blizzards and drifts could quickly shut off essential supplies if train service was disrupted.

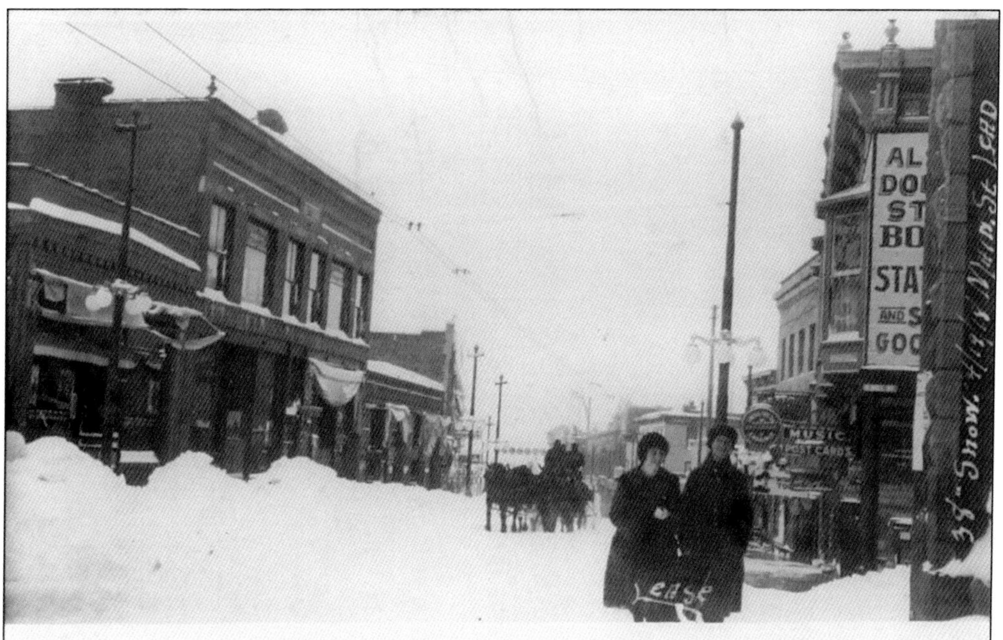

A late spring snow in 1918 left 38 inches in Lead and created a "general blockade of traffic." The storm affected only the area about 10 miles around the city.

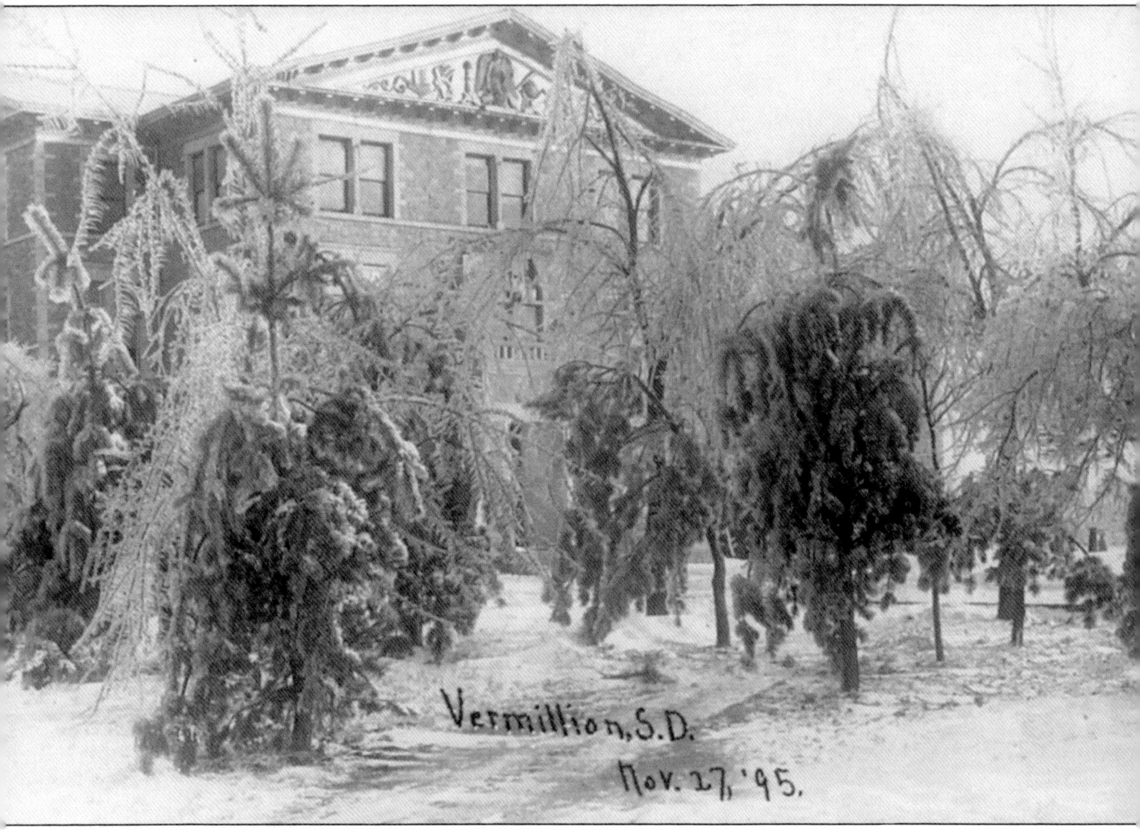

An ice storm turned these trees into beautiful sculptures, but it could also pose serious danger to people and animals, and in later years could create disaster by downing power and telephone lines.

Eight

On a Personal Note

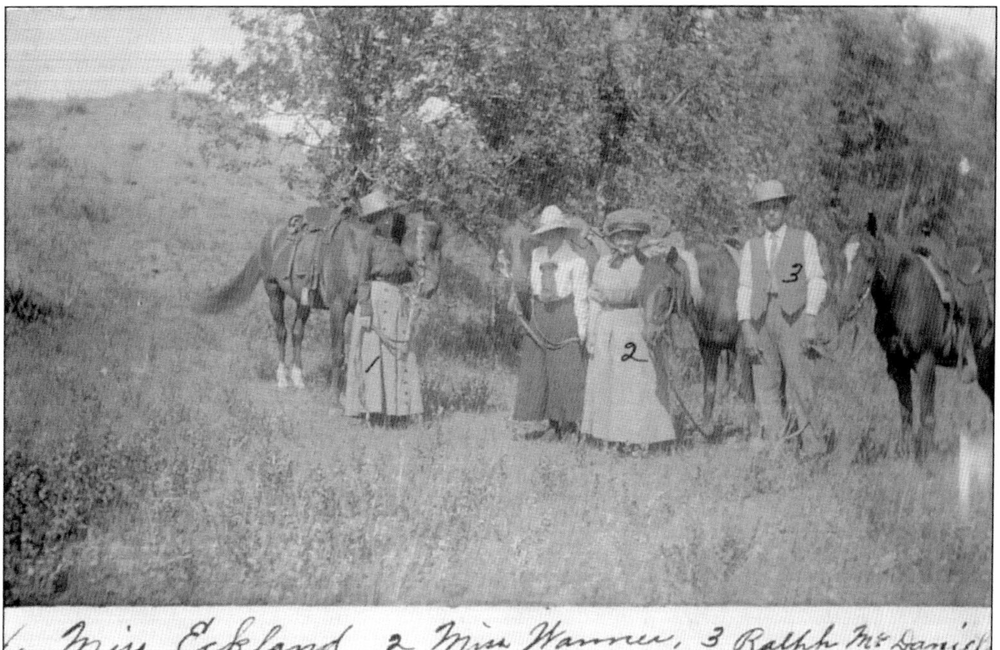

Postmarked in Eagle Butte in 1911, the message on the back of this postcard explains: "Dear Mamma, This is a picture of those girls that lived in that cottage over by Lantry. You remember we drove right past the house the day we drove over there."

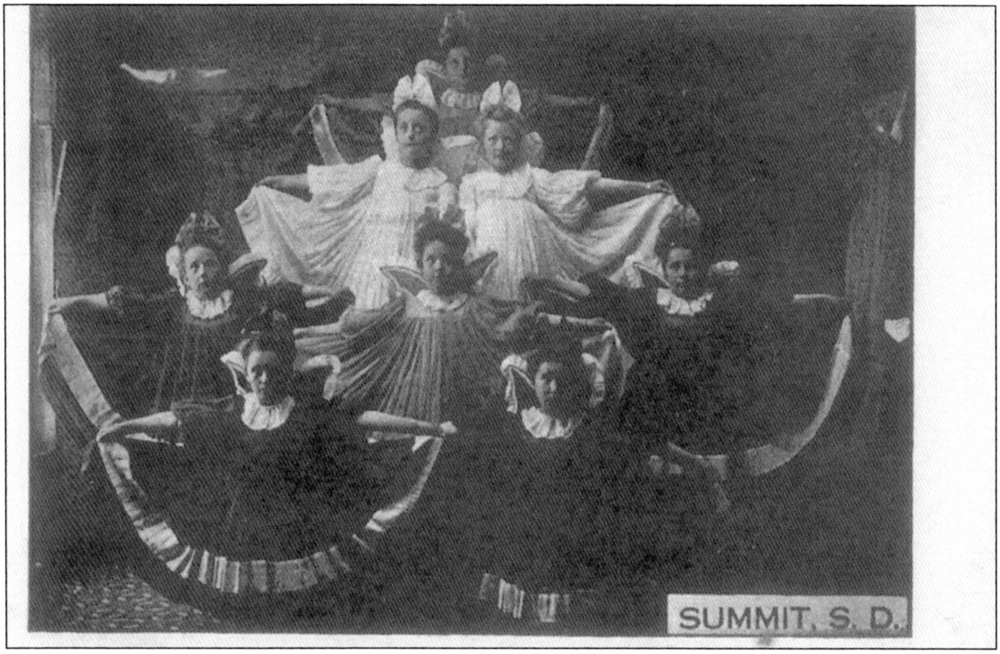

A pyramid of young angels poses for the camera in Summit in 1908.

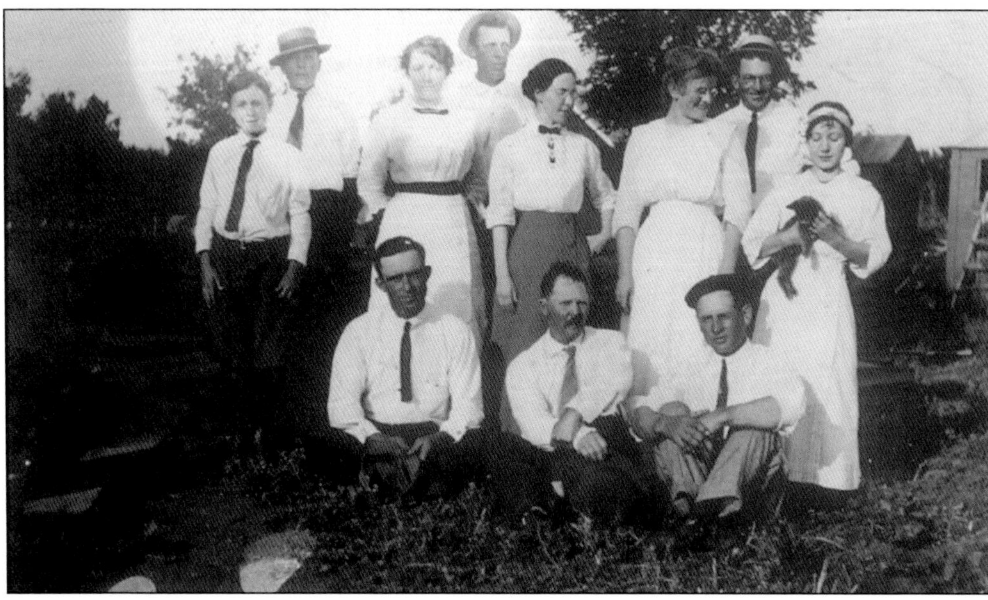
A pleasant group poses with a cat in Hayti in 1913.

During the heyday of penny postcards, formal portraits could be printed with postcard backs so that they could be sent to friends and relatives. This unidentified portrait came from the studio of S. Trad in Marion.

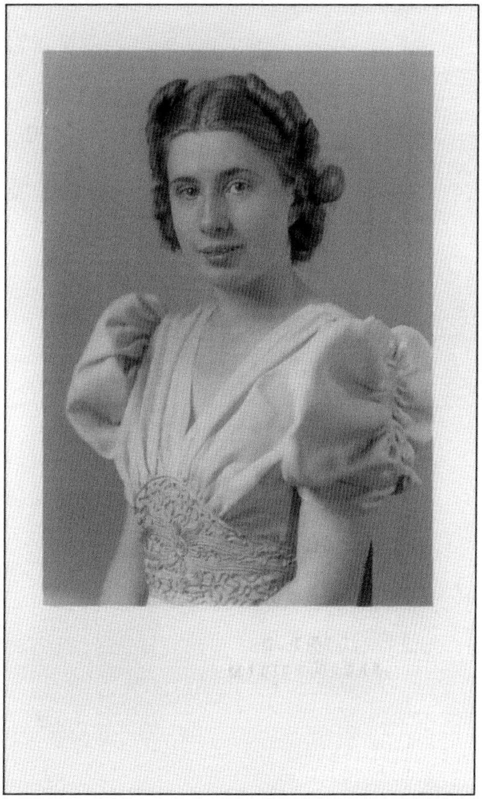

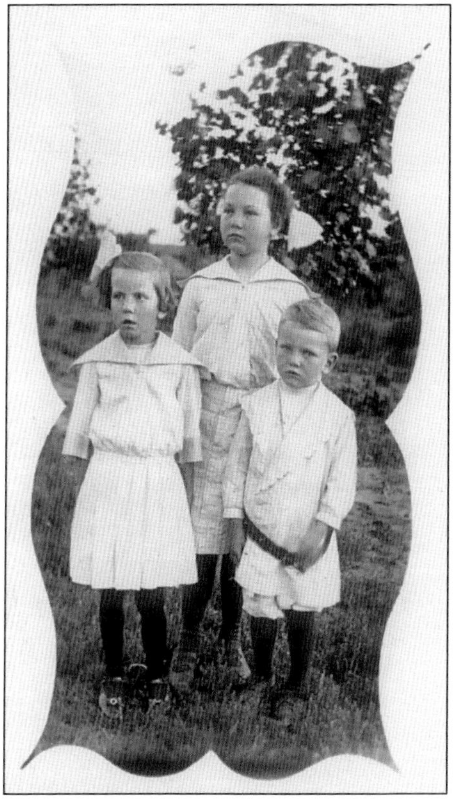

This photo of Iva, Edna, and Raymond Lloyd was taken near Reliance about 1913. State census records show that the Lloyd children were born in Nebraska and probably moved to South Dakota with their family to homestead a year earlier.

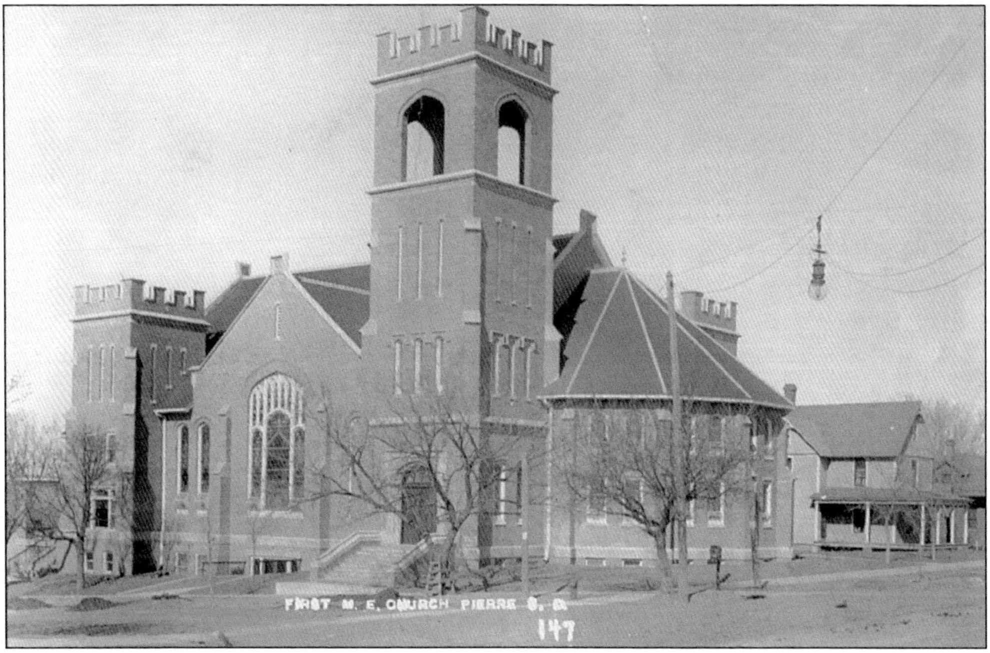

The message on this card included a mixture of English and German, explaining some land dealings near Bixby in Perkins County in the spring of 1912: "Moe's land ist offen für filing. Er hat ein anders genommen nah Lemmon. Mutter hat das vom Mrs. Larson gehört. I'm going to S.S. school. Wonder who will be there. Wunder of Moe nicht ein ander claim contested hat und hat warten müssen."

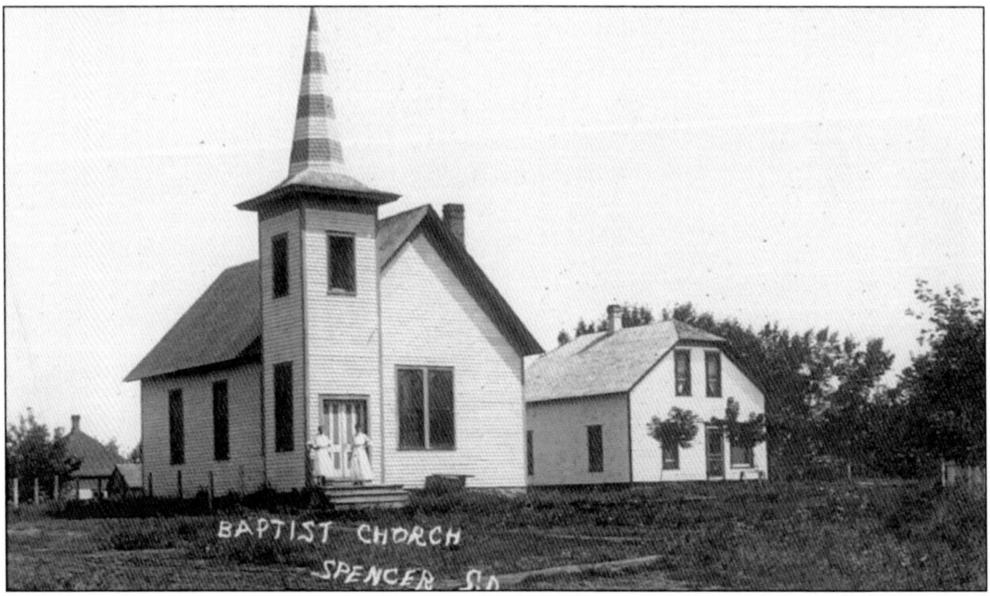

A note to Ella Jones in DeSmet reported quilting news from her sister Lethe in Spencer in 1908: "This is Thurs eve and beautiful too. The society tied out a quilt for the juniors and got Mrs. Pughs started a quilting. Ma and Mrs. Lang.—quilted this P.M. thought you would like this card."

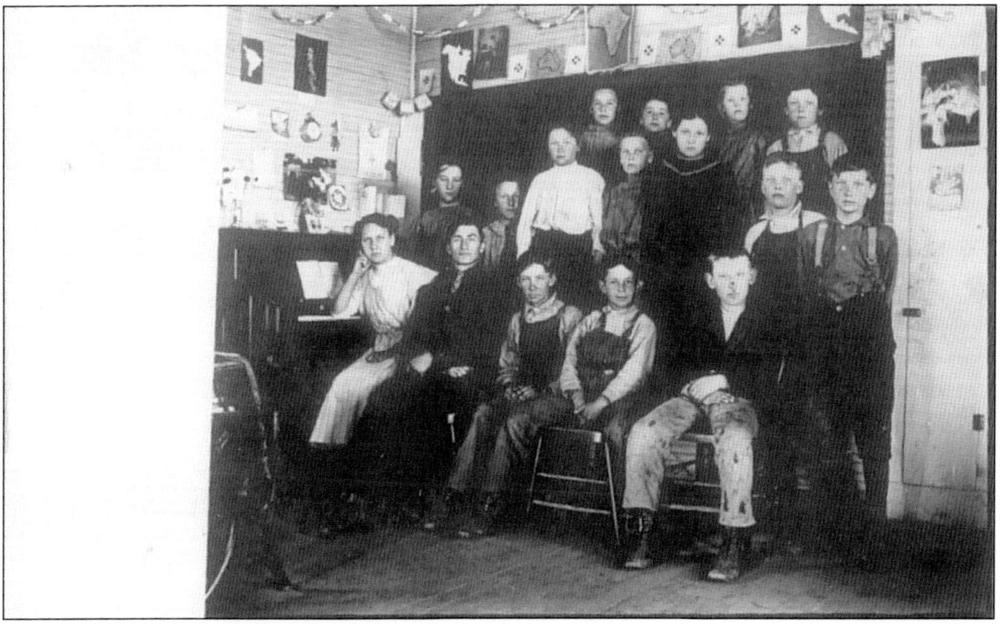

This group photo, from a rural school near Selby in 1908, shows some of the class projects displayed on the walls.

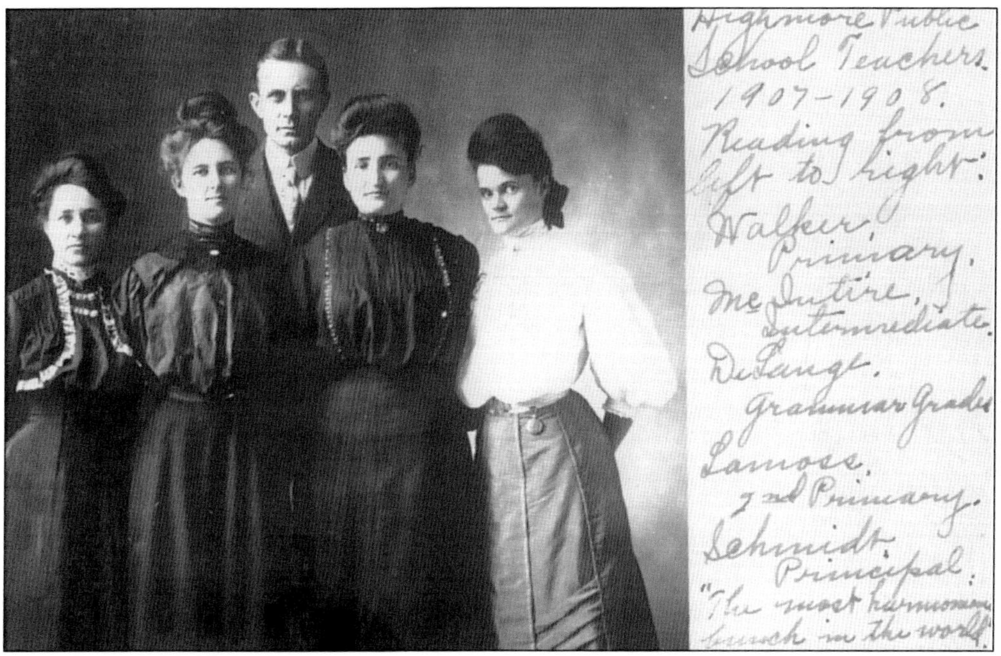

The staff of the Highmore School posed for a group picture in 1907, "the most harmonious bunch in the world."

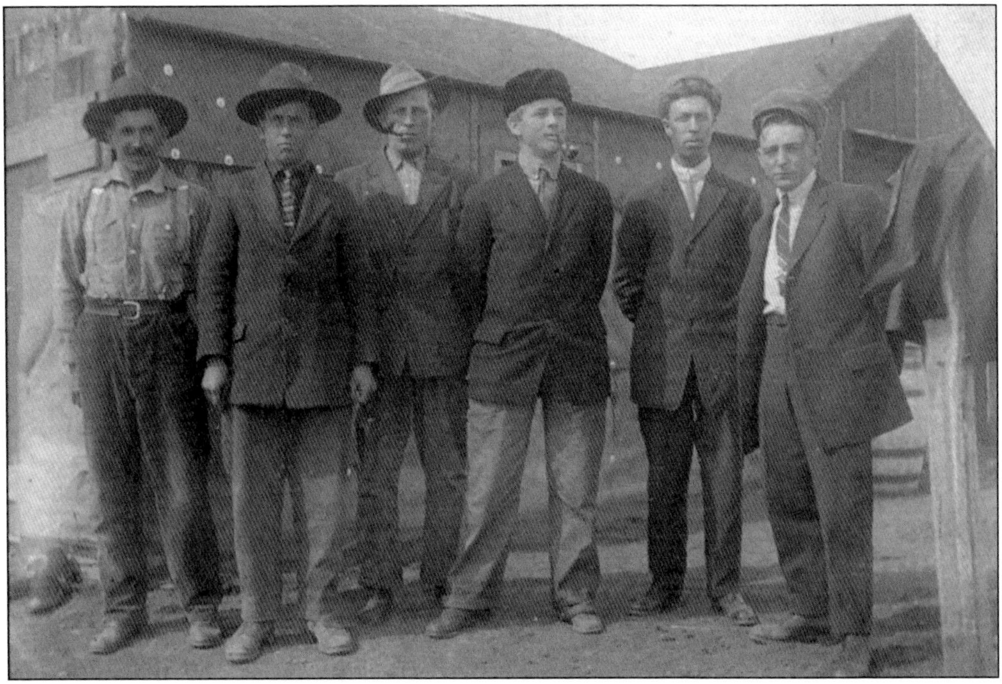

This postcard was made from a "cyanotype," an inexpensive type of photograph with a characteristic blue tint. Labeled simply "Dakota Farmers," this group included Gust Marks, Julius Marks, Simm Dahl, Jim Clausen, Andrew Anderson, and Andrew Syvert. Information from state census records indicates that the picture was probably taken near Vale sometime before 1915.

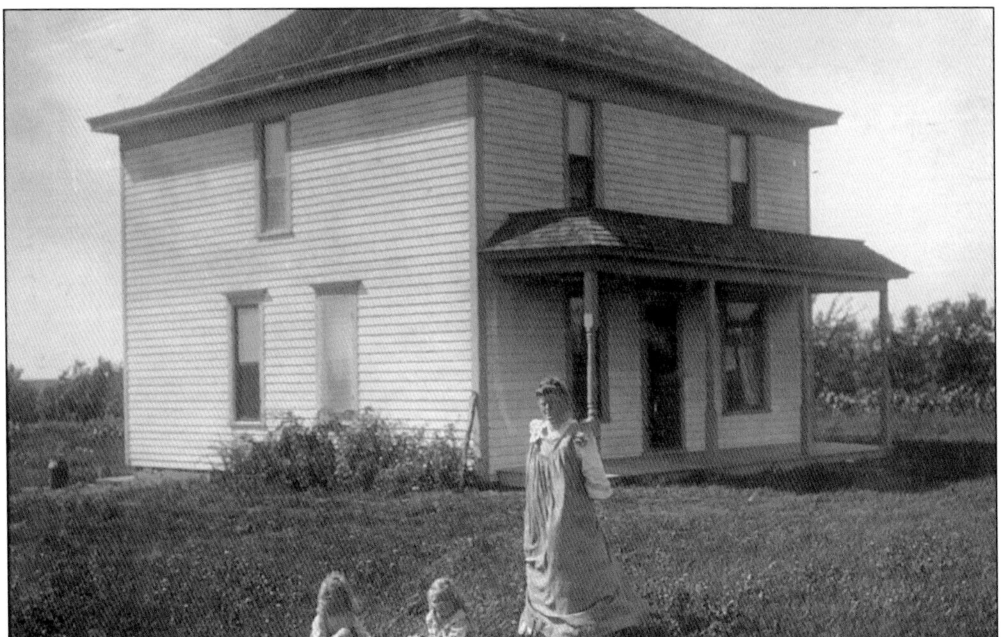

"This is 'Our House' me & the Kids on a washday," wrote Margaret Williams in DeSmet to a friend in Meers.

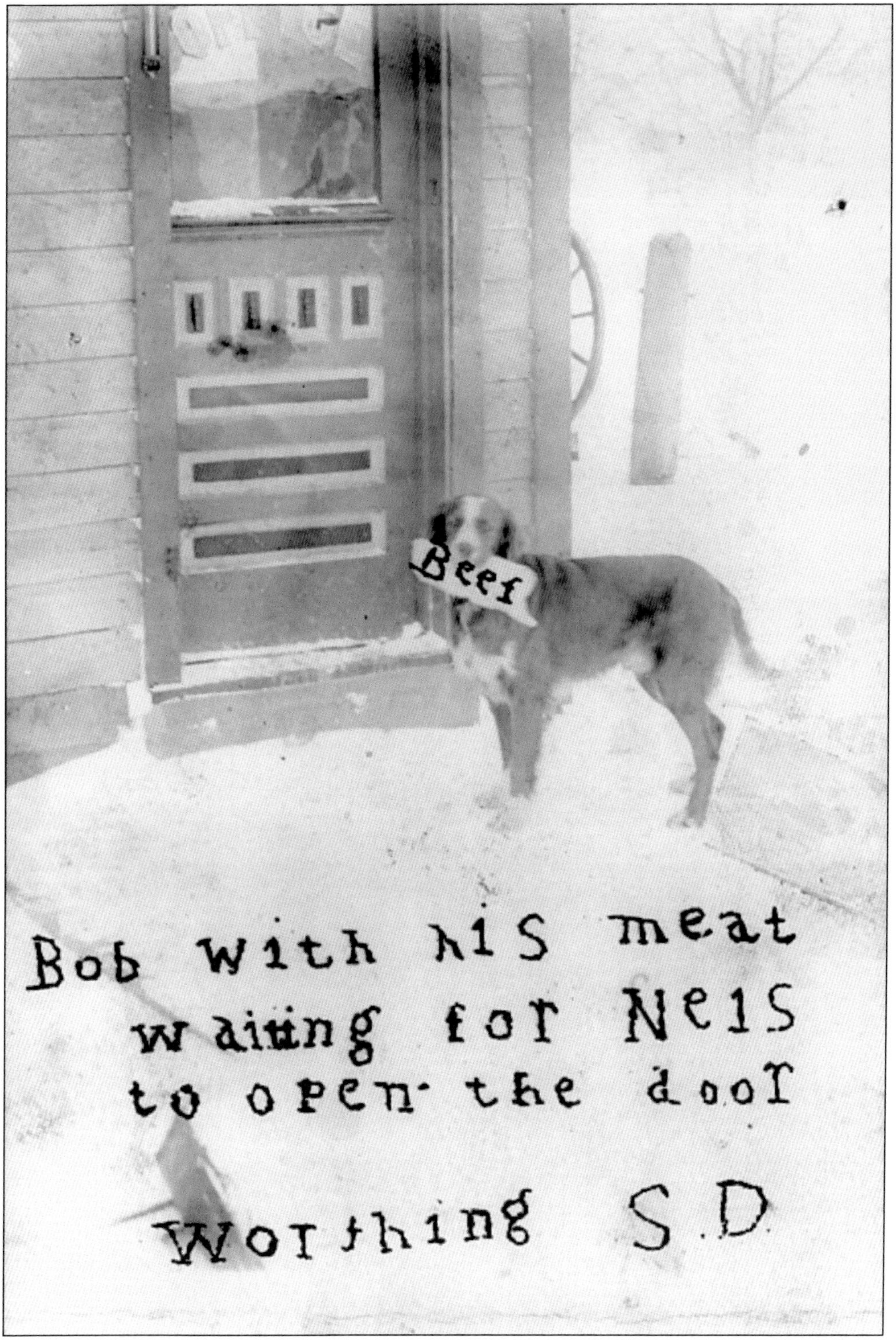

Bob the dog waits on a snowy porch in Worthing.

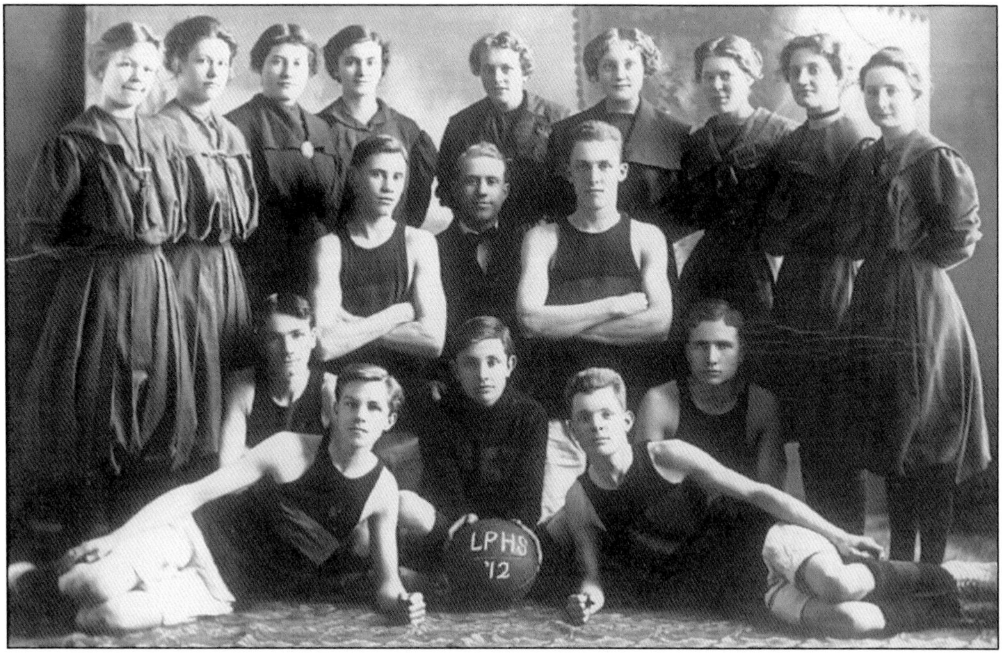

Men's and women's basketball teams from Lake Preston High School posed together for this group portrait in 1912.

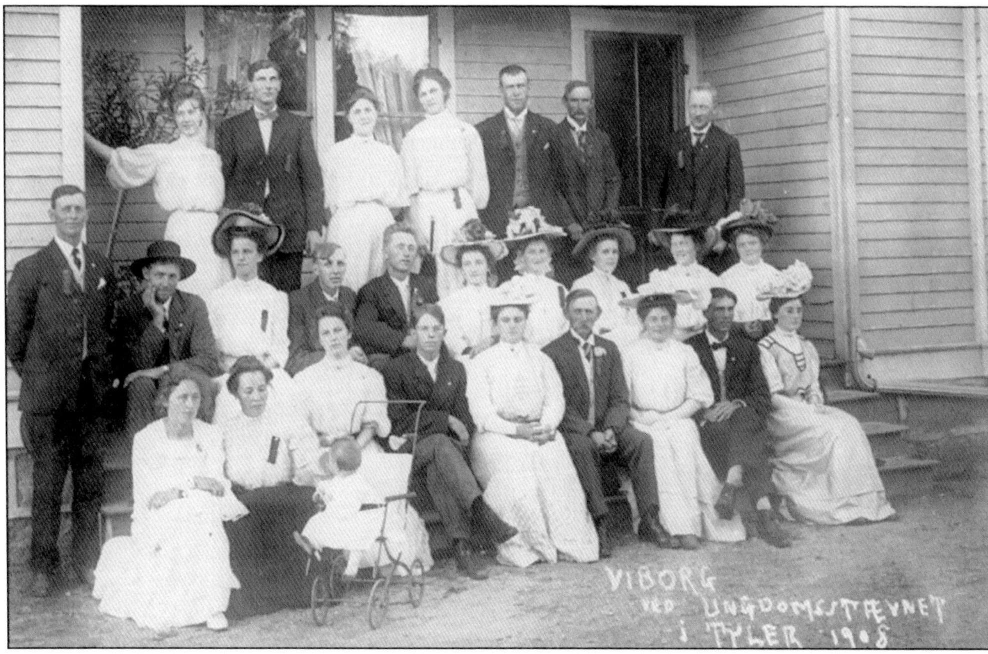

Cecilia wrote to her cousin Carl Smith in Wall in 1908: "Expect you are rather lonely out there so I will send you some of our good looking sober people to cheer you."

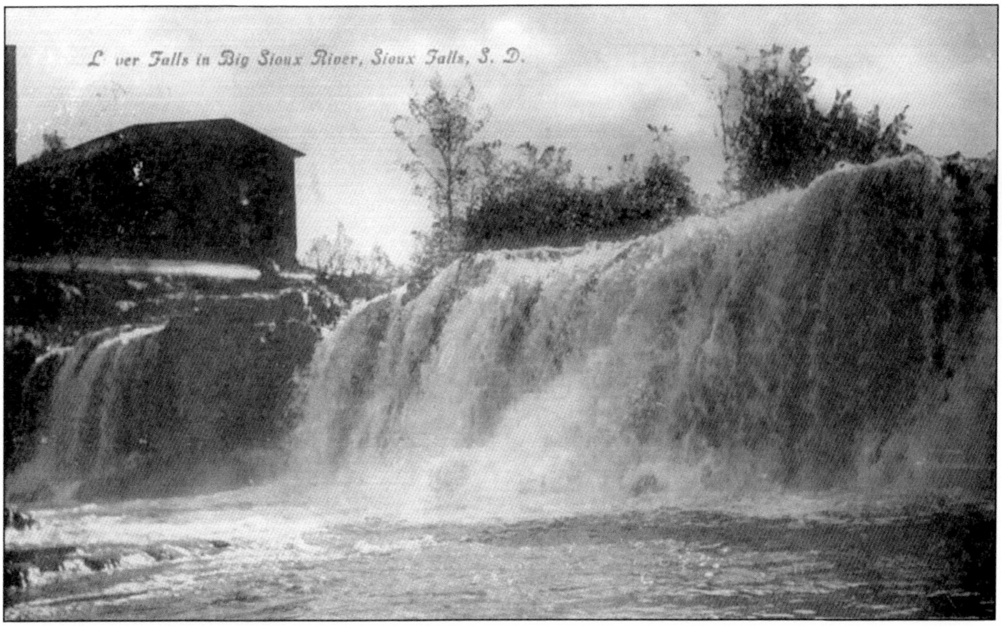

Melinda Seater wrote to a friend in Flint, Michigan, in 1909, while visiting in Sioux Falls: "I am out with the Cleveland Ladies Orchestra for the summer playing at different Chautauquas. The work and the trips are very interesting. Shall be home Sept."

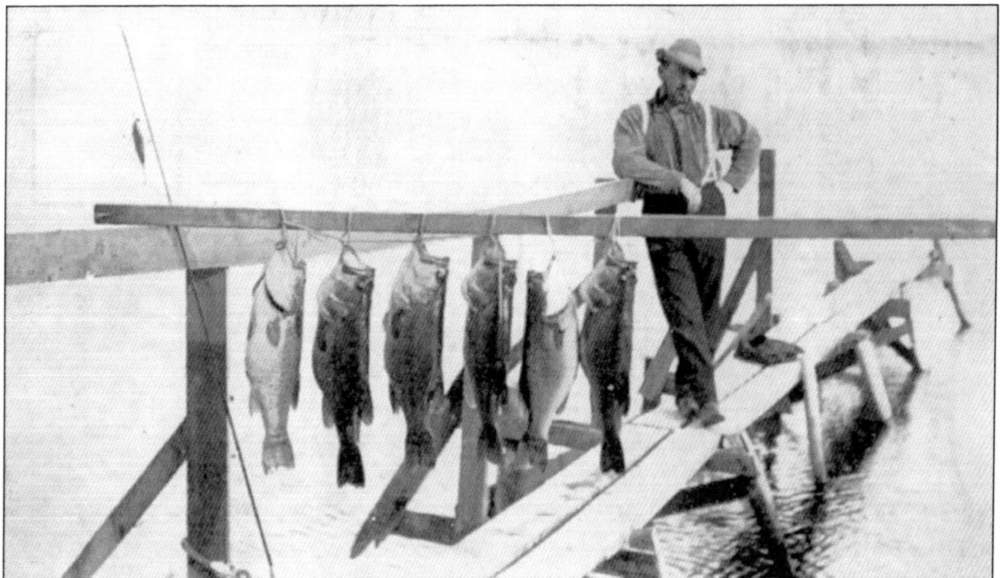

An early mornings catch on Lake Andes, Ravinia, S. D.

Some men always had time to go fishing in South Dakota.

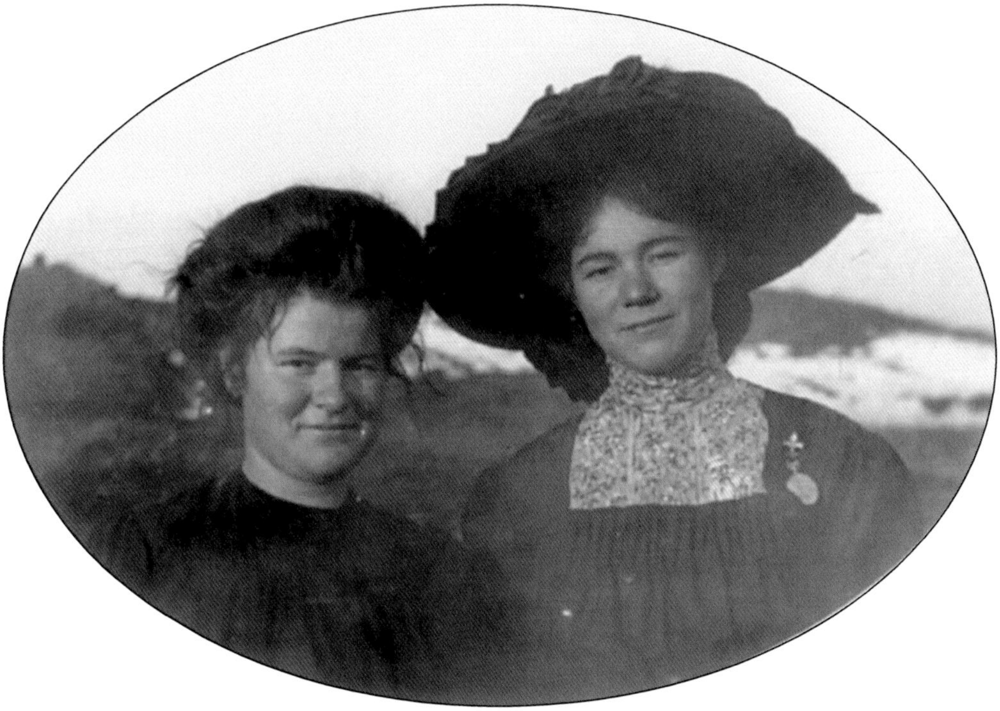

Gustav M. Johnson moved from his homestead to Philip in 1907, when the first town lots were sold. He began a photography business, taking pictures of homesteaders and settlers—including these two lovely ladies.

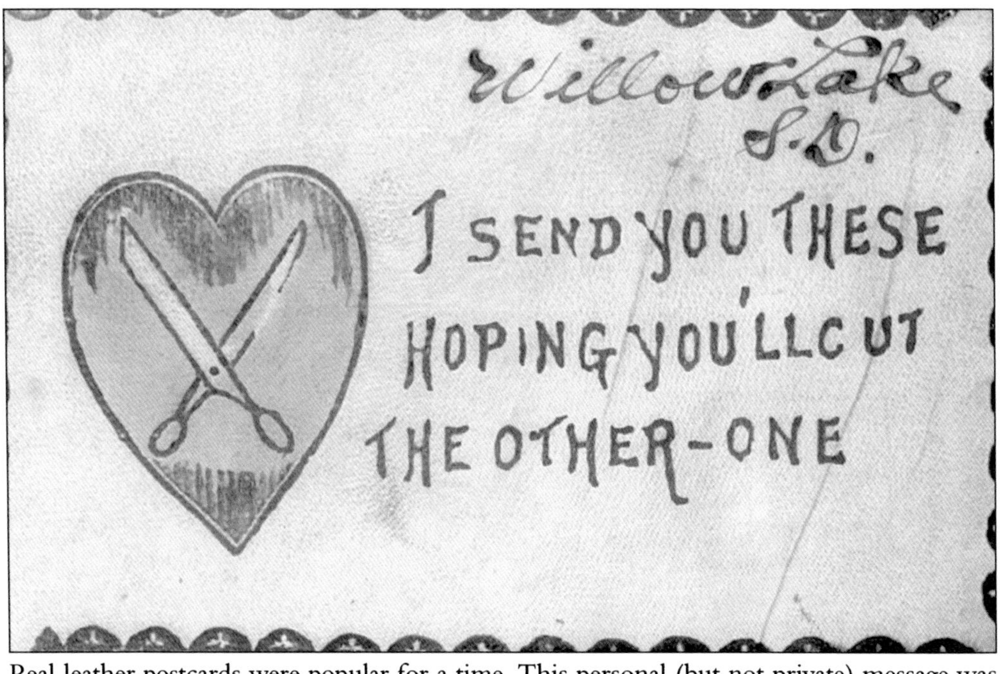

Real leather postcards were popular for a time. This personal (but not private) message was sent from Willow Lake to a young lady in Henry in 1907.

Nine

NATIVE AMERICANS

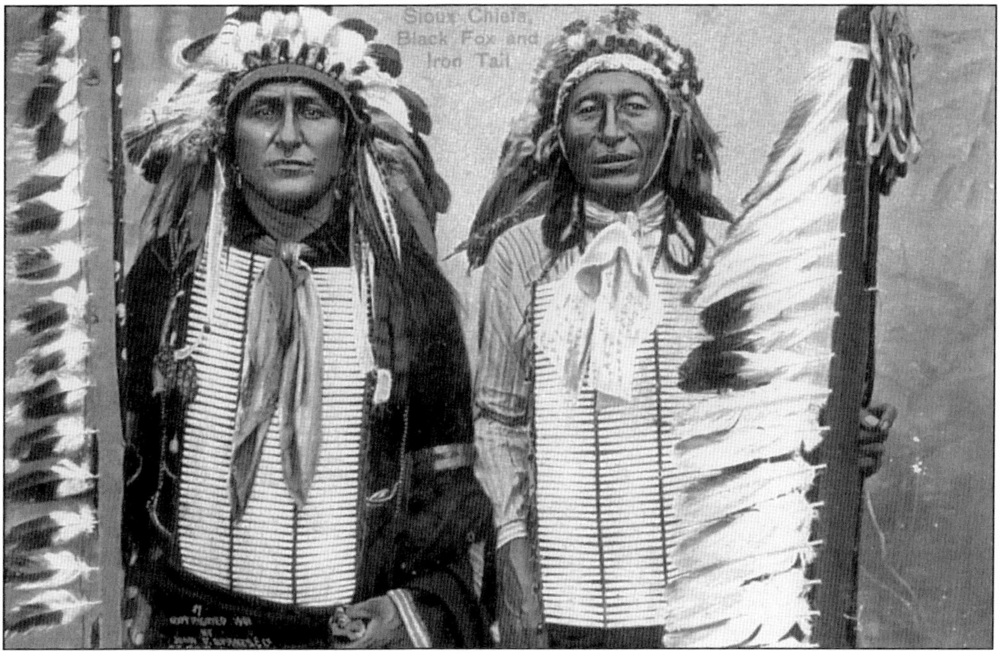

The golden age of postcards was not a golden age for Native Americans. Popular postcards in the early 1900s pictured them mostly as curiosities left over from a bygone era. Pictured here are Black Fox, believed to be the first to fire a shot at Wounded Knee, which precipitated the massacre of Big Foot's band in December 1890, and Iron Tail, who toured with Buffalo Bill's Wild West Show in Europe and was one of the models used in the design of the Indian head nickel.

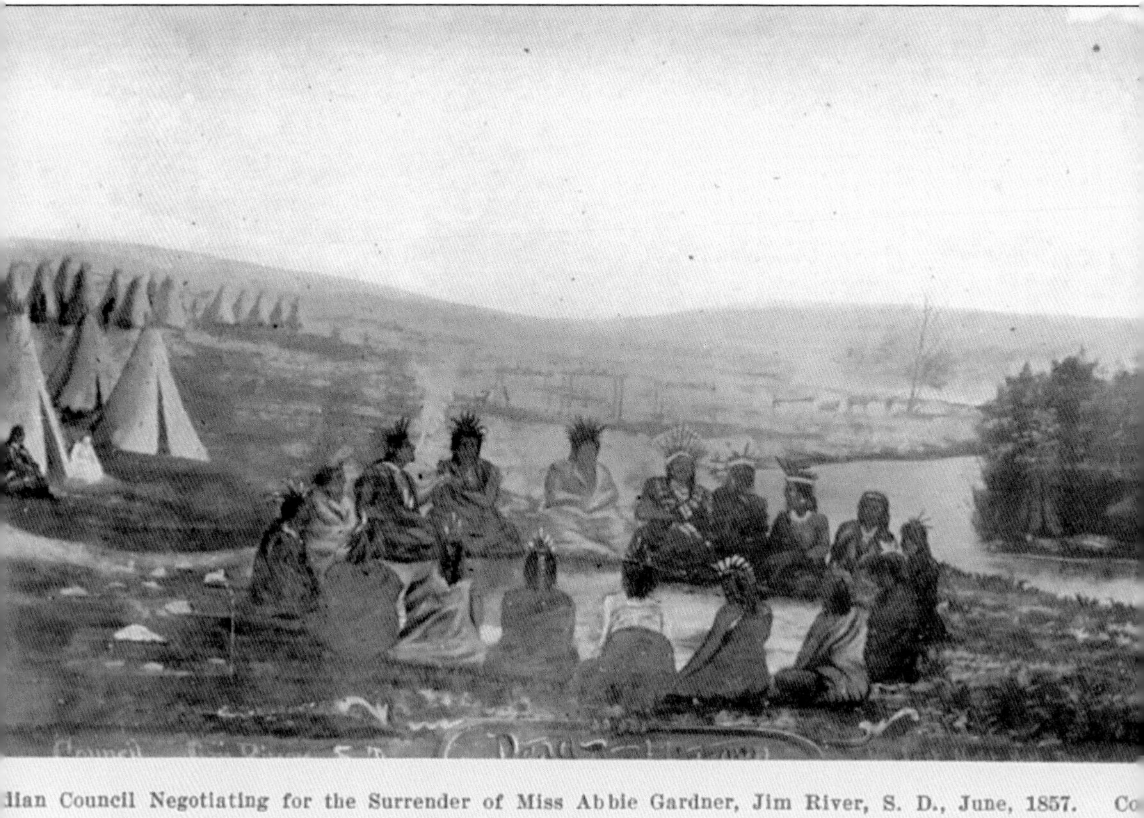

After a raid by Inkpaduta in 1857, in which four women were taken captive from a settlement in Minnesota, missionaries provided trade goods to a group of Christian Native Americans who then negotiated for their release. Thirteen-year-old Abbie Gardner survived the 83-day ordeal and returned home. The Daughters of the American Revolution sponsored a monument that marks the spot of Abbie Gardner's release, 3 miles north of present-day Redfield.

Sitting Bull's picture was widely used both to glorify traditional Native American culture and to symbolize its ultimate defeat at the end of the 19th century. Born in what is now South Dakota, Sitting Bull led his people to victory at the battle of the Little Bighorn, spent several years in exile in Canada before surrendering to United States authorities in 1881, and in 1885, toured with Buffalo Bill's Wild West Show as a live relic from the Old West.

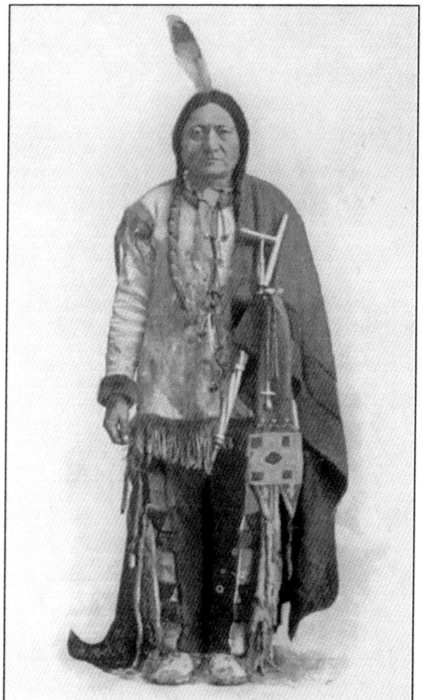

SITTING BULL, SIOUX.

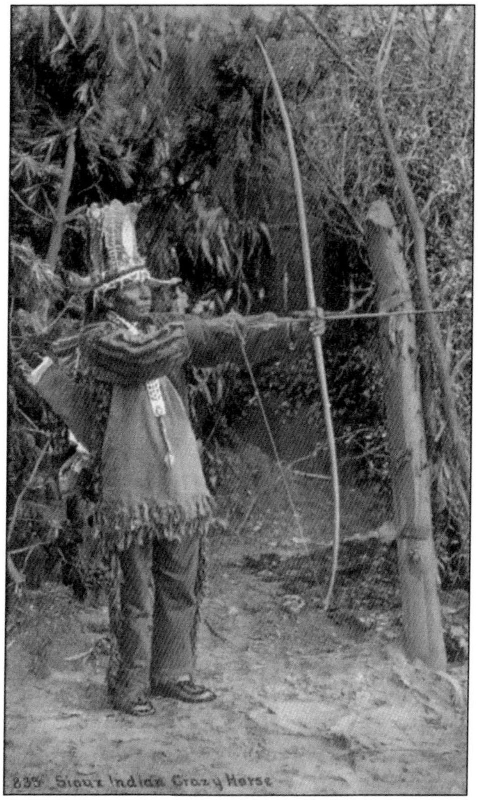

Crazy Horse, the famous warrior who led his Oglala band at the battle of the Little Bighorn, was killed at the age of 35, shortly after surrendering at Fort Robinson in 1877. It has never been documented that a photograph was ever taken of him. This postcard might show another person also named Crazy Horse, but more likely the caption was added by the publisher, hoping to increase sales.

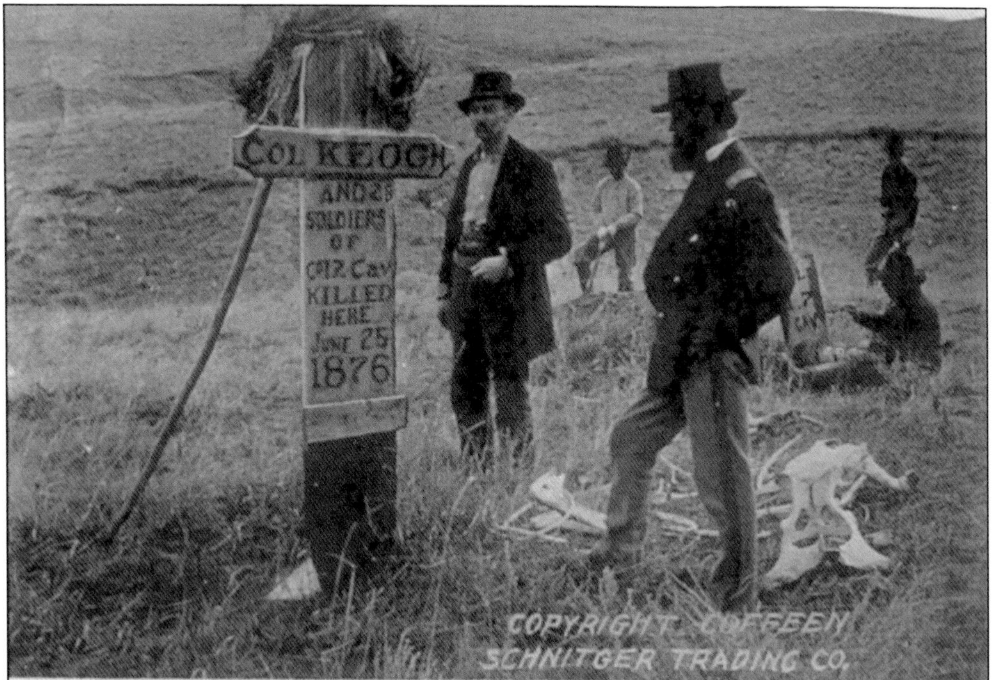

Col. Keogh and 28 Soldiers of Comp. I, 7th Cav., Killed in Custer Battle, June 25, 1876.
From Photo Taken One Year Later.
Copyright, 1906, Coffeen Schnitger Trading Co., Sheridan, Wyo.

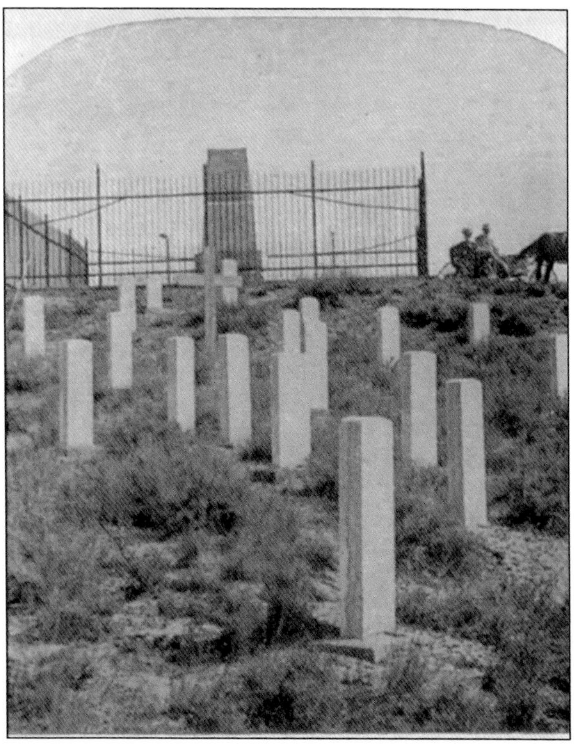

The battle of the Little Bighorn took place in Montana, but involved many of the tribes residing in Dakota Territory. The 1876 battle was also connected to the gold rush in the Black Hills, which began after General Custer announced the discovery of gold by members of his expedition in 1874. A year after the battle, in 1877, Captain Myles Keogh's reconstituted Company I returned to the battle site to bury the soldiers' remains and to mark their graves with wooden stakes.

In 1881, the bodies of the soldiers buried at Little Bighorn were dug up and moved to a mass grave underneath a huge stone monument, pictured in the background. Later, marble markers were placed where the bodies were originally found.

Red Cloud fought the United States Army to a standstill, helped negotiate the Treaty of Fort Laramie that gave the Sioux tribes all of western South Dakota and more, and then encouraged his Oglala band to settle peacefully at Pine Ridge. He lived until 1909, and had to watch as first the Black Hills and then most of the Lakota lands were taken by white settlers.

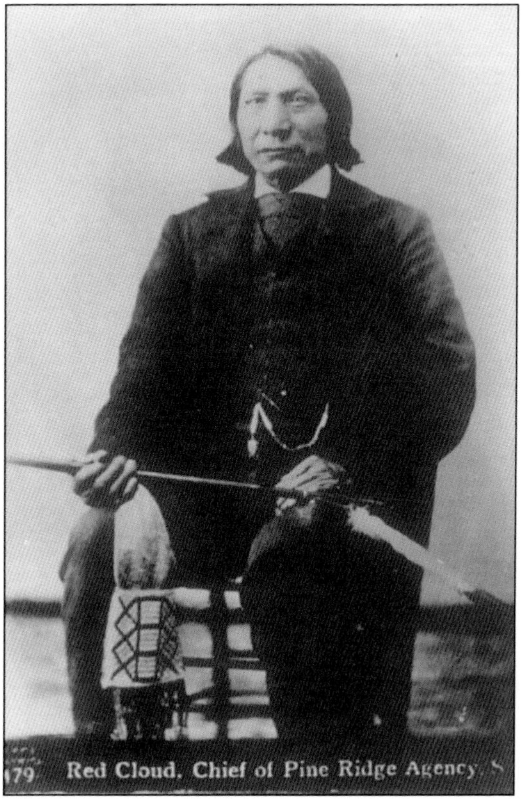

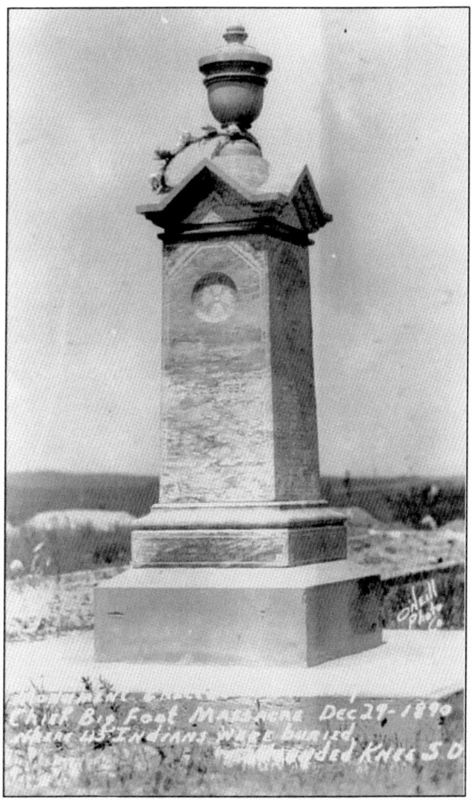

The stone monument at Wounded Knee was erected by surviving relatives and other Oglala and Cheyenne River Sioux Indians, in memory of those who died there on December 29, 1890.

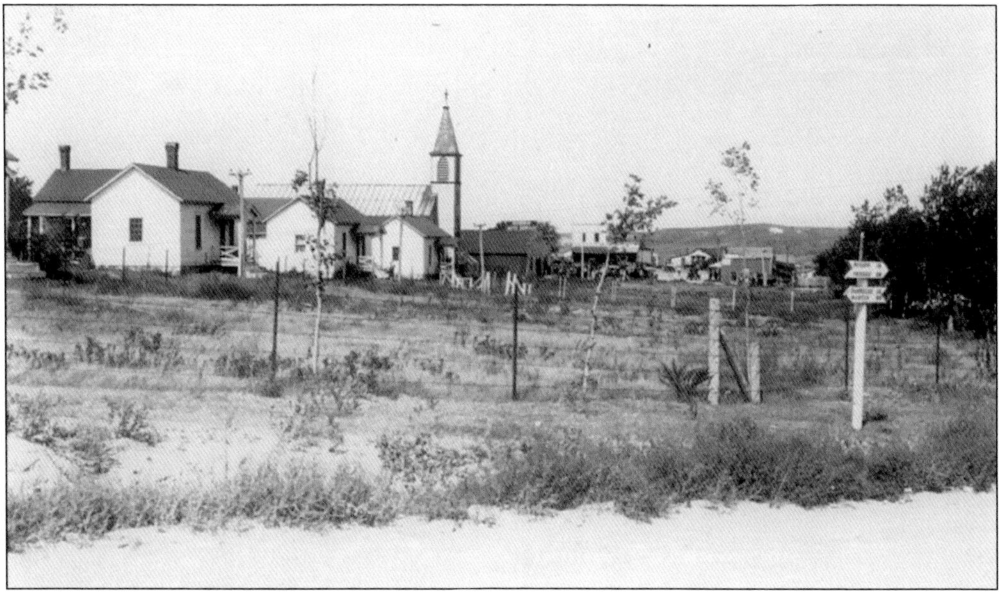

Most of South Dakota's Native American population resided in isolated reservation communities, such as this one at Rosebud.

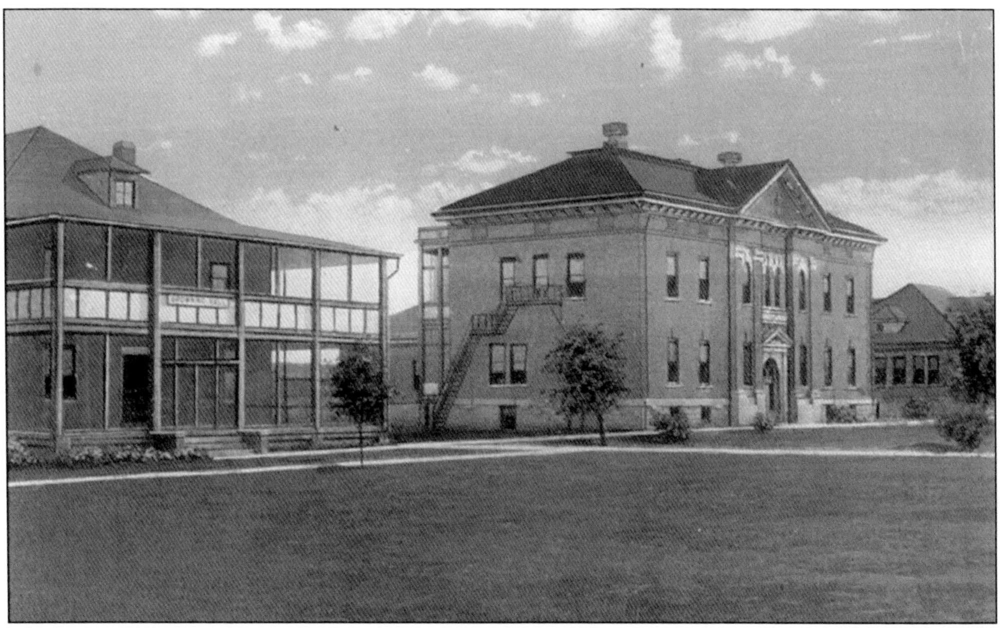

The Pierre Indian Industrial School opened in 1890, at the east edge of town on land donated by the Pierre Board of Trade. In 1974, it became the Pierre Indian Learning Center.

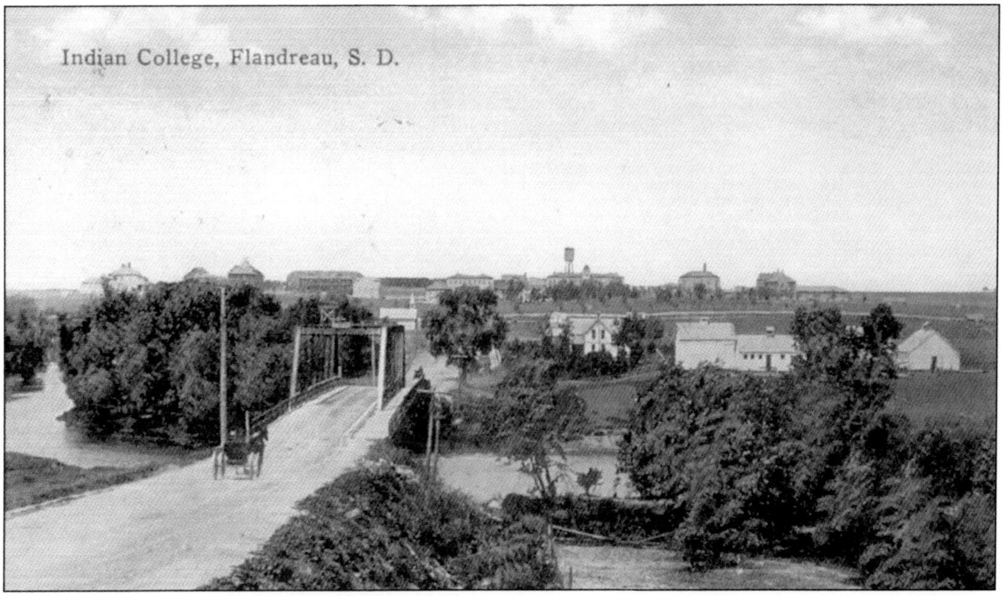

Between 1869 and 1873, the Flandreau band moved from the Santee reservation in Nebraska and homesteaded on land in Moody County. With support from Senator R.F. Pettigrew, the federal government established a vocational boarding school in Flandreau in 1893, built on land that Pettigrew sold to the government.

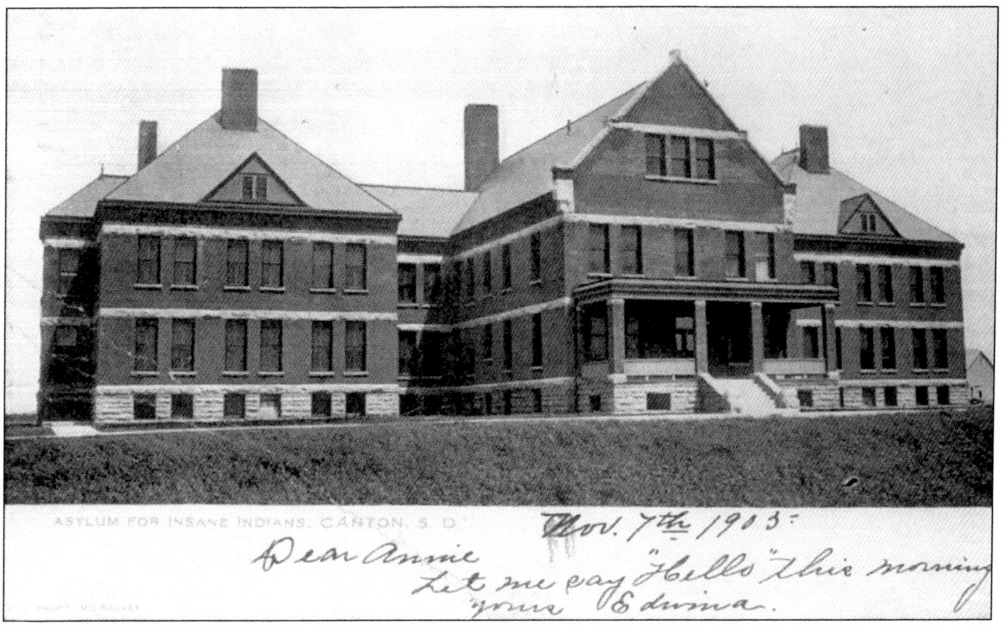

The Hiawatha Asylum for Insane Indians opened in Canton in 1902, the result of pork-barrel legislation pushed by Senator R.F. Pettigrew and Congressman O.S. Gifford. After several federal reviews, even officials within the problem-ridden Bureau of Indian Affairs agreed that it was one of the most poorly operated institutions in the country. After the hospital closed in 1933, the 337-acre site was sold to the City of Canton and used for a municipal hospital, gun club, 4-H fairgrounds, and a golf course.

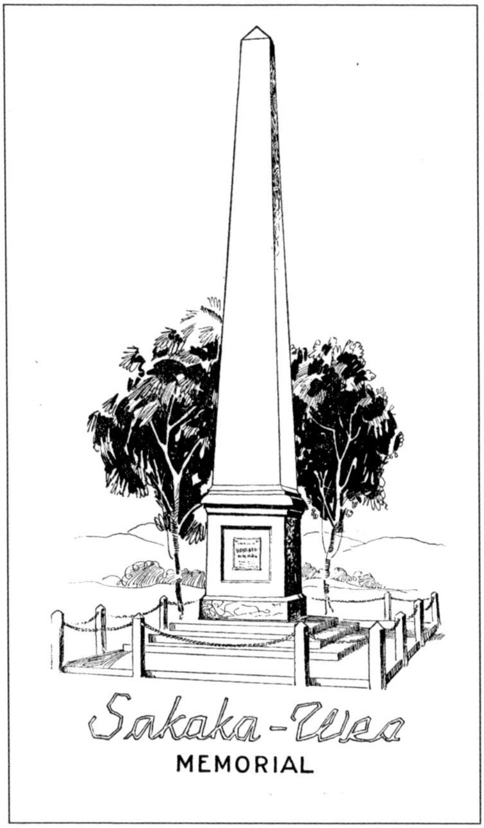

This monument was erected in 1929, across the river from Mobridge to honor Sacagawea, the Shoshone guide who helped Lewis and Clark cross the Rocky Mountains. According to a journal kept by John C. Luttig, a clerk for fur trader Manuel Lisa, she died in 1812 at Fort Manuel, 30 miles north of this site.

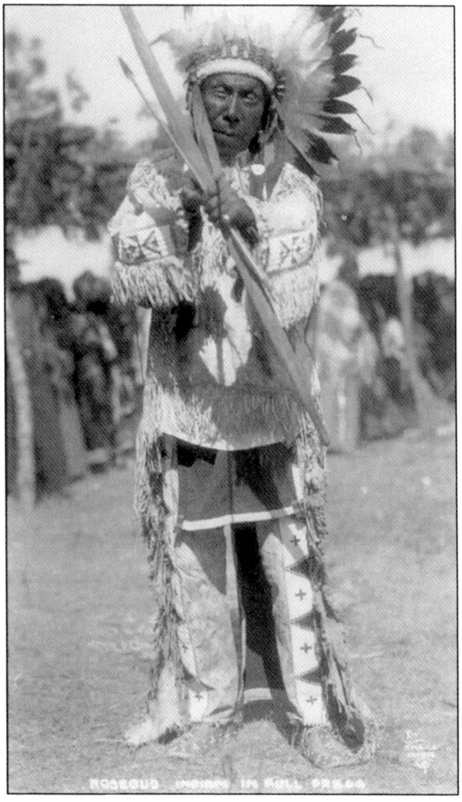

Local Native Americans appeared in traditional costume for parades, Fourth of July festivals, and other special events in many South Dakota towns, and sometimes they could make a little money posing for photographers or tourists.

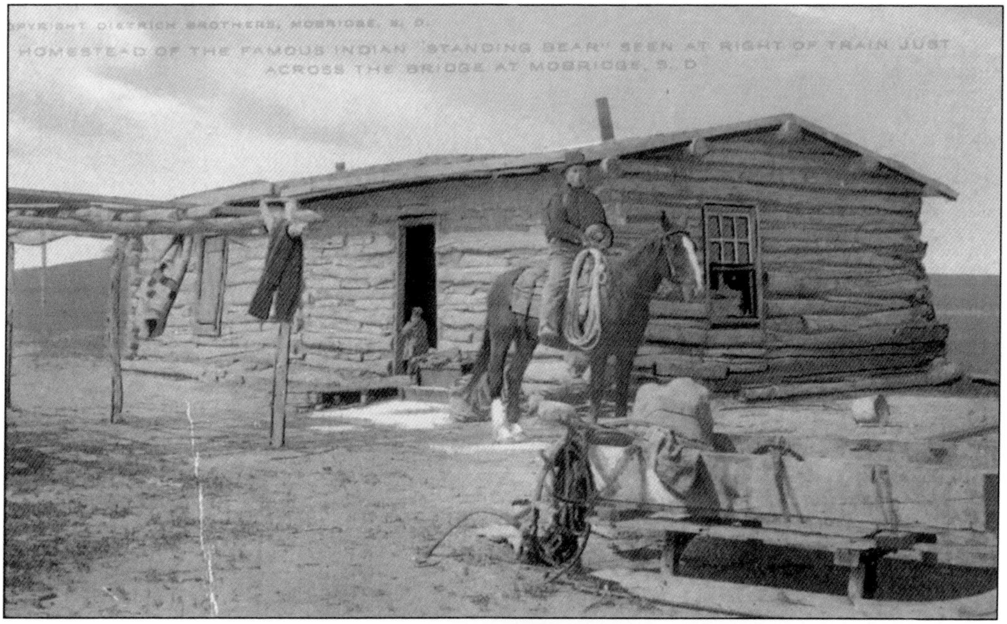

Passengers on the west-bound "Olympian" and east-bound "Columbian" trains on the Milwaukee Road were apprised to watch for this house of a "real live Indian" as they crossed the Standing Rock reservation.

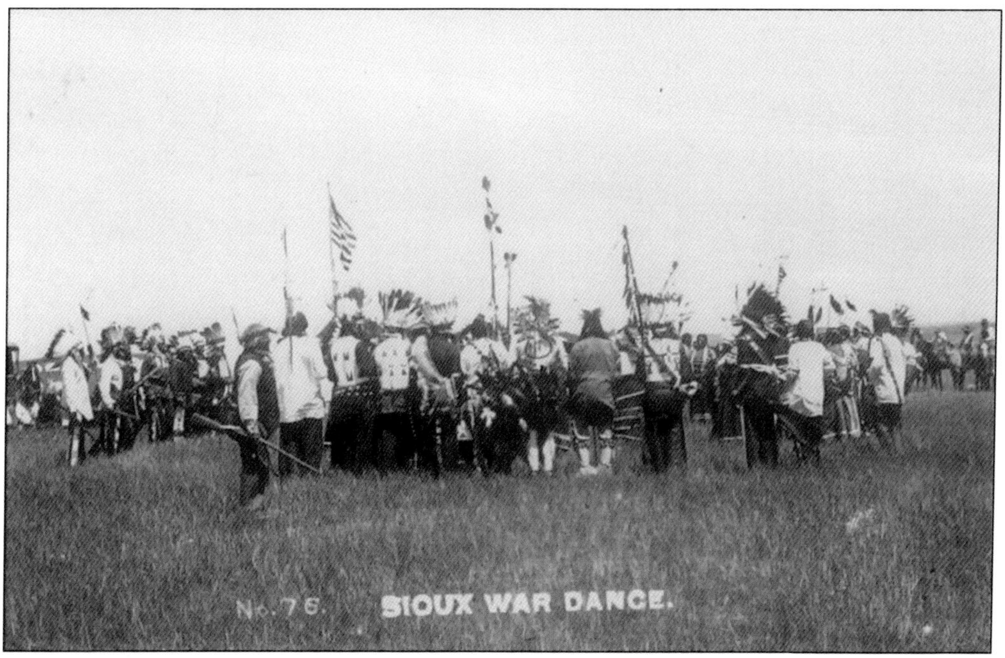

The sun dance, ghost dance, and some other religious ceremonies were prohibited on the reservations for many years, but other kinds of dances attracted crowds at pow-wows and other local events.

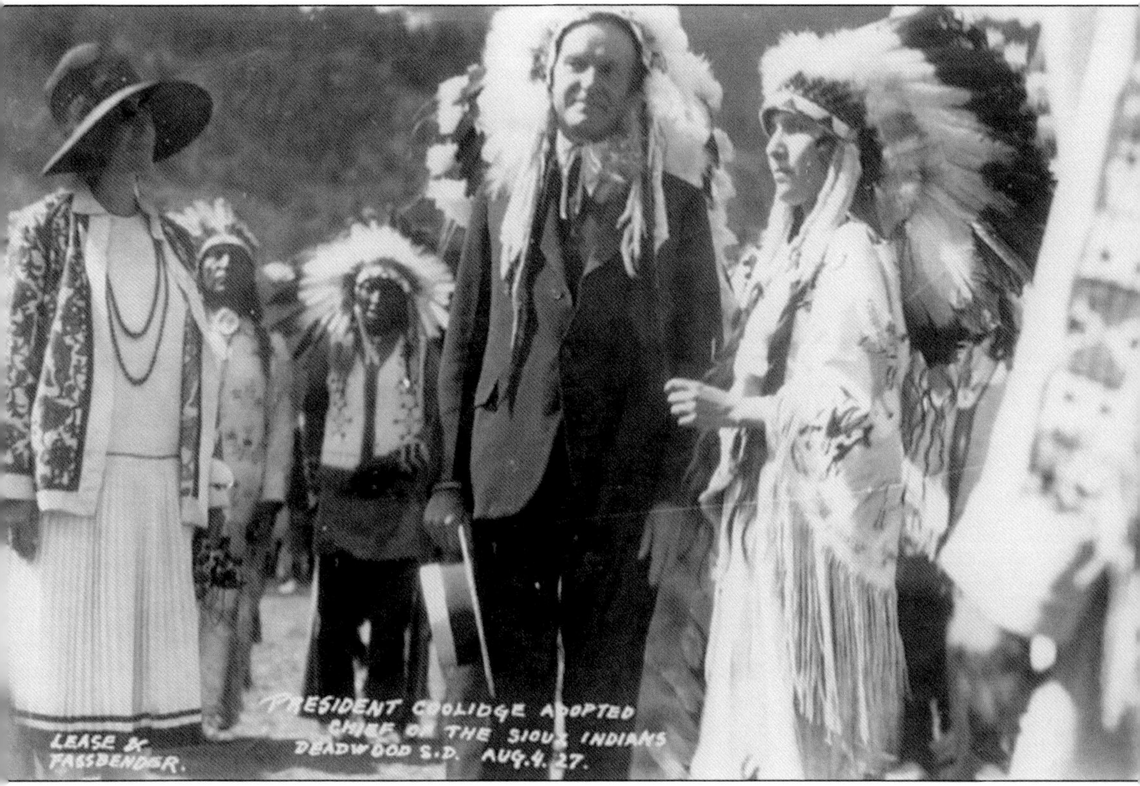

President Calvin Coolidge spent most of the summer of 1927 at the State Game Lodge in the Black Hills. He and his wife Grace made friends throughout the area. At the Days of '76 celebration in Deadwood on August 4, Coolidge was adopted as high chief of the Sioux tribe and named "Leading Eagle, Wamblee-Tokaha." Rosebud Yellow Robe, standing next to President Coolidge, presented him with his bonnet.

Ten

THE WESTERN MYTH IN CREATION

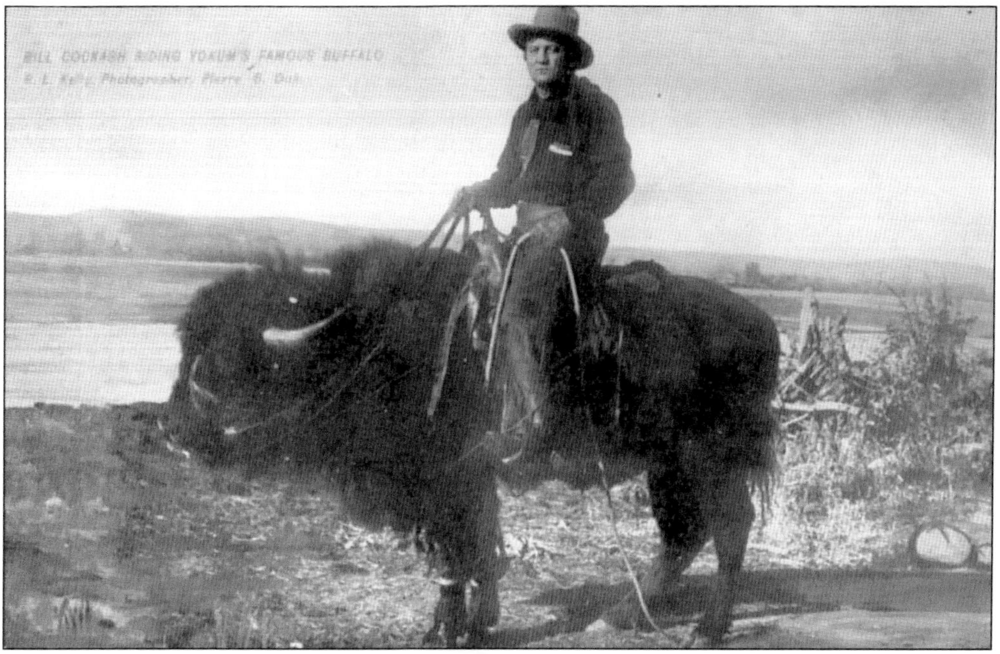

The image of the West held by most Americans was largely created by dime novelists and journalists, and later by Hollywood screenwriters and directors. However, westerners not only accepted mythical versions of their region, but they actively perpetuated and expanded them. R.L. Yokum of Fort Pierre trained two young buffaloes to pull a two-wheeled wagon, and fitted this one out with a saddle as well. Yokum showed off his buffalo cart in eastern cities, including Cincinnati and Baltimore.

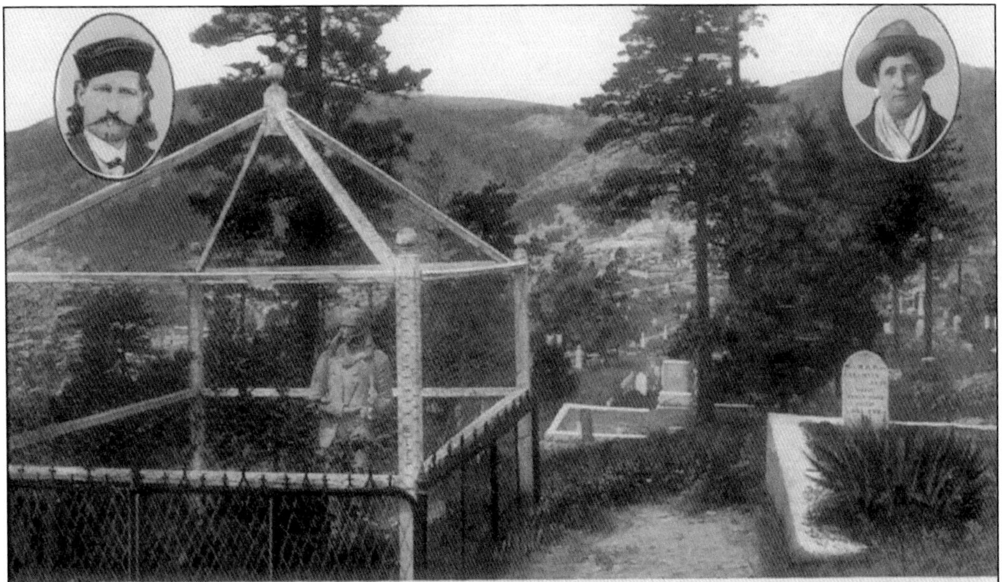

88. Tombs of "Wild Bill" and "Calamity Jane", Mt. Moriah Cemetery, Deadwood, Black Hills, S. D.

COPYRIGHTED 1911 BY W. B. PERKINS.

The grave of Wild Bill Hickok in Deadwood quickly became a popular pilgrimage spot, and fans paid their respects by taking pieces of the grave marker with them. This statue by Alvin Smith was installed in 1903, to replace another statue whittled down to its base, which in turn replaced the original grave marker that had vanished by 1891. The bottom photo shows the Smith statue already missing a hand and disappearing piece by piece. The nearly unrecognizable stump was removed to the Adams Museum in 1955.

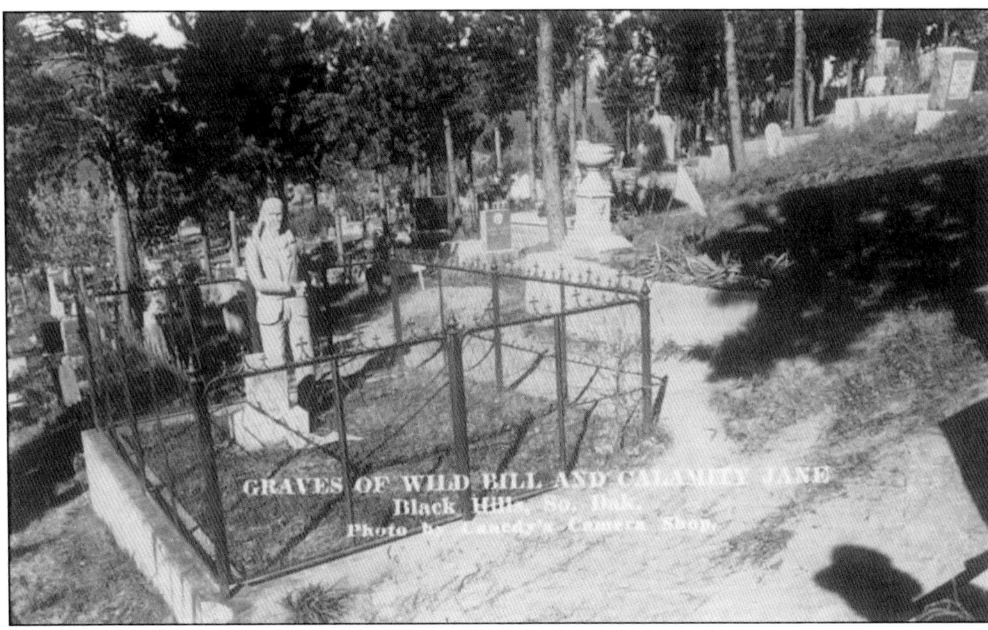

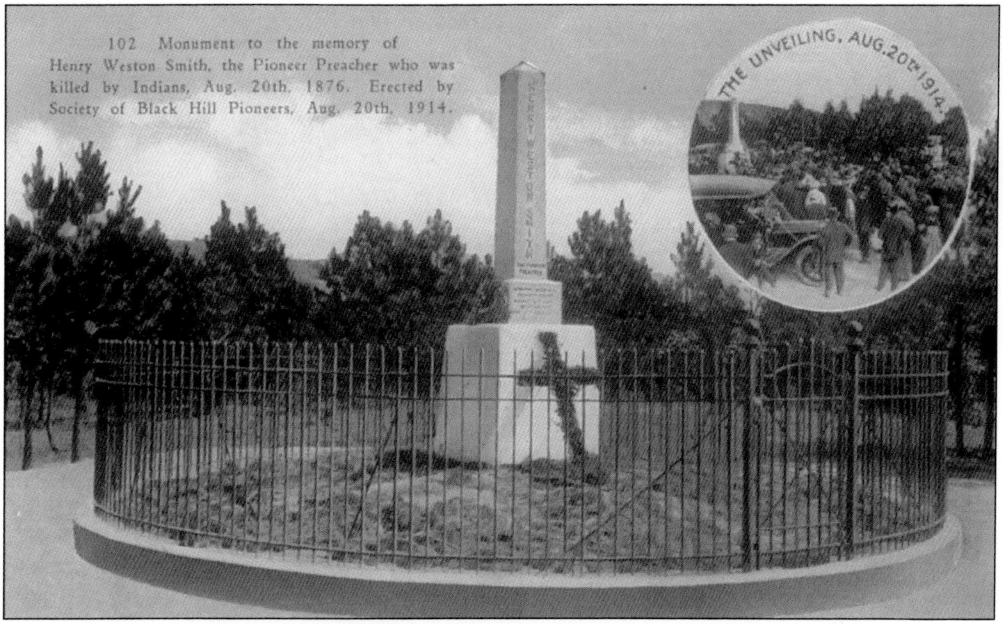

Henry Weston Smith's career as the first minister in Deadwood ended only a few weeks after it began in August 1876, when he was murdered on the road to Crook City by an unknown assailant. A full-size statue placed on his grave in 1891 was hacked to pieces by memento hunters. This monument was placed on the highway 3 miles north of Deadwood to mark the spot of Smith's "martyrdom," although the actual murder site was 2 miles further into the woods.

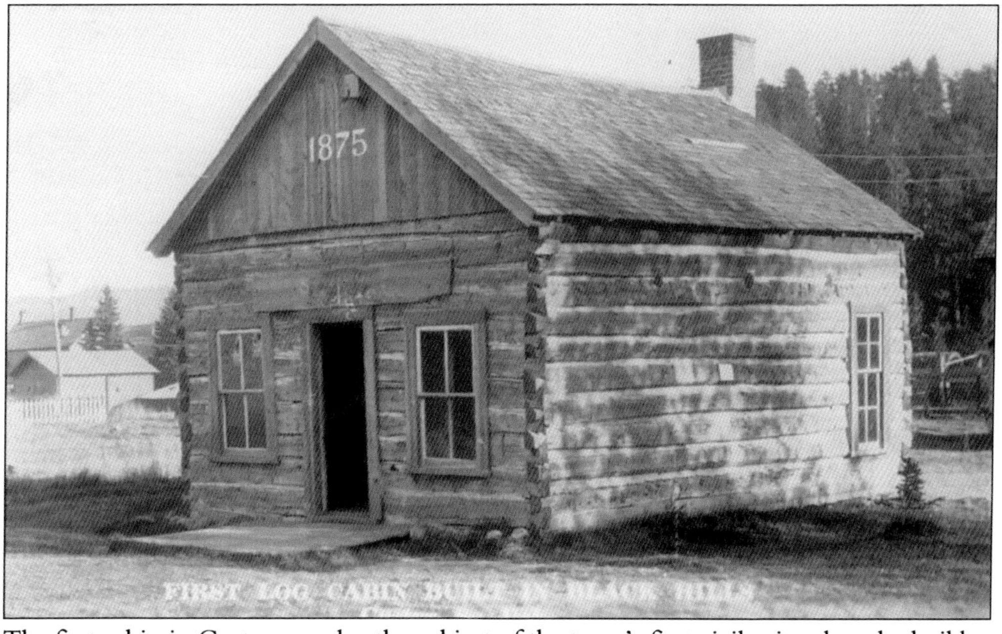

The first cabin in Custer was also the subject of the town's first civil suit, when the builder, Dr. D.W. Flick, returned to Custer in 1876, to find the cabin inhabited by Captain Jack Crawford, the area's first poet. The cabin eventually became a museum in Way Park, which was located in front of the Custer County Courthouse and dedicated in 1921.

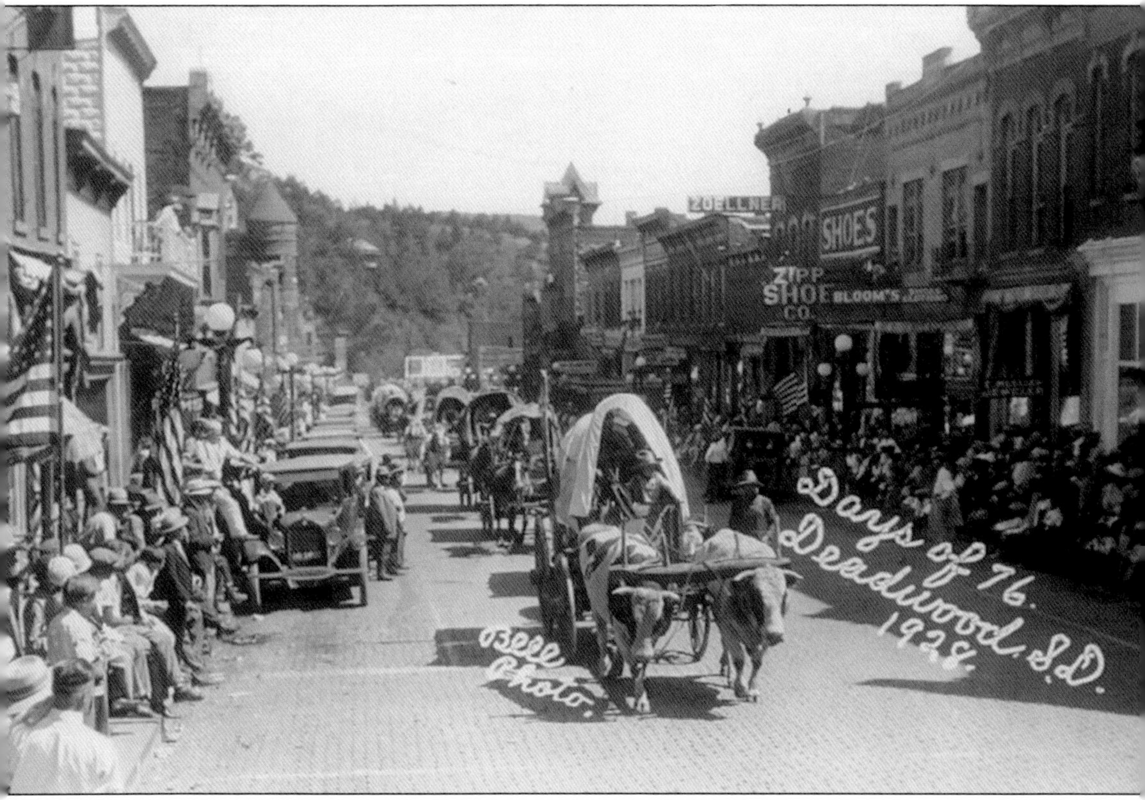

By the 1920s, Deadwood had become a flourishing town with brick storefronts and law-abiding citizens. The wild days of the gold rush era were recreated in the "Days of '76" celebrations, which began in 1924.

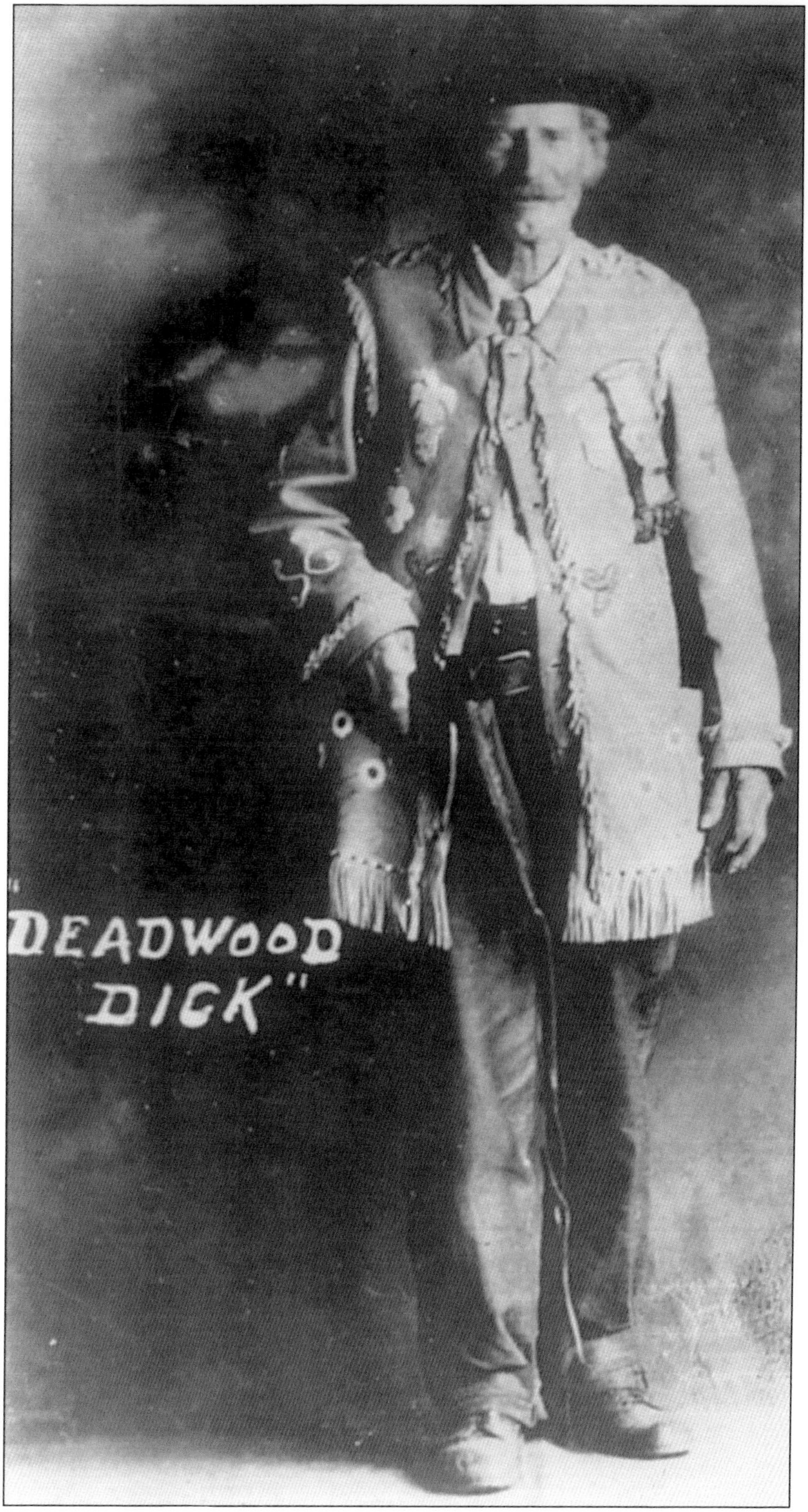

Created as a character in one of Ned Buntline's dime novels in 1877, Deadwood Dick was brought to life in the 1920s by Richard Clark, who was hired by the Deadwood Chamber of Commerce to play the role in the annual "Days of '76" celebrations.

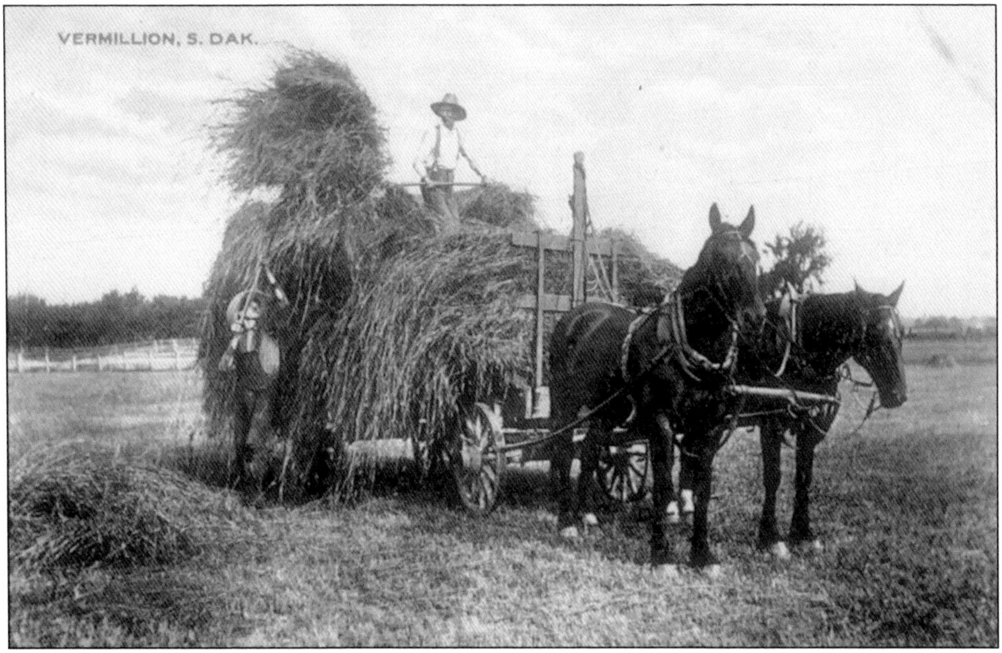

The sender of this postcard liked the image enough to buy it but knew it was probably a stock photo provided by the New York publisher, as indicated in the message on the back: "Although these farm scenes are marked Vermillion, we don't believe they are, for they don't have fences like this here you know."

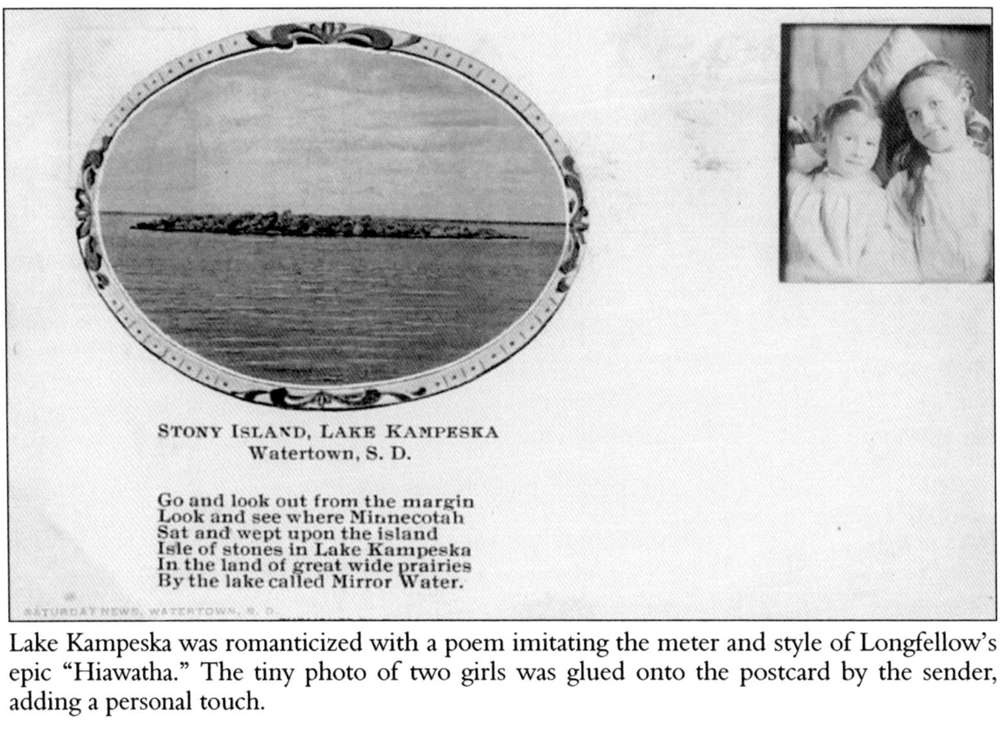

Lake Kampeska was romanticized with a poem imitating the meter and style of Longfellow's epic "Hiawatha." The tiny photo of two girls was glued onto the postcard by the sender, adding a personal touch.

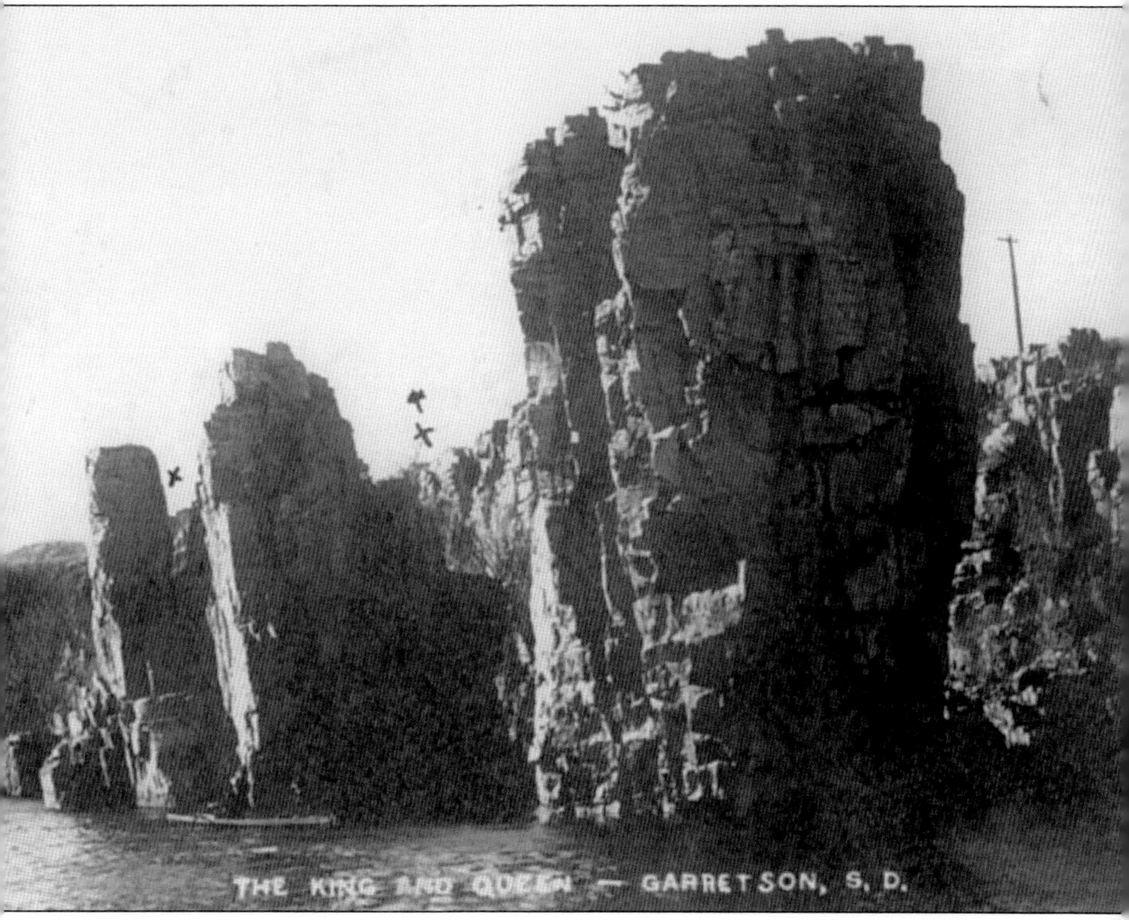

Local tales report that Frank and Jesse James visited Dakota Territory while on the run after the disastrous Northfield, Minnesota, raid in 1876. This postcard shows that their visit to Garretson had already passed into legend at an early date. The message reads: "The 2 cross shows wear I and you clumb down to see Jessie James hole wher he was hid the one x showes where they never reach bottom of the watter. This stone is 1500 feet high."

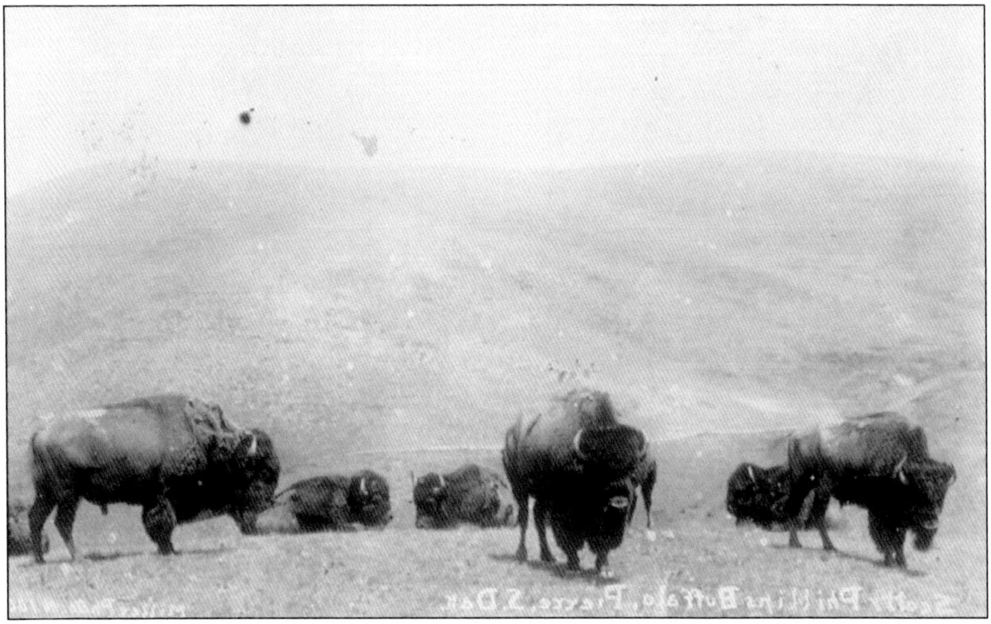

Scotty Philip's real-life exploits read better than some dime novels. Farmer, gold prospector, army scout, banker, and real estate man, Philip became best known for his efforts to save the buffalo from extinction. His buffalo ranch eventually covered 15,000 acres north of Fort Pierre, and visitors could take special river ferries or trains to see the herd. This postcard was printed backwards at the photo studio.

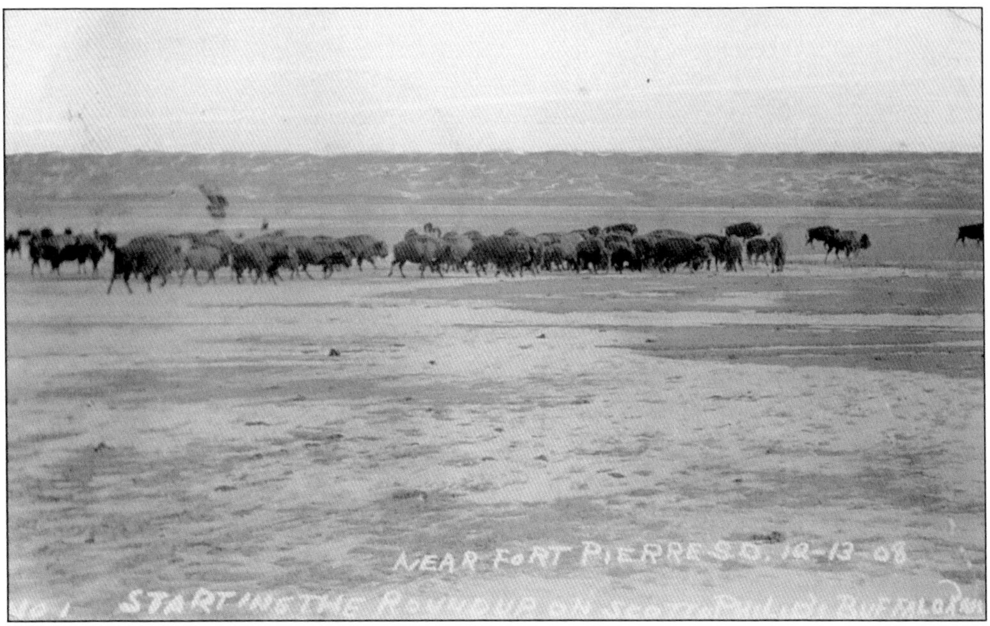

Scotty Philip had 400 head of buffalo on his ranch when he died in 1911. In the 1920s, part of the herd was moved into the new game preserve at Custer State Park.

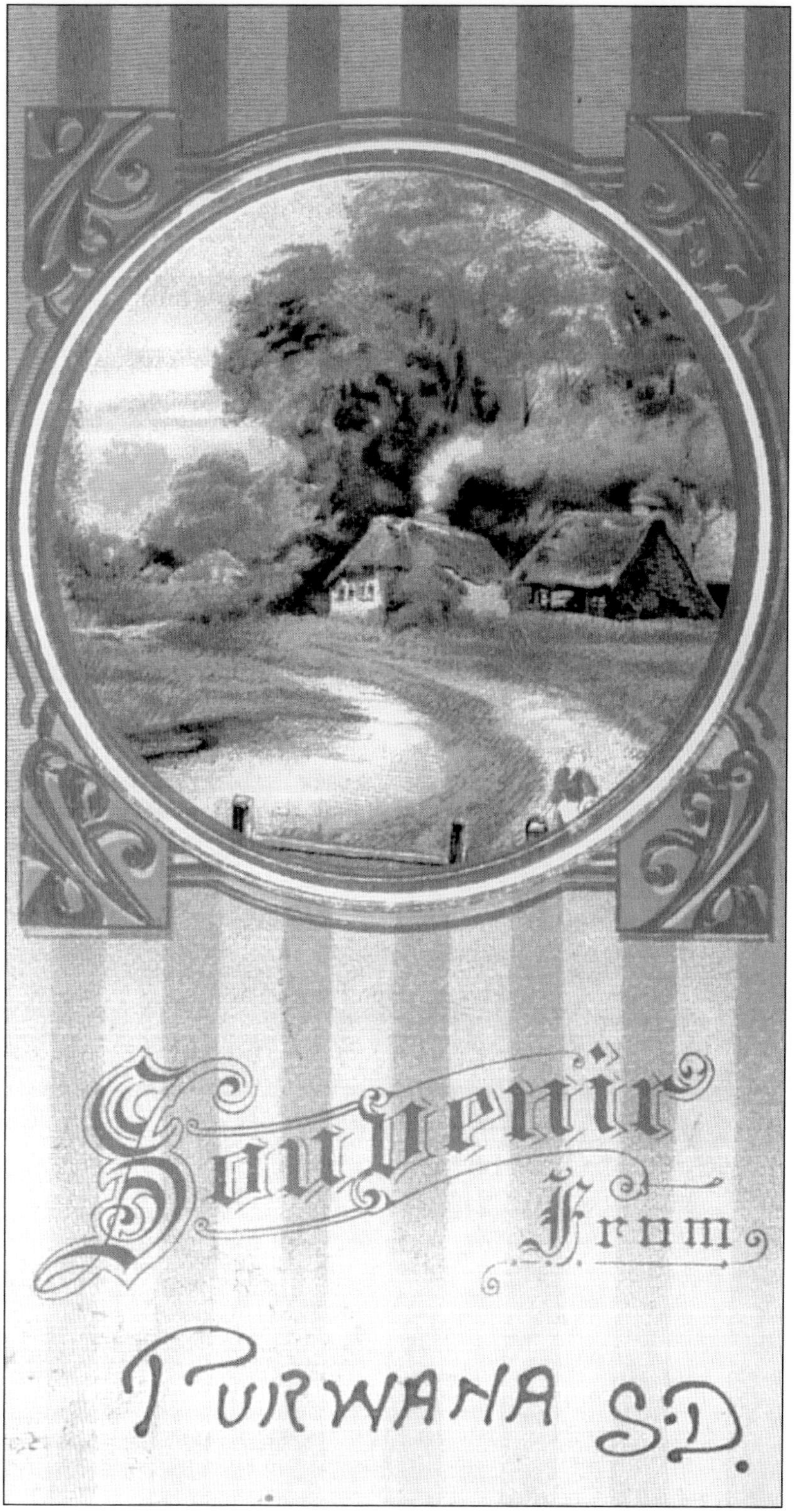

This souvenir of Pukwana featured a farm scene with thatched-roof cottages. It was not uncommon at this time for postcards with scenes of lakes, rivers, and trees that could not be found in South Dakota to say "Greetings from Cresbard" or "Near Beresford, S. Dak."

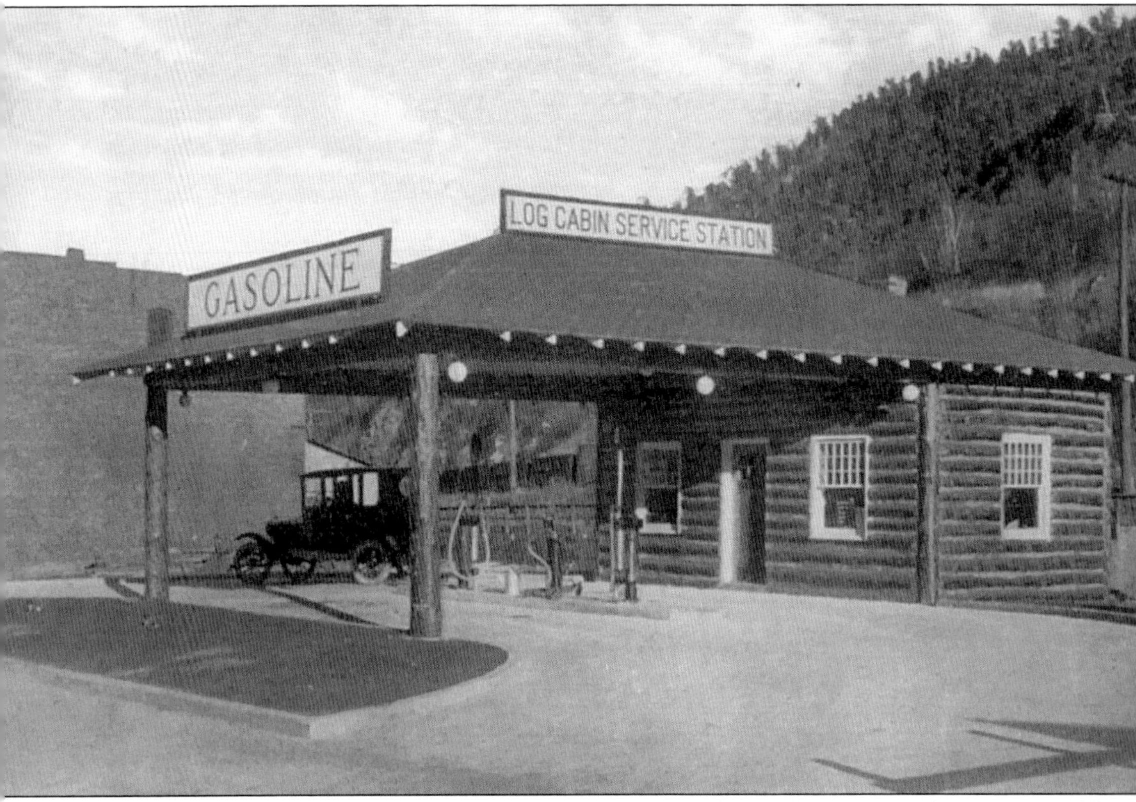

This gas station in Deadwood was constructed in log-cabin style to give it the proper "Old West" look, to appeal to tourists and the locals as well.